Cordial
Concurrence

PRAEGER SERIES IN POLITICAL COMMUNICATION
Robert E. Denton, Jr., General Editor

Enacting Political Culture: Rhetorical Transformations of Liberty Weekend 1986
David E. Procter

Within These Walls: A Study of Communication Between Presidents and Their Senior Staffs
Patricia D. Witherspoon

Continuity and Change in the Rhetoric of the Moral Majority
David Snowball

Mediated Politics in Two Cultures: Presidential Campaigning in the U.S. and France
Lynda Lee Kaid, Jacques Gerstle, and Keith R. Sanders

Crime and the American Press
Roy Edward Lotz

A Shining City on a Hill: Ronald Reagan's Economic Rhetoric, 1951–1989
Amos Kiewe and Davis W. Houck

The Cold War As Rhetoric: The Beginnings, 1945–1950
Lynn B. Hinds and Theodore O. Windt, Jr.

Presidential Perspectives on Space Exploration: Guiding Metaphors from Eisenhower to Bush
Linda T. Krug

Political Campaign Communication, Second Edition
Judith S. Trent and Robert V. Friedenberg

Ethical Dimensions of Political Communication
Edited by Robert E. Denton, Jr.

Cordial Concurrence

Orchestrating National Party Conventions in the Telepolitical Age

Larry David Smith
and Dan Nimmo

Praeger Series in Political Communication

New York
Westport, Connecticut
London

Library of Congress Cataloging-in-Publication Data

Smith, Larry David.
    Cordial concurrence : orchestrating national party conventions in
the telepolitical age / Larry David Smith, Dan Nimmo.
       p.   cm. — (Praeger series in political communication)
    Includes bibliographical references and index.
    ISBN 0–275–93863–8 (alk. paper). — ISBN 0–275–93864–6 (pbk. :
alk. paper)
    1. Political conventions—United States.   2. Television in
politics—United States.   I. Nimmo, Dan D. II. Title.
III. Series.
JK2255.S65   1991
324.5 '6' 0973—dc20   91–3549

British Library Cataloguing in Publication Data is available.

Library of Congress Catalog Card Number: 91–3549
ISBN: 0–275–93863–8 (hb.)
     0–275–93864–6 (pb.)

First published in 1991

Praeger Publishers, One Madison Avenue, New York, NY 10010
An imprint of Greenwood Publishing Group, Inc.

Printed in the United States of America

The paper used in this book complies with the
Permanent Paper Standard issued by the National
Information Standards Organization (Z39.48–1984).

10 9 8 7 6 5 4 3 2 1

To Robert E. Petersen,

who understands the Great Barbecue as V. L. Parrington
did, and appreciates barbecue as no one else can

Contents

About the Series by Robert E. Denton, Jr.   ix

Series Foreword by Robert E. Denton, Jr.   xiii

Preface   xvii

Prelude   National Party Conventions: The Political
             Orchestration of Cordial Concurrence   1

Chapter 1   From Concert Halls to Opera Houses:
             The Evolution of National Convention
             Orchestration   25

Chapter 2   Political Impresarios: Parties, Media, and
             Galleries as Orchestrators   51

Chapter 3   Picturesque Stages and Patriotic Programs:
             Concurrence in Orchestrating Places, People,
             and Events   81

Chapter 4   Stages, Pits, Floors, Balconies, and Boxes:
             The Parties' Productions at National
             Political Conventions   105

Chapter 5   Melodies and Discords: TV Coverage of the
             Democratic Convention in Atlanta   137

Chapter 6   Grand Old Party or Ruptured Harmony?:
             TV Coverage of the Republicans in New Orleans   165

Chapter 7   The Number of Genuine Music Lovers Is
             Probably Very Low: Chanties of Criticism and
             Reform   189

    Finale   Voices in Concert: The Interinstitutional
             Orchestration of Politics   215

             References   229

             Index   241

About the Series

Those of us from the discipline of communication studies have long believed that communication is prior to all other fields of inquiry. In several other forums I have argued that the essence of politics is "talk" or human interaction.[1] Such interaction may be formal or informal, verbal or nonverbal, public or private but it is always persuasive, forcing us consciously or subconsciously to interpret, to evaluate, and to act. Communication is the vehicle for human action.

From this perspective, it is not surprising that Aristotle recognized the natural kinship of politics and communication in his writings *Politics* and *Rhetoric*. In the former, he establishes that humans are "political beings [who] alone of the animals [are] furnished with the faculty of language."[2] And in the latter, he begins his systematic analysis of discourse by proclaiming that "rhetorical study, in its strict sense, is concerned with the modes of persuasion."[3] Thus, it was recognized over two thousand years ago that politics and communication go hand in hand because they are essential parts of human nature.

Back in 1981, Dan Nimmo and Keith Sanders proclaimed that political communication was an emerging field.[4] Although its origin, as noted, dates back centuries, a "self-consciously cross-disciplinary" focus began in the late 1950s. Thousands of books and articles later, colleges and universities offer a variety of undergraduate and graduate coursework in the area in such diverse departments as communication, mass communication, journalism, political science, and sociology.[5] In Nimmo and Sanders's early assessment, the "key areas of inquiry" included rhetorical analysis, propaganda analysis, attitude change studies, voting studies, government and the news media, functional and systems analyses, tech-

nological changes, media technologies, campaign techniques, and research techniques.[6] In a survey of the state of the field in 1983, the same
authors and Lynda Kaid found additional, more specific areas of concerns
such as the presidency, political polls, public opinion, debates, and advertising to name a few.[7] Since the first study, they also noted a shift away
from the rather strict behavioral approach.

Today, Dan Nimmo and David Swanson assert that "political communication has developed some identity as a more or less distinct domain of
scholarly work."[8] The scope and concerns of the area have further expanded to include critical theories and cultural studies. While there is no
precise definition, method, or disciplinary home of the area of inquiry, its
primary domain is the role, processes, and effects of communication
within the context of politics broadly defined.

In 1985, the editors of *Political Communication Yearbook: 1984* noted that
"more things are happening in the study, teaching, and practice of political
communication than can be captured within the space limitations of the
relatively few publications available."[9] In addition, they argued that the
backgrounds of "those involved in the field [are] so varied and pluralist
in outlook and approach, . . . it [is] a mistake to adhere slavishly to any set
format in shaping the content."[10] And more recently, Swanson and
Nimmo called for "ways of overcoming the unhappy consequences of
fragmentation within a framework that respects, encourages, and benefits
from diverse scholarly commitments, agendas, and approaches."[11]

In agreement with these assessments of the area and with gentle encour-
agement, Praeger established the series entitled "Praeger Series in Political Communication" in 1988. The series is open to all qualitative and
quantitative methodologies as well as contemporary and historical studies.
The key to characterizing the studies in the series is the focus on communication variables or activities within a political context or dimension. Scholars from the disciplines of communication, history, political science, and
sociology have participated in the series.

I am, without shame or modesty, a fan of the series. The joy of serving
as its editor is in participating in the dialogue of the field of political communication and in reading the contributors' works. I invite you to join me.

Robert E. Denton, Jr.

NOTES

1. See Robert E. Denton, Jr., *The symbolic dimensions of the American presidency*
(Prospect Heights, IL: Waveland Press, 1982); Robert E.Denton, Jr., & Gary Wood-
ward, *Political Communication in America 2nd ed.* (New York: Praeger, 1990);
Robert E. Denton, Jr. & Dan Hahn, *Presidential Communication* (New York:
Praeger, 1986); and Robert E. Denton, Jr., *The primetime presidency of Ronald Rea-
gan* (New York: Praeger, 1988).

2. Aristotle, *The politics of Aristotle*, trans. Ernest Barker (New York: Oxford University Press, 1970), p. 5.

3. Aristotle, *Rhetoric*, trans. Rhys Roberts (New York: Modern Library, 1954), p. 22.

4. Dan Nimmo & Keith Sanders, Introduction: The Emergence of Political Communication as a Field, in Dan Nimmo & Keith Sanders (Eds.), *Handbook of political communication* (Beverly Hills, CA: Sage, 1981), pp. 11–36.

5. Ibid., p. 15.

6. Ibid., pp. 17–27.

7. Keith Sanders, Lynda Kaid & Dan Nimmo, eds., *Political communication yearbook: 1984* (Carbondale: Southern Illinois University Press: 1985), pp. 283–308.

8. Dan Nimmo & David Swanson, The field of political communication: Beyond the voter persuasion paradigm in David Swanson & Dan Nimmo, (Eds.), *New directions in political communication* (Beverly Hills, CA: Sage, 1990), p. 8.

9. Sanders, Kaid & Nimmo, p. xiv.

10. Ibid., p. xiv.

11. Nimmo and Swanson, p. 11.

Series Foreword

There is probably no single topic that receives more attention in American politics than presidential campaigns. It is a uniquely American "spectacle" that is both entertaining and sustaining. "Every four years," according to James Barber (1980), "a gong goes off and a new presidential campaign surges into the national consciousness: new candidates, new issues, a new season of surprises. But underlying the syncopations of change there is a steady, recurrent rhythm from election to election, a pulse of politics, that brings up the same basic themes in order, over and over again" (p. 3). Although exciting, do presidential campaigns matter? Are they simply constructed spectacles of symbols, rituals, and "mere rhetoric" resulting in what Kenneth Burke (1969) calls "a secular variant of prayer" which serves "to sharpen up the pointless and blunt the too sharply pointed"? (p. 393).

The dominant view of scholars of the impact of campaigns upon voters for nearly forty years was the "limited effects model" based upon the early research of Paul Lazarsfeld, Bernard Berelson, and Hazel Gaudet (1948). They argued that most voter decisions were based upon attitude predispositions, group identification, and interpersonal communication. Thus, mediated messages and full campaign activities contribute little to the actual conversion or persuasion of voters favoring one candidate over another.[1] Today, however, scholars are recognizing a variety of factors that influence voter preferences partially as a result of the decline of political parties, the increase of single issue politics, the prominence of mass media, and the sophistication of social science research.

Despite the problems in attempting to analyze political communication in relation to audiences (Morley, 1990), today the most widely accepted model of campaign effects is basically the "uses and gratifications" model (McLeod & Becker, 1981). This approach argues that campaign effects upon voters depend upon the needs and motivations of the individual voter. Voters may attune to campaign messages for a variety of reasons—information, issue discussion, position validation, candidate appeal, or pure entertainment—to name only a few. Thus, the impact of exposure to campaign communication results from the interaction of message and individual. David Morley (1990) asserts that we have largely ignored "the fundamental role of the media in articulating the public and private spheres and in the social organization of space, time, and community, as the framework through and within which the dynamics of political communication are constructed" (p. 123).

This perspective is consistent with Bruce Gronbeck's (1978, 1984) "functional model of campaign research." In his model, Gronbeck recognizes instrumental and consummatory functions. Instrumental functions of campaigns include behavioral activation, cognitive adjustments (issue positions, etc.), and legitimation of the process and newly elected leaders. Often forgotten are consummatory functions embodied in the communication processes that go beyond candidate selection and legislative enactments. They encompass the metapolitical images and social-psychological associations that provide the glue that holds our political system together. Campaigns, as Gronbeck (1984) argues, "get leaders elected, yes, but ultimately, they also tell us who we as a people are, where we have been and where we are going; in their size and duration they separate our culture from all others, teach us about political life, set our individual and collective priorities, entertain us, and provide bases for social interaction" (p. 496).

The value of a communication approach to campaign analyses is in the recognition that campaigns are exercises in the creation, recreation, and transmission of significant symbols through communication. Communication activities are the vehicles for social action. Thus, despite the difficulty in identifying or measuring impact, campaign communication activities are important elements in the voter decision-making process.

Of the general phases of a presidential campaign (preprimary, primary, conventions, and general campaign), little systematic analysis has been given to the brief but important convention periods. Larry David Smith and Dan Nimmo make a wonderful contribution in demonstrating the role and importance of political conventions in our age of media politics. Today, conventions do more than nominate the party's candidate. In essence, conventions serve as the center stage for the nominee to present issues and self to the American voters. They are, in the eloquence of the authors, "the political orchestration of cordial concurrence."

This study focuses on how leaders orchestrate the event which is viewed as a process of give-and-take among party members, the news media, and various governmental institutions. As telepolitical events, Larry Smith and Dan Nimmo recognize the value of political conventions as social drama presenting "a microcosm of all that *is* American politics."

Cordial Concurrence: Orchestrating National Party Conventions in the Telepolitical Age is an important contribution to the study of politics and political communication for several reasons. Smith and Nimmo offer one of the few systematic studies of the process of political conventions. Their analysis goes beyond what conventions do to include how they fulfill metapolitical and social-psychological functions of American campaign politics. The authors provide genuine insight into how the news media approach covering conventions, thus further enhancing our understanding of the process of the creation of "mediated realities." Finally, this study provides a useful discussion and analysis of the role, function, and future of political conventions in contemporary American politics.

As you will very quickly note, the authors use the recurring metaphor throughout the book of "musical orchestration." The analogy encompasses the complexities of opera, musical composition, and elements of harmony and melody. But, I must confess, to the lover of American politics, it's all just "rock-n-roll!"

Robert E. Denton, Jr.

NOTE

1. See also Garrett O'Keefe, "Political Campaigns and Mass Communication Research," in *Political Communication: Issues and Strategies for Research*, Steven Chaffee, Ed. (Beverly Hills, CA: Sage, 1975), pp. 129–64; and Garrett O'Keefe and Edwin Atwood, "Communication and Election Campaigns" in *Handbook of Political Communication*, Dan Nimmo and Keith Sanders, Eds. (Beverly Hills, CA: Sage, 1981), pp. 329–58.

REFERENCES

Barber, J. (1980). *The Pulse of Politics.* New York: W.W. Norton.
Burke, K. (1969). *A Grammar of Motives.* Berkeley: University of California Press.
Gronbeck, B. (1978). The Functions of Presidential Campaigning. *Communication Monographs, 45,* 268–80.
Gronbeck, B. (1984). Functional and Dramaturgical Theories of Presidential Campaigning. *Presidential Studies Quarterly, 14,* 487–498.
Lazarsfeld, P., Berelson, B. & Gaudet, H. (1948). *The People's Choice,* 2nd ed. New York: Columbia University Press.
McLeod, J. & Becker, L. (1981). The Uses and Gratifications Approach. In D. Nimmo and K. Sanders (Eds.), *Handbook of Political Communication.* Beverly Hills, CA: Sage.
Morley, D. (1990). The Construction of Everyday Life: Political Communication and Somestic Media. In D. Swanson and D. Nimmo (Eds.), *New Directions in Political Communication.* Newbury Park, CA: Sage.

Preface

When television first came upon the political scene in the 1950s there was considerable speculation among politicians, journalists, and scholars about the likely impact on the body politic of sending pictures through the air. The early verdict was that this all-powerful medium would transform politics. When research discounted the effects of TV upon the individual political preferences of citizens, speculation centered on the "marginal" impact of the medium. The contemporary judgment returns to the quality of the first one—namely, as a scholar of our acquaintance insists, "it's all TV."

There is little question that television's current political role is a major one, so much so that we accept the proposition that this is a telepolitical age. Saying that, however, is not to say that politics is nothing but TV. To say that television mediates political realities is not to insist that TV is politics. What people currently take for granted as "television" is, after all, but one of numerous diverse and pluralistic institutional complexes that figure in the fashioning of what citizens encounter as politics in their daily lives. As Kurt and Gladys Lang (1959) implied in a prescient way at the outset of speculation about TV's political role, and continued to suggest almost a quarter of a century later (1983), to take political communication seriously is not only to examine the effects the media have upon people but to consider the transactions the media as social institutions have within the context of a host of other institutions involved in politics. TV's mediation of political realities is but the product of an interinstitutional process.

This book endeavors to take seriously the role of institutions in the study of political communication. It does so within the context of one institutional setting of long historical standing—the quadrennial national party conventions. The focus is the orchestral process that brings together for the only time in American political life specific institutional complexes. That process is, in part, what Aronson (1983) borrowed as James Joyce's "method of a symphony of fragments—styles stridently struck against one another—to make a perfect harmony of hyperbole" (p. 191). However, we argue that convention orchestration strives for more than a harmony of hyperbole. By exploring what that orchestration is all about we seek to broaden our understanding of the interinstitutional mediation of politics.

This book not only examines orchestration; it derives from an attempt to orchestrate the contributions of numerous individuals who gave their time, energies, and gracious cooperation to the project. Foremost is the superintendent of the U. S. Senate Press Gallery, Robert E. Petersen, to whom we dedicate this book. Bob Petersen mentored the first-named author of this work through an internship in the Senate Press Gallery. Later, first in 1984 and then in 1988, he provided press credentials to each political party's conventions that afforded observation of convention activities from the vantage point of front-row seats of the press gallery.

The bulk of this study examines the orchestration of the 1988 Democratic National Convention in Atlanta, Georgia, and the Republican National Convention in New Orleans, Louisiana. We are indebted to a hardworking and imaginative research team that learned quickly to pay attention and go with the flow at both sites—Kaylene Barbe, Perry Kennedy, and Melinda Talbert. At Atlanta we were also encouraged, aided, and abetted by a consultant to the team, Jack Douglas. Mark Wattier, who was undertaking his own research at both conventions, generously shared portions of videotapes of backstage proceedings he made at both sites. We thank as well Dale Wilman of CBS Radio and National Public Radio for his on-location assistance in Atlanta and New Orleans, and Randy Hooker for his guidance in New Orleans.

In addition to personal observations, discussions, and interviews conducted at each party's convention, this study relies on analysis of network TV coverage of each assembly. Without the voluntary efforts of friends, colleagues, and others who recorded that network coverage (on ABC, CBS, CNN, C-SPAN, and NBC), that analysis would have been impossible. Many of those same individuals, as well as others, collected newspaper and magazine accounts of coverage as well. We express thanks to Robert Bellamy, Kevin Brown, Cindy Cooper, John Gray (and the University of Arkansas at Little Rock), Mike Hemphill, Barbara Monfils, Robert Savage (and the University of Arkansas at Fayetteville), Don Singleton, Glenn Smith, Marshall Stephenson, Charlie Stewart (and Purdue University), and David Swanson (and the University of Illinois at Urbana-Champaign) for their archival and collection efforts.

A final data source for this work consists of interviews conducted following the conventions with representatives of political parties, network news organizations, and congressional galleries. We appreciate the time and patience they took to respond to our questions. We cite each such individual in the reference list of this book. For assistance with the transcriptions of the postconvention interviews we extend our gratitude to Karen Varney and, for other administrative assistance, Diana Cable.

We have strived to represent fully in our orchestration the contributions made by each of the musicians we have acknowledged. If our efforts to do so with one voice yield discordant sounds blame not the musicians. As H. L. Mencken (1956) said, "Music is hard for musicians, but easy for pedants and quacks" (p. 548).

Cordial Concurrence

National Party Conventions: The Political Orchestration of Cordial Concurrence

Technically, the first national nominating convention of a political party took place in 1808. The declining Federalists, no longer able to claim that the party's congressional caucus that heretofore had nominated presidential candidates was representative of the party as a whole, turned to a party convention to do its work. That first convention scarcely foreshadowed the arrival or character of the quadrennial gatherings we know today. The Federalist convention was closed to all but those specifically invited and only half of the states sent representatives (Morison, 1911). So it was not until 1831 that the movement toward national nominating conventions began in earnest. In September of that year the little remembered Anti-Masons met in Baltimore to name William Wirt their standard-bearer. And in December, the more formidable National Republicans convened in the same city to nominate Henry Clay. The following year the first national nominating convention of a still surviving political party gathered, also in Baltimore.

That convention of the Democratic party (then also called variously Republicans or Democratic Republicans) had before it but one matter that might spark controversy. It was not whom to nominate for president; the Democratic presidential candidate in the person and persona of Andrew Jackson had already been "endorsed" (i.e., nominated) by several state legislatures. What was at issue was the selection of a vice-presidential candidate, Martin Van Buren or John C. Calhoun. Jackson and his forces realized that the preferred candidate, Van Buren, would have less difficulty being selected via the convention route than any other nominating method, hence used the conclave for that purpose. A final item remained—namely, to formulate measures to reelect Jackson as president.

To that end Democrats drafted an "address" (what today is called the party platform) congenial to Jackson's candidacy. It contained but one resolution:

The convention reposes the highest confidence in the purity, patriotism and talents of Andrew Jackson, and most cordially concurs in the repeated nominations which he has received in various parts of the Union as a candidate for reelection to the office he now fills with so much honor to himself and usefulness to this country.

Substitute George Bush or Michael Dukakis for Andrew Jackson, delete from the address the phrase "for reelection" and insert "election," and the resolution would have provoked no rancor if included in the platform of the Republican or Democratic parties at their national conventions in 1988. Just as the first national convention of a major political party in 1832 did not "nominate" a candidate for president, but instead cordially concurred in repeated endorsements by various state legislatures, so too in 1988 neither major party convened to nominate, but instead to legitimate endorsements by voters in statewide presidential primaries. Democrats meeting in Atlanta in July, and Republicans in New Orleans in August, cordially concurred in "repeated nominations . . . received in various parts of the Union."

In fact, cordial concurrence has been the norm and not the rarity of national nominating conventions since their inception in 1832—at least if the number of roll call votes required to select a presidential candidate are any indicator. Consider, for instance, the Democratic party. In the period 1832–1988 Democrats gathered in convention 41 times to select a party candidate for president of the United States (one convention was deadlocked, forcing a second one the same year). In only slightly less than two-thirds of those conventions (27 out of the 41) the delegates did so on the first roll-call vote. Since the 1936 abolition of the party rule that a two-thirds vote of the delegates, rather than a simple majority, was required to select a presidential nominee, the Democrats have had but one (in 1952) of their total of 15 multiballot conventions between 1832 and 1988. Since their first party convention in 1856 the Republicans have gone to a second or later ballot to select the nominee in but 9 of 34 conventions, the last being in 1948.

First-ballot nominations, of course, do not necessarily mean convention leaders and delegates conduct themselves in a spirit of cordiality, harmony, and charity. For example, in 1948 delegates to the Democratic convention in Philadelphia overwhelmingly concurred in the nomination of Harry Truman for reelection, but the concurrence was scarcely cordial. Intensely bitter conflicts over a civil rights plank in the Democratic platform split the party, resulting in the formation of Strom Thurmond's rival Dixiecrat candidacy during the general election. Two decades later Hubert

Humphrey's 1968 candidacy won the concurrence of two-thirds of Democratic convention delegates on the first roll call, but today we remember the convention for the violence outside the meeting hall and the acrimony within, not for cordiality. First-ballot victories for Republican nominees have also periodically reflected anything but cordial concurrence. Dwight Eisenhower's 1952 nomination on the initial roll call by better than a three-to-one margin came only after a harsh but decisive struggle with the forces of rival Robert Taft in what news headlines bannered as the "Contested Delegate Battle." Similarly, in 1964 the tightly controlled majority bloc of delegates cordial to Barry Goldwater's first-ballot nomination booed his chief challenger, Nelson Rockefeller, a loud reminder of the limits of cordial partisanship.

Yet, no matter how intense the preconvention, convention, and postconvention factional strife, since the era of national nominating conventions began, more often than not the respective parties have departed their quadrennial gatherings voicing for public consumption what the Democrats did in 1832—the "highest confidence in the purity, patriotism, and talents" of their nominee. And, more often than not, they have endeavored to advance the impression that their concurrence in the party's choice was cordial, if not in the beginning then certainly once the selection had been made. Such public voicings and proffered impressions, however, do not just happen. As Niccolò Machiavelli taught, the superficial appearance of things so vital in politics must not be left to chance but instead be the subject of princely calculation.

"MUSIC, THOUGH PRECISE, IS NOT ARTICULATE": TAKING SERIOUSLY THE IMPORTANCE OF POLITICAL ORCHESTRATION

This is a study of how political, media, and professional leaders in a telepolitical age orchestrate the appearance of cordial concurrence at the national nominating conventions of the two major political parties. Given two facts—namely, that (1) it has become increasingly fashionable in recent years for many politicians, scholars, political journalists, and others to dismiss the national political conventions of the two major parties as relics of a bygone age; and (2) several book-length studies of the convention process already exist—a few words are in order regarding why an examination of political orchestration is important and what it adds that other volumes do not.

First, consider the often-repeated dismissals of conventions as "political dinosaurs," a point we return to in far greater detail in Chapter 7. The claim takes several forms. Two were articulated a week after the 1984 Democratic convention by David Burke, a vice-president at ABC News, in an interview conducted on the "CBS Morning News." Attempting to justify ABC's broadcasting of a rerun of an entertainment series, "Hart to Hart," on Tuesday evening of the convention—then abruptly cutting away from the program to cover the address of Jesse Jackson—rather than airing live convention coverage prior to Jackson's address, Burke dismissed the significance of conventions on grounds that presidential primaries, not conventions, are the decision makers and, moreover, "partisan political events that are sculptured for the very fact that we have our cameras there may not be truly a service to the public" (Joyce, 1988, p. 382).

That the party conventions are not decision *makers* is, in itself, not new. Conventions have always tended to be decision *ratifiers*—that is, they put the party label on decisions made elsewhere: compromises and deals struck in state legislatures in an earlier era, then in state conventions run by party machines, in smoke-filled rooms, but rarely openly on the floor of a national convention. Furthermore, they have been decision *publicizers* as well, "sculpturing" convention events for dissemination by newspapers, then radio, now television. As columnist Howard Rosenberg (1988a) noted in coverage of the 1988 Republican conclave, "undoubtedly, these conventions are mainly festivals of propaganda and persuasion aimed at swaying the home audience" (p. 1). We agree in large part with Rosenberg's assessment and with what he adds—namely, that "TV and the election process are now inseparable, with each party's candidate traditionally getting a sizable boost in the polls after its convention is televised." If Rosenberg's appraisal (and others like it) is correct, then inquiry bearing on *how* leaders orchestrate ratification and publicity to achieve an impression of cordial concurrence can enhance understanding of the vital and dynamic relationship among political parties, the mass media, and the electoral process in a teleconvention era.

Another form the dismissal of conventions as dinosaurs takes, however, challenges such a view. Political journalist David Broder (1985) offers a typical expression of this form:

In some respects, it's probably not much of an exaggeration to say the political conventions have become as much a show case for the rival television news organizations as they have a forum where the parties can work out their internal differences, choose their leadership, or project their own issues and appeals to the public. . . . It is no longer the politicians who set the agenda, the timetable, the schedule, or who decide what is perceived by the public from the convention hall. It is largely those television networks. (pp. 5–6)

Broder makes a valid point: TV news organizations (network, cable, regional, and local) exploit party conventions to showcase their talents, styles, and state-of-the-art electronic gadgetry. But, as we shall see in the pages that follow, to say that TV controls agendas, timetables, schedules, impressions, and other aspects of convention politics goes too far. The orchestration of cordial concurrence is a joint process involving the combined efforts of party, news media, professional, and governmental institutions in a continuous give-and-take. As Chapters 5 and 6 describe, the results of that orchestration may sometimes be melodious, sometimes harmonious, sometimes discordant. But they are never determined by a single orchestrator.

Whether convention events are "sculptured" for the TV cameras (the view typified by David Burke), "set" by the TV networks (the widely shared view expressed by David Broder), or the conjoint activities of several institutions, there is little doubt that they are telepolitical events. That telepolitical character contributes to another view that dismisses conventions as being extinct as dinosaurs. It takes the form of carping that telepolitical conventions are prolonged, dull, and out of step with audience viewing tastes and habits. Allegedly buttressing that view, and the contentions that flow from it, are long-term declines in the proportion of the viewing audience tuning into TV network coverage, producing an all-time low of 48 percent for the 1988 Democratic convention, 47 percent for the Republican. Since people do not watch, argue some TV executives, journalists, and critics, there should be drastic cuts in coverage. Said ABC News president Roone Arledge during the 1988 Democratic convention, "the time is clearly here" for changing network coverage: "The two political parties should sit down on their own or maybe with the networks to come up with something more appealing to the American people" (Donlon, 1988, p. 1A). And, "It's hard to justify on purely news grounds preempting a week of prime time" (Hansen, 1988g, p. 19C). NBC News president Lawrence Grossman concurred: "Unless there is a major story there, it could very well be that we would cut back on the amount of time that we would provide for our coverage" (Hansen, 1988g, p. 1C).

We explore these and other proposals for change in the party conventions and their coverage in Chapter 7 and in our Finale. Here, however, we insist that it is premature to fret about the extinction of party conventions on grounds that television audiences are turned off and tune out. A viewing audience with a 47–48 percent share is scarcely meager, either in proportions (only slightly below the average voter turnout in presidential elections) or calculated as total number of viewers. Moreover, that share underestimates the proportions of Americans who follow the party conventions on TV via the Cable Satellite Public Affairs Network (C-SPAN), Cable News Network (CNN), regional TV consortia including Continental United States Communications (CONUS) and Potomac Communications, the plethora of local TV news organizations originating coverage from convention sites, and the established TV news services of each political party, the Democrats' Convention Satellite News Service (CSNS) and the GOP's RNC Network (RNCN). It also ignores sizable radio audiences, readers of daily newspapers and weekly news magazines, and the world-wide audiences of foreign news organizations covering the conventions.

Finally, even if the total numbers of persons exposed to the cordial concurrence orchestrated at national party conventions were small (and we
contend it probably is much larger than guessed), one must also realize
that many within that audience are political activists, opinion leaders, and
influentials. Summary dismissals of conventions as irrelevant to their interests may fall on deaf ears. As Edwin Diamond (1988b) reminded critics
of the Democrats' orchestrated 1988 conclave who, "presumably . . . miss
the blood in the streets" drama of, say, coverage of the 1968 Democratic
convention, there is, after all, this other audience:

If anything, though, this week's convention has demonstrated the value of traditional conventions. Party workers and the volunteers who will run phone banks
and October vote drives have been energized. A sleek herd of prime contributors
have been rounded up by party fund raisers; they are being feted and prepared
for milking. And, the fall campaign begins tonight. (p. 18)

"Some chicken, some neck" Winston Churchill supposedly said during
the Battle of Britain in responding to Adolf Hitler's boast that he would
wring the neck of Britain like a chicken. We suspect that if one could esti-
mate the total size and composition of the viewing, listening, and reading
audience of national party conventions, the conventions too would prove
to be "some chicken, some neck."

The justification for detailed examination of attempts to orchestrate cordial concurrence in telepolitical conventions, however, need not lie solely
in countering claims that conventions themselves are relics of a bygone
political era. Party conventions are, and have been from their earliest days,
elaborate gatherings of the party faithful to rejuvenate their political
juices, celebrate their partisan loyalties, and gird their loins for, as Diamond noted, "the fall campaign [that] begins tonight." In this sense the
national conventions of the two major parties are political spectacles. And
in a deeper sense they are a vital *part* of what political scientist Murray
Edelman (1988) calls "the political spectacle." Spectacle construction, he
writes, consists of:

the contriving of events and the dissemination of news about them to create anxi-
eties and aspirations, insecurities and reassurances, that fuel a search for legitimat-
ing symbols . . . The spectacle is unpredictable and fragmented, so that individuals
are always vulnerable and usually can do little more than react, chiefly by keeping
abreast of the news that concerns them and by acquiescing in the realities it creates.
(p. 123)

In this book we analyze such spectacle construction in the orchestration
of cordial concurrence in the convention setting as, to use Edelman's
words, "the contriving of events and the dissemination of news about
them." Edelman argues that spectacle serves as both political tactic and

mystification, a drama that enhances selected interests over others while both focusing and displacing the attention of spectators. Moreover, the construction of spectacle takes on a life, an imperative, of its own that outlives the drama itself. Historian, music, and social critic Jacques Barzun (1941) wrote well before Edelman that "this drama is also musical, and music, though precise, is not articulate. It does not state or inform, but rather impresses or conveys meanings" (p. 237). This study concentrates on the "precise" but "not articulate" political orchestration that is contemporary conventions in "the political spectacle," an orchestration that we contend, like music, does less to state and inform than it "impresses or conveys meanings."

ORCHESTRATED MELODY VERSUS ORCHESTRATED HARMONY

This focus on the process of convention orchestration sets our study apart from other book-length efforts that have examined the politics of national nominating conventions. It serves no purpose here to review in detail those earlier and contemporary studies, although we will make reference to them as relevant in our discussion of the evolution of convention orchestration in Chapter 1. It is, however, useful to categorize the general subjects dealt with by those studies. Many have examined the origins and history of party nominating conventions (for example, Thomson, 1956; Bishop, 1916; Eaton, 1964; Chase, 1973; Cook, 1976). Others have analyzed nominating conventions as part of the overall electoral process, particularly with an eye toward describing the shifting importance of conventions within a changing political climate (including, among others, Stoddard, 1938, 1948; Davis, 1972, 1983; Pomper, 1963; Chase, 1974; Marshall, 1981; Shafer, 1988). There have also been noteworthy efforts to compile the key proceedings of party conventions (McKee, 1906; Bain, 1960; Bain & Parris, 1973). Certainly the most ambitious study to date that gathered and analyzed evidence pertaining to the nominating process per se at conventions was the comprehensive study of David, Goldman, and Bain (1960a, 1960b). There have also been accounts, some anecdotal and others systematic, of particular conventions, including H. L. Mencken's (1932, 1956) biting commentaries; Murray's (1976) study of the 103 ballots it took Democrats to nominate a candidate in 1924; an anthology of separate studies pertaining to convention politics in 1960 (Tillett, 1962); Farber's (1988) detailed description of the 1968 Democratic convention; and Reeves's (1977) recollections of the 1976 Democratic convention.

Finally, a few of the aforementioned studies contain abbreviated accounts of how convention politics has changed in the electronic age, especially as a result of televised proceedings (noteworthy are Davis, 1983; Shafer, 1988). Two that address that topic specifically are Thomson's

(1956) account of the first widely televised conventions in 1952, and the personal recountings of J. Leonard Reinsch (1988), radio and TV director for Democratic national conventions in three decades, depicting how conventions sought to exploit the electronic media from radio in the 1940s through TV in the 1980s. Joining these book-length studies is a host of academic articles by communication and political science scholars that explore convention voting, rules, delegate selection, oratory, and more.

These various histories, records of proceedings, empirical analyses, case studies, and anecdotal renditions are a rich source of the decisions made at party conventions, how, and why; they also recount shifts in journalistic practices that influence those decisions, how, and why. Examples of political controversies and intrigues, bargains struck, how electoral reform influenced convention politics, and the impact on convention decision making and on public impressions of the televising of conventions abound. The process that emerges is linear: first, party factions conflict (over nominees, platform planks, etc.); second, party leaders (be they candidates, bosses, managers, or others) forge compromises between factions; third, party leaders publicize resulting pre-, ongoing, and postconvention decisions to political journalists via a variety of techniques; and, fourth, journalists report the decisions, then probe for the reasons behind them and/or whether such decisions are "real" or only facades masking unresolved and bitter rivalries and self-seeking motives.

There is much to be learned from linear accounts of convention politics, just as there is much to be learned, and enjoyed, in listening to music simply for the sake of the melodies. In a musical melody score, one note follows another to form a tune. Enjoyable as that may be to the ear, there is also something to be learned and enjoyed in listening to harmonies, when different instruments of diverse types and numbers make simultaneous noises heard in combination. To the extent that previous accounts of the politics of national conventions inform us about orchestration politics it is primarily about the orchestration of melody. Our concern, by contrast, is with the orchestration of harmony, of cordial concurrence.

The research underlying this volume consists of a detailed analysis of the orchestration of cordial concurrence in the 1988 national nominating conventions of the two major parties. We supplement that case by a less detailed analysis of orchestration at each party's conventions in 1984 and by piecing together evidence from previous studies suggesting cases of convention orchestration. That research indicates to us that the political process that is the orchestration of cordial concurrence is not linear but transactional, not melody but harmony. It is a process demanding the fashioning and refashioning of a concurrence, beginning years in advance of any given convention. For example, the Democrats formally began searching for the site of the 1992 convention more than two years before the event, and decided upon New York City in July 1990; Republicans announced Houston's Astrodome as their 1992 site in January 1991. That process takes into account and involves exchanges between party leaders, convention managers, governing officials, news executives, working journalists, and a host of diverse interests. The degree that orchestration of cordial concurrence is harmonious, or at a minimum is not cacophonous, has a great deal to do with the what, how, and why of the party gathering and its nominee depicted in news accounts prior to, during, and after the week of each party's national convention.

"TO WRITE A SUCCESSFUL OPERA A KNOWLEDGE OF HARMONY AND COUNTERPOINT IS NOT ENOUGH; ONE MUST BE ALSO A SORT OF A BARNUM"

So penned the iconoclastic journalist H. L. Mencken (1956, p. 546), who was prone to write about all of politics in precisely the same vein. Politics, of course, is not music and music is not politics. However, even though *orchestration* is a term more familiar to the musical art form, it is no stranger to the political art form as well. Musical orchestration can, and often does, consist of nothing more elaborate than scoring a simple tune or rehearsing a barbershop quartet. But orchestration is certainly key to more elaborate productions—for example, cantatas, chorales, oratorios, and the most lavish of all, operas. In similar fashion political orchestration can consist of something as familiar as the prepared remarks of a speaker, or arranging a dinner between a lobbyist and a legislator, yet extend to elaborate ceremonies, inaugurals, coronations, and most certainly national political conventions.

Given the parallels between musical and political orchestration, we contend that it will advance our understanding of the fashioning of cordial concurrence at national political conventions if we begin by exploring how such orchestration occurs in an equally elaborate art form, the opera. Let us therefore introduce our search for how cordial concurrence is orchestrated by a brief comparison of the parallel elements in musical operas and political conventions, a comparison that will prove useful in each ensuing chapter of this volume.

Writing "in defense of politics" as an activity that is autonomous in its own right—one that can't be deduced from or reduced to economic, social, psychological, or spiritual sources—political scientist Bernard Crick (1962) spelled out the logic of politics:

Politics arises from accepting the fact of the simultaneous existence of different groups. . . . The political method of rule is to listen to these other groups so as to consolidate them as far as possible, and to give them a legal position, a sense of security, some clear and reasonably safe means of articulation, by which these other groups can and will speak freely. Ideally politics draws all these groups into each other so that they each and together can make a positive contribution toward the general business of government. (p. 14)

Thus considered, orchestration politics in national conventions also, if cordial concurrence is to emerge, accepts the simultaneous existence of different groups, listens, provides them a legal voice, and consolidates a "positive contribution" toward the general business.

Writing about the "magic of opera" and the logic that characterizes musical opera in its own right, Knapp (1972) observes how musical "discursiveness [a discursiveness already noted in Barzun's remark that music "though precise, is not articulate"] is given form and balance by repetition . . . by anticipation of what is to come, by endings or breaks that signify a small or large section" (p. 14). Unlike dramatic verse that requires only a few lines to establish its point, or visual art forms that require even less, musical composition—especially operatic—demands time for the synchronization and consolidation of diverse instruments, voices, and motives. Thus is operatic orchestration, which requires lengthy staging of acts and scenes that may take hours, even days for audiences to view, likened to a political convention requiring, in 1988, four full days of attendence by delegates and four evenings of prime time for TV viewing audiences.

Orchestration in music and politics consumes time, time to balance in delicate ways the diverse elements that constitute an opera or a convention. We will be identifying those elements throughout this work, but consider here the various types of musical-political conduct involved in elaborate orchestrations. Critical theorist Theodore Adorno wrote treatises on music and on politics, as well as many other subjects. In his *Introduction to the Sociology of Music* (1976) he describes various ways people enter into the music experience. All are pertinent to opera; notice how each has a political parallel in national conventions as well.

Adorno builds his typology of musical conduct on the basis of how well people listen to music and what they can hear. Even in the case of elaborate musical productions such as opera, what one can detect in the inner composition by one's listening influences impressions of the visual spectacle manipulated via staged settings, costumes, props, and so on. This is a point not lost on students of other forms of conduct—for example, commercial advertising. Thus Ries and Trout (1983) offer evidence to support their argument that "the mind works by ear," and continue, "We're not saying that the visual doesn't play an important role. Of course it does. What we are saying is that the verbal should be the driver and the pictures should reinforce the words. All too often [in commercial advertising] the opposite is the case" (p. 6). In a similar vein political conduct requires a capacity for listening. As many scholars insist, "politics is talk" and "talk about talk" (Roelofs, 1967; Hall, 1972; Bell, 1975). Detection of the inner composition of political talk, although that talk may not always be "music to the ears," places a premium on discerning the difference between politicians who "say what they mean" and those who "mean what they say."

With that caveat—to which we will return from time to time—on Adorno's use of listening conduct as basic to music, and by extension to politics, consider his typology of listeners for what it can tell us about convention orchestration. The first type is the *expert*. Here is, says Adorno (1976), "the fully conscious listener who tends to miss nothing and at the same time, at each moment, accounts to himself for what he has heard" (pp. 4–5). This is a discerning student of orchestration, melodic and harmonic: "Spontaneously following the course of music, even complicated music, he hears the sequence, hears past, present, and future moments together so that they crystallize into a meaningful context." And, who are these experts? "Today this type may be more or less limited to the circle of professional musicians," and "not all of them meet its criteria."

Expertise in political listening too calls for "spontaneously following the course" of events, hearing sequence and "past, present, and future moments together." In the orchestration of cordial concurrence that is convention politics the expert listener is, as in music, a professional. In the telepolitical age that translates to professional orchestrators; and, like musical professionals, not all of them meet the criteria of expert. As we shall see in this volume, they have diverse titles: the convention's chief executive officer, convention manager, director of communications, director of news media operations, director of satellite news service, and the like. Titles aside, the respective political parties seek out these professionals for their experience. They have a record of every four years engaging in harmonizing overall convention activities, listening for discords, adjusting to changes in tempo, and managing an impression of convention cordiality.

"Making experts of all listeners," writes Adorno, "would of course be an inhumanly utopian enterprise" (p. 5). The absence of a professional musical education, formal or via experience, pressures of making a living in nonmusical ways, and other time-consuming demands render the impossibility. But it is possible to be a *good listener* "as opposed to the expert." The good listener too "hears beyond musical details, makes connections spontaneously, and judges for good reasons, not just by categories of prestige and by arbitrary taste, but he is not, or not fully, aware of the technical and structural implications." For, "having unconsciously mastered its immanent logic, he understands music about the way we understand our own language even though virtually or wholly ignorant of its grammar and syntax" (p. 5).

In convention politics good listeners are to be found among some, but not all, persons who are *partisan* and *media* orchestrators as contrasted with *professional* orchestrators. Partisan orchestrators are party leaders working on behalf of contending candidates and/or factions seeking to manage a victorious outcome in struggles for nomination and/or the platform, and, if not victory, at least a face-saving result within the atmosphere of cordial concurrence. Media orchestrators include, first, professional media personnel: executive producers of convention coverage for the three commercial over-the-air television networks; cable networks such as CNN or C-SPAN; regional TV consortia (CONUS, Potomac); local TV news outlets; producers of pooled coverage available to network and cable stations; and the managing editors for convention coverage of daily newspapers, newsweeklies, political journals, and other publications. A second set of media orchestrators are not part of the media at all but are paid employees of the federal government. These are the superintendents of the House and Senate press galleries responsible for the critical task of credentialing news organizations; lobbying on their behalf for floor passes, podium passes, and work space; and assigning that work space. Like good musical listeners, partisan and media orchestrators judge "for good reasons, not just by categories of prestige and an arbitrary taste" but are not always aware of the technical and structural implications of their acts for cordial concurrence.

Adorno's third type of listener is the *culture consumer*: "a copious, sometimes a voracious listener, well-informed, a collector of records." And, "he respects music as a cultural asset, often as something a man must know for the sake of his own social standing; this attitude runs the gamut from an earnest sense of obligation to vulgar snobbery" (p. 6). For the culture consumer the "joy of consumption . . . music 'gives' to him outweighs his enjoyment of the music itself as a work of art that makes demands on him" (p. 7). Hence, the culture consumer is inclined to bend with the wind, liking and not liking compositions as they happen to be in vogue; "conformism and conventionality largely mark" the consumer. If the operas of Richard Wagner are "in," the culture consumer is there applauding; if "out," the consumer is there but likely to "call Wagner names" (p. 7).

Culture consumers occupy seats and tread the foyers at political conventions just as they do at operatic performances. Some are party members moving from one bandwagon to another. More likely, however, we find culture consumers among members of the working news media—print journalists, still photographers, TV floor correspondents, and network anchors. As voracious listeners they turn their ears to convention controversy; endeavoring to be well-informed they pick the brains of politicians and delegates; and as collectors of records they accumulate one-liners, sound-bites, and gossip. For sake of "social standing" (i.e., career advancement), the journalist often relates to politics as Adorno says musical consumers do to music, with a "fetishistic touch" whereby "the standard he consumes by is the prominence of the consumed" (p. 7)—that is, the story that is a "good story" by virtue of its conformism and conventionality. Thus, for example, responding to journalists' judgments prior to the 1988 Democratic National Convention that it would be "dull and boring," the leader of the Ohio delegation retorted, "unless there is blood running on the floor, you people aren't satisfied," thereby asserting that the standard consumed by journalists is but the prominence of the consumed!

The fourth type of musical conduct described by Adorno is the *emotional listener*. For this listener music triggers "instinctual stirrings." This type "may indeed respond with particular strength to music of an obvious emotional hue," is "easily moved to tears," "fiercely resists all attempts to make him listen structurally" (pp. 8–9). It is not hard to discover the emotional listeners at a political convention. They are the delegates whose convention experience, as with an emotional listener's presence at opera, works "to cover the drudges and notorious 'tired businessmen' who seek, in a realm that will not affect their lives, to compensate for what they must deny themselves otherwise" (p. 9). Certainly not all convention delegates listen purely emotionally to politics. Yet, as we shall see in Chapters 5 and 6, the chanting response at the 1988 Democratic convention to Senator Edward Kennedy's "Where was George?," the tears of delegates when Jesse Jackson urged that "you don't know the me that makes me me," and the crescendo at the Republican convention for George Bush's "I am that man!" bravado provide more than a mere hint of the emotional dimension of convention conduct.

Resentment listeners constitute Adorno's fifth type, and they too populate convention halls as well as opera houses. What is a resentment listener?

He scorns the official life of music as washed-out and phantasmic, but he does not strive beyond it; rather, he flees back of that life, back to times which he fancies are proof against reification, against the dominant commodity character. In his rigidity he pays tribute to the very reification he opposes. (p. 10)

Substitute *politics* for *music* in Adorno's statement and we have a particular type common to convention listening; that is, the political critic who disdains the official life of politics as the musical critic often scorns the official life of music. Critics (billed variously as commentators, political analysts, seasoned veteran journalists, political experts, media critics, resident pundits) appear on the convention floor, in anchor booths, on the press podium, off the speaker's podium, and in the columns of news dailies and newsweeklies. They provide instant analysis of what did and did not happen, whether it was spontaneous or stage managed, and the prospects of events for the party, election, nation, and Free World. More frequently than not their dismay and resentment at the whole performance is apparent to one and all.

Next, "the quantitatively most significant of all the types," according to Adorno, is the *entertainment listener* for whom music is entertainment "and no more" (p. 14). Given the large proportions of this type among the general population, along with the fact that musical extravaganzas must appeal to vast numbers to survive financially, there is little surprise that musical compositions and spectacles seek to entertain more than elevate sensibilities or enlighten tastes.

Compare operas and conventions in the age of TV. Often, in viewing opera on TV the pace seems slow, set design superficial, representations of life silly. Knapp (1972) laments: "In a telegenic age when visual appearance has become as important as the brain or message behind it, the contradiction between image and reality on the operatic stage is often painful" (pp. 10–11). Television inverts the artistic emphasis of opera. On stage the *balance* of sound and vision is, in order, (1) singing line and orchestra, (2) picture, and (3) intelligibility of words. On TV the order becomes (1) picture, (2) singing line and intelligibility of words, and (3) orchestra (Bornoff, 1968). *Opera is no longer construed as opera; it becomes television.* The balance between listening and viewing is replaced by the dominance of viewing. So too do national conventions shift from partisan events as such to television programs, with the logic of TV imposing action on its political subject matter just as televised opera imposes action on musical subject matter. In an opera house music is the priority, but on television the picture must entertain; in a convention hall politics are the priority, but on television, again, the picture must entertain.

Finally there are the "musically *indifferent, the unmusical,* and the *antimusical*" (Adorno, 1976, p. 17). And, as any observer of U.S. campaigns and elections would testify, there are the politically indifferent, apolitical, and antipolitical. For them the orchestration of cordial concurrence goes unheard, unseen.

A comparison of Adorno's types of musical conduct with those in convention orchestration suggests the similarities of musical and political listeners. Elaborate musical spectacles, such as opera, and political spectacles, such as national conventions, are parallel in other ways as well. To begin with both musical operas and political conventions originated as elitist creations predicated on nostalgic longings for days gone by. With opera, the Florentine *camerata* sought to recreate Greek theatre by setting poetry to music. For conventions, the political elite endeavored to extend democracy's participatory qualities (or at least the illusion thereof) through a widely heralded forum for the expression of the people's will. When opera originated as an art form in the 16th century, music was in an embryonic stage. By the same token, when party conventions originated in the early 19th century, American democracy was in its infancy. Interestingly, neither musical operas nor party conventions achieved their original objectives. Opera moved from simplistic music designed simply to celebrate poetry, to a form consisting of elementary poetry surrounded by elaborate music. The national convention, by comparison, facilitated an unexpected evolution from a faction-oriented construction of democracy toward a party-oriented view that consolidated competing factions under the umbrella of a two-party system.

Chapter 1 provides detail on the historical evolution of the orchestration of cordial concurrence via convention politics. A few words are appropriate here comparing these developments with those of operatic orchestration. Just as the convention's evolution helped the two-party system define American democracy, opera's emergence was a pivotal point in the history of music. The movement away from the choral compositions of the church toward secular solo voices is directly attributable to the *camerata's* innovation. For subject matter the Florentines turned to mythology; they relied on harpsichords, lutes, and flutes to provide a light musical background for poetic readings. Ewen (1972) tells us Rinuccini's *Dafne* (the first opera) consisted of merely a prologue and six scenes. More important, however, is the fact that the three characters in the opera "sang rather than spoke their lines" with brief interludes of "dance or a choral number" (p. 9) to relieve the monotony of continuous singing.

With time, these simplistic productions shifted from emphases on poetry to instrumentation. Still, the extent of this movement was wholly contingent upon cultural context: the Italians continued to stress singing over instrumentation; the Germans emphasized the production's instrumental qualities. Relatively simple plots dominated both schools for some time, yet their diversity of emphases not only represented turning points in opera's development but they had implications for all of music as well. The American Founding Fathers were no more prescient in anticipating the emergence of a two-party system than the *camerata* in foreseeing the rise of instrumentally dominated opera. Certainly the first nominating convention of a major party in 1808, the Federalists—like Rinuccini's *Dafne*—did not even hint at the arrival or character of the elaborate spectacles we know today in the telepolitical, teledramatic age.

Although the principal focus of both opera and conventions has remained constant across the ages (i.e., dramatic portrayal through music and the cordial concurrence behind a predetermined candidate), each spectacle has evolved from a talent-based entity to a vast bureaucratic production. During the early days of opera and of conventions, virtuoso talents were free to do as they pleased. The show was built around stars with few (or no) standardized performances. This is no longer the case. The contemporary party convention, like the musical opera, follows a tightly woven script that dictates virtuoso performances; if they occur at all, they do so under controlled circumstances. Just as the appearance of printed music created a series of "standards" for composers, directors, and talents to adapt to their artistic ends, the party convention invokes similar "standards" designed to strike identical responsive chords among loyalists of diverse coalitions. "We want them all singing out of the same hymnal," a comment made by the manager of the 1988 Republican National Convention when interviewed for this study, capsulizes how standardization has replaced spontaneity in the orchestration of cordiality. Prime-time TV still focuses on political celebrities, but these prima donnas sing notes carefully scored well in advance in cooperation with the convention's orchestrators.

These orchestrators (i.e., nonperforming and ancillary personnel associated with conventions), as is the case with operas, constitute bureaucracies as elaborate in scope as the spectacles they stage. The orchestration of any production—be it an opera, a dramatic stage play, a political convention, or a summit meeting of world leaders—moves through preproduction, production, and postproduction stages. Each phase requires the coordination not only of the performing artists but of numerous off-stage personnel as well. For example, in a manner paralleling that wherein technical innovations in lighting, sound reproduction, and stage design added a host of nonperforming artists to the opera company or house, political parties now employ set designers, stage directors, and TV producers for the staging of their spectacles.

To suggest the scope of the techno-bureaucratic complex involved in the orchestration of both musical and political spectacles, consider here in a preliminary way three sets of personnel. (We describe the phases and personnel involved in convention politics in greater detail in Chapters 2, 3, and 4.) There are, of course, the *performing artists*. In opera these include conductors, singers, and musical critics. In political conventions, the conductors are the professional managers and media consultants alluded to earlier who are retained by both parties to direct the show; political singers are the various presiding officers, speakers, and the delegates (who often act as members of the chorus or as "extras," as they do in operatic productions); and critics consist of media critics, journalistic pundits, and, occasionally, scholars—the resentful listeners in Adorno's typology.

Reflect on each singly. That conventions have evolved to a point that professional producers and directors control the event is, of course, beyond question. As a conductor directs the music from the conductor's pit, so a party-selected director controls the convention's unfolding score, usually from a TV control room. Convention speakers, the equivalent to operatic singers, appear in three roles: solo performances from the rostrum, solo and choral appearances by delegates, and in video creations of party filmmakers. Assuredly, talent is talent and, therefore, some performers are easy to direct, others are not. Convention conductors are deeply frustrated, as we shall see later, when their singers improvise and deviate from the strategically scored script. Moreover, as with their operatic counterparts, conductors encounter difficulties in executing their choral segments. Though the chorus's harmonizing contributes considerably to the show's aesthetics, the presence on the set of the delegate-chorus is difficult to manage. Finally, critics abound in the convention setting. Opera never had as many self-styled and professional critics, perhaps to opera's benefit. To the degree that virtually every journalist covering a national convention may feel compelled to critique some aspect of the spectacle, critics far outnumber any other single group of conventioneers. No doubt the presence of such a large critical community sometimes poses problems for the performing, nonperforming, and ancillery personnel associated with the spectacular show. We address the critic's role in Chapter 7.

A second key set of convention personnel consists of nonperforming artists. In musical opera these include composers, stage directors, and stage designers. In party conventions composers constitute orchestral teams under the direction of the chief executive officer (for the Democrats) and the convention manager (for the Republicans). A variety of specialists handle technicalities of stage direction and design. The Republicans function much like an established opera house with a host of experienced orchestrators operating within a rich tradition of stage production; the Democrats in recent conventions have changed their personnel with regularity as well as their theories of dramatic production. As a result, the GOP maintains a small group of seasoned professionals who design sets and coordinate stage direction, a cadre not available to Democrats.

Both parties, however, have elaborate composing operations orchestrating a coherent set of themes throughout the four-day party production. Central speech units, message committees, and "choral hymnals" are the products of composing artists. Since conventions have moved away from being talent-dominated productions, the composer's role has increased proportionately. The translation of established "standards" (the political equivalent of the musical "golden oldie" or the operatic leitmotif) into popular renditions places considerable demands on convention composers. Like the librettist who must subordinate personal writing inclinations to the musician's work, party speech writers and film producers must conform to the tune that is the product of the convention composer's pen.

A third set of convention personnel vital to the production are the ancillary personnel. The ancillary personnel consist of party personnel—administrators, managers, and staff—as well as administrative units external to convention personnel per se. Party personnel include party leaders and professional consultants responsible to the respective parties. The administrative structures of the national chairs and the national committees, along with professional consultants and the various campaign organizations, function as operatic boards of directors and impresarios. They are responsible for financing, facilities coordination, promotion, and evaluation. External administrative units essential to convention orchestration are numerous. The superintendents of the House and Senate press galleries, radio and television galleries, photographers' galleries, and periodical galleries join the television network pool producers, the executive structures of the five TV networks (ABC, CBS, CNN, C-SPAN, and NBC) and other media organizations (local, state, national, and foreign), and the host committees of the cities holding the convention to coordinate convention logistics with the parties and representatives of the various presidential campaigns. These activities typically differ in their orchestration for Democratic and Republican conventions, yet, as we will see, there are areas where interparty coordination is emerging.

The following pages describe how these three sets of convention personnel interact in different ways in the three stages of convention orchestration. As a brief prelude to that discussion, in the *preproduction* phase managers and administrators struggle over the logistics of where to hold the convention (site selection) and the distribution of hotels and work space, communications arrangements, transportation, security, entertainment, labor-management negotiations, and much, much more. Nonperforming artists are also extremely active during preproduction. Composers and stage directors coordinate set design, the performers' movements, camera locations, lighting, audio, and—eventually—the score itself. Although the two parties undertake these preproduction activities differently, activity among both Democrats and Republicans during this phase is intense. While performing artists are not quite as active in preproduction, there is movement. Critics attend the party-media walk-throughs (early visits to the convention hall and work areas months in advance) once the site has been determined; speakers lobby for performance times; and filmmakers produce their creations.

Of course, the intensity of activity increases as show time nears, the *production* phase. For both internal and external ancillary personnel, much of their work is completed by show time. The score and script are set, the actors are in place, the critics are seated, and the curtain rises. Primary attention shifts to the performing artists as the ancillary and nonperforming artists sit back, try to anticipate what can go wrong, and make plans to cope accordingly. Once the show is over *postproduction* activities wrap up the spectacle. During this phase critics reflect on their daily reactions and offer thoughtful responses; opinion polls indicate the show's success or failure; and ancillary personnel assemble to evalute the overall production. In fact, in 1989 a blue ribbon commission was formed to examine the effectiveness of and recommend changes in convention orchestration. We examine their deliberations in Chapter 7.

Thus, not only have both productions moved away from improvisation toward standardization, they have spawned intricate bureaucracies with specialized roles and divisions of labor that must be coordinated in the shows' mulitiphased orchestration. In the process both the musical opera and the party convention have evolved into techno-bureaucratic spectacles in ways the founders of neither could have prophesied. Aside from their evolution from elitist gatherings to technological spectacles, party conventions and musical operas share other features. First, both are culturally bound phenomena. The content and form of opera is wholly contingent upon its cultural context. That Italian opera differs from its French, German, and English counterparts is certain. Standards of evaluation recognize this: to interpret Italian *opera buffa* in terms of, say, German *singspiel*, though both are comic operas, one must accept that their content and delivery differ immensely owing to cultural heritages. Similarly, U.S. conventions are radically different from, say, the annual party conferences that occur in Great Britain, Australia, or Canada. They pursue distinctly U.S. ends through distinctly U.S. rituals. Consequently, in order to appreciate the intricacies of convention demonstrations, roll calls, and media coverage, the critic must accept the production's cultural independence.

Second, both musical operas and party conventions are ritually oriented and ritual laden. An opera displays particular organizing features that contribute to both its artistic expression and its interpretation. Operas open with preludes or overtures; scenes flow through combinations of recitatives and arias; music provides scenic transitions; audiences applaud and critics carp. These ritualistic acts manifest themselves differently owing to cultural context, yet they create common expectations within everyone—ranging from composers or conductors to performing artists to audiences and critics. The convention's podium oratory, platform debates, demonstrations, roll calls, films, and so on also feature ritualistic traits. These activities *are* the convention. Just as the presentation of drama through music gives us opera, the symbolic constructions generated through convention oratory, films, demonstrations, and voting constitute conventions. These ritual enactments represent the organizing principles of spectacle construction. Although they have evolved over time, these rituals are raw materials shaped, within limits, by production planners.

Third, both conventions and opera are products of delicate organizational balances. An opera results from a multilevel series of cooperative labors. The coordination of musical arrangement, theatrical content and movement, and set design requires conductors, directors, and stage managers working together toward a single artistic goal. The administrative personnel associated with an opera house or company must understand the needs of both performing and nonperforming artists. This systemic symmetry between ancillary personnel, performing artists, and nonperforming artists is the focal point of the production process. Conventions, too, are cooperative productions. Party officials or administrators, campaign operatives, media representatives, governmental entities, and a variety of professional consultants orchestrate convention planning. Though parties—like opera companies—work in different ways, the diversity of elements involved in this interinstitutional production reflects the spectacle's magnitude.

Lastly, both a convention and an opera are representational expressions;

therefore, they may extend toward the absurd. Opera's reliance on fantas-
tic situations and supernatural acts is central to its artistic expression.
Characters die on stage only to rise again and recant their demise, or turn
to the audience and utter their most private thoughts by way of asides. Unlike the more naturalistic portrayals of movies or television shows, opera
condones chaos, which, of course, provides for both a diversity of expression and interpretation. The convention shares this representational quality through its very existence. The "national party" does not exist (and
never did), but every four years the convention orchestrates a reality that
suggests it does. To demonstrate the inclusive qualities of this nonentity,
convention orchestrators resort to representational acts. For instance,
groups with little influence within the party's reigning coalition receive
special attention in platforms, roll calls, and demonstrations. These representational rituals operate as music applied to movement, shaping strategically conceived realities for the artistic and persuasive ends of operas
and conventions, respectively.

PROBING THE ORCHESTRAL EXPERIENCE: DATA
SOURCES FOR THE STUDY

This study rests on a substantial body of data. That data consist principally of direct observations; extensive interviews with convention orchestrators, journalists, and critics; content analysis of news media coverage,
print and televised, of conventions; and published documents. Although
the principal focus of the study is upon the national conventions of the
Democratic and the Republican parties in 1988, it is buttressed by similar
data from both party conventions in 1984, primary and secondary analyses of materials pertaining to conventions held since the ushering in of the
televised conventions beginning in 1948, and historical materials dealing
with the evolution of party conventions.

Conducting the direct observation was a research team consisting of the
co-authors of this volume and four additional members. The team attended both the Democratic National Convention in Atlanta, Georgia, for
a week-long period in July 1988 and the Republican National Convention
in New Orleans, Louisiana, for a similar period in August 1988. At each
convention members had press credentials to the convention work site
(the World Congress Center in Atlanta, the Hyatt Regency Hotel and the
Louisiana Superdome in New Orleans) and shared credentials for seats
and working space in the press gallery in each convention hall (the Omni
in Atlanta and the Superdome in New Orleans). Members of the research
team attended all convention sessions, selected press conferences and
press briefings, and conducted conversations with convention managers,
media liaisons, working journalists of the U.S. and foreign press, delegates, and party leaders. In addition, four members of the research team

attended hearings of the Commission on National Political Conventions, held in Washington, D.C., in April 1989.

During the week of each party's 1988 national convention members of the research team conducted focused interviews with working journalists covering the convention and with media critics assigned by their news organizations to analyze print and TV coverage of each convention. Team members conducted interviews with 84 such journalists and/or critics at the two convention sites. Following the convention, in 1989, the co-authors conducted extensive, focused personal interviews with 21 key convention orchestrators—convention managers, consultants, party press directors, party satellite news directors, executive producers of the various television networks, and officials of the U.S. House and Senate press and radio/TV galleries.

The research team also taped and analyzed all televised convention coverage of both the 1988 Democratic and Republican National Conventions for five national networks—ABC, CBS, CNN, C-SPAN, and NBC. In addition, logs of coverage by the Democrats' Convention Satellite News Service were available to the authors. The research reported here is also supplemented by analysis of the content of televised coverage of each party's convention in 1984 by ABC, CBS, C-SPAN, and NBC and by thematic analysis of 1988 convention coverage by major daily newspapers and news services.

Finally, this research draws upon a variety of documents made available to the authors including transcripts of convention addresses; convention press guides, schedules, and organization charts; seating, work space, and budget plans employed by credentialing authorities; TV network notebooks describing details of planned coverage of both major party conventions in 1988; and videotape and transcript records of testimony given at hearings conducted before the Commission on National Political Conventions in 1989 as well as commission reports.

A PROGRAM GUIDE TO THE APPRECIATION OF CONVENTION ORCHESTRATION

This study of the orchestration of cordial concurrence in the telepolitical age derives from the view that such orchestration is the joint activity of a host of convention planners. Orchestrators are not limited to workers of candidates and parties but the interinstitutional mediation of three key complexes: (1) professional convention managers and consultants; (2) media personnel (in executive and reportorial positions) from print and electronic journalism, and drawn from national, regional, state, local, and foreign news organizations; and (3) public officials charged with representing the plural, diverse, and competing interests of working journalists in a partisan milieu. How that orchestration occurs and the results it produces constitute the subject of this volume.

Associated with the key theme in this volume of interinstitutional mediation are several others introduced in this Prelude: national party conventions are integral to primary-general election campaigns, not relics of the past; cordial concurrence, with the emphasis on producing the *cordial* describes today, as it has more frequently than not, the major function of conventions rather than that of nominating; image building via conventions, for both the party and candidates, incorporates manipulations of processes and proxemics as well as of manifest message content; imperatives emerge from party conventions that continue to operate long after the final gavels sound; and orchestrated teleconventions are a portion of a larger teleparty politics that is party politics in the age of mass media.

We address these various themes, or leitmotifs, as follows. We begin in Chapter 1 with a selective history of party conventions, emphasizing how the orchestration process has evolved. We describe in greater detail the movement away from virtuoso-dominated concert halls toward the vast bureaucratic opera houses that minimize improvisation in favor of standardization. As concert halls excited the aural senses, the shift to opera houses excited the visual; we shall see that the aural-to-visual shift appears politically in the continuing effort to discover convention sites amenable to sophisticated staging.

Chapter 2 examines the intricate networks of production personnel briefly described earlier. We examine how the constituent components of our three institutional complexes—parties, media, and press galleries—parallel the ancillary, performing, and nonperforming artists in musical orchestration. The major parties differ in how they coordinate the production effort and, as we shall see, the orchestration differences carry political consequences.

The three phases of the convention production's development introduced earlier occupy our interest in Chapter 3. From site selection and assorted preproduction activities through the staging of the production itself and finally the postproduction, we present the inner workings of the vast interinstitutional mediation that constructs the quadrennial convention spectacle.

Chapter 4 analyzes the separate Democratic and Republican orchestrated stage productions at each party's four-day convention. What happens on stage both reflects and refracts the continuing relations among convention conductor-leaders on the podium, working journalists in the pit, delegates on the floor, spectators and hangers-on in the balconies, and TV anchors and analysts in the boxes. This chapter mirrors the on-stage presence of a convention as it unfolds, sometimes following the orchestration smoothly, sometimes with discordant sounds.

In Chapters 5 and 6 we turn to the qualitative and quantitative analysis of news media coverage of the 1988 Democratic and Republican conventions. Although each party's set of convention conductors strive to present a four-night extravaganza unified in song and story—for example, comparable to Richard Wagner's ambitious four-night operatic *Ring* cycle—what viewers at home witness varies—sometimes an oratorio, a chorale, a chanty, a chorus, a chant, or a solo, depending upon the TV network of preference covering the spectacle.

Any evening's performance, and the entire four-night production, as with a musical spectacle, is subject to review and criticism. Chapter 7 examines the reviews of convention proceedings and coverage by various political, media, and reformists critics—namely, editorial, op-ed, and columnist responses; TV network analysts; party spin specialists; media critics of the dailies and weeklies; and media watchdog organizations. With a focus on calls for reform of the national convention process, the chapter reviews the hearings of the 1989 Commission on National Political Conventions that brought together party leaders, convention personnel, executive and working journalists, and governing officials.

We close this volume with a Finale that considers the implications of our analysis for understanding the orchestration of cordial concurrence, the place of convention politics in presidential elections, and interinstitutional mediation as a vital feature in the construction of the contemporary political spectacle—as it is in the construction of entertainment spectacles, especially musical. Our curtain rises with scenes from convention history as we examine the evolution that produced our telepolitical assembly.

Chapter One

From Concert Halls to Opera Houses: The Evolution of National Convention Orchestration

Opening their comprehensive account of the politics of national party conventions, David, Goldman, and Bain (1960a) note how "in a world of constant political change" conventions "are among the oldest important political institutions to be found in any country" (p. 1). The convention has endured, the authors argue, because of its ability to adapt to the changing political environment by responding both to "conscious action" and "unrecognized pressures." They contend that "the more clearly" convention activities "are seen and understood, the more readily it will be possible to devise efforts designed to improve their effectiveness . . . and the easier it will be to stave off changes that might be adverse to the general welfare" (p. 7).

The purpose of this book is to see and understand a particular convention activity "more clearly"—one that political scientist Pendleton Herring pointed to a half-century ago, well before television arrived on the convention scene. Herring (1940) spoke of the convention as "an indigenous institution" that "can be best evaluated with respect to our own peculiar needs" (p. 228). The principal such need, wrote Herring, is "to unify a party not inherently unified." Consequently, the convention's purpose "is not to examine intellectual differences but to seek terms of agreement" and "when differences cannot be reconciled" to promote "unity in the face of disagreement" (p. 229)—that is, to seek and publicize what we have described as cordial concurrence. To achieve that end Herring noted that the convention devised techniques for forming coalitions. Those techniques lend themselves to the spectacular:

Experience indicates that prizefights, football games, and similar sporting spectacles have characteristics that please the populace. Debating societies have a more limited following. The intellectually inclined may view this as an unfortunate situation. If a political spectacle is the way to arouse public attention, that is reason enough for the average politician. (p. 230)

The chapter that follows charts the beginnings and growth of the national political convention as an indigenous spectacle. The focus is selective—namely, our concern is with the evolution of the convention as an orchestrated partisan gathering rather than upon the details of personalities, issues, and conflicts at each quadrennial conclave. Our appeal is in part to the casual music lover who wishes a historical guide to convention orchestration that is devoid of needless details, but we also summarize sufficient sources of convention history to appeal to what Adorno labeled the expert listener, who might wish to examine the nuances of partisan give-and-take in convention settings. Our historical sketch is fourfold. We begin by exploring the various ends served by national party conventions within the American polity. We then turn to each of three historical stages in the development of convention orchestration—the periods of group mediation, mass mediation, and contemporary telepolitical mediation.

Key criteria associated with orchestration permit us to highlight major turning points in orchestral development. We consider, first, the matter of *who controls the show*. An understanding of how the convention moved from a show dominated by an impresario (i.e., the party boss) to a performance that was talent dominated, then an event managed by production companies, is essential to grasping how the convention evolved as an administrative entity. Second, a review of how the *nature of the show's content* shifted from lengthy improvisations, to performances by talented artists, to the current emphasis on visually attractive scripts suggests evolving standards of what are "good" and "bad" partisan musical scores. Third, any musical spectacle involves a relationship between those who stage the extravaganza, the production company, and those who comment on the performance, the news media. This *company-media relationship* in partisan spectacles consists of that between party politician and political reporter—one that has shifted from being party controlled, to cooperative, to adversarial through a gradual progression from print to aural to visual means of mediation. Finally, we examine shifts in *production formats as expressive modes*: elaborate oratory, ornate party platforms, and spontaneous demonstration in a period of group mediation; the demise of favorite-son candidacies, floor fights, and repeated roll calls in the period of mass mediation; and an emphasis on acceptance speeches, scripted demonstrations, and party-produced visuals in a telepolitical era.

THE NATIONAL PARTY CONVENTION AS AN AMERICAN POLITICAL INSTITUTION

To map out the appearance of the nominating convention is, in many respects, to plot the development of American democracy itself. That the formation of the American approach to governance was not an overnight sensation may be seen through William Nisbet Chambers's (1963) colorful prose: "Revolution on Monday, independence on Tuesday, a constitution on Wednesday, political parties on Thursday, orderly elections on Friday, stable democratic government by Saturday, and rest on Sunday—any such conception of political creation is the stuff of dreams" (p. 10). Chambers's Genesis metaphor provides a feel for the turning points in the system's "creation." Of principal concern here is from Thursday through Saturday—that is, how party leaders created and maintained national coalitions through the promotion of an illusion (i.e., the *national party*).

Fundamental is an appreciation for the two-party system's role in American democracy. Schattschneider (1942) argues the parties "created" the American system to an extent that "democracy is unthinkable save in terms of" those organizations (p. 1). Reliance on checks and balances places a major emphasis on the parties' abilities to maintain coalitions. Separation of powers rests on the parties' capacity to meet the requirements of the electoral college; otherwise, the House of Representatives assumes responsibility for the selection of the chief executive—a clear violation of separation of powers. Party mobilization, then, is a major part of the American electoral process and, subsequently, the convention's *prime* purpose.

If the country "had more than two major parties, a system such as the national party conventions might never have developed" (Pomper, 1963, p. 13). In the absence of a two-party structure, the competing interests that are a natural consequence of representative democracy could easily stifle the electoral process. This situation is further complicated by our "federal system of government, in which states, and therefore state parties, have independent power" (Pomper, p. 13). Thus, some entity was required to promote active debate, yet simultaneously encourage compromise. The convention provides that occasion and, in so doing, "totally split Congress off from the presidential succession and established for the first time an institutionalized, real separation of powers" (Davis, 1983, p. 25).

Ernest Meyer (1902) describes four phases of the party convention's emergence. The initial period (which begins during "the first quarter of the eighteenth century and closes with the Revolution") saw the caucus move from "a secret, private, unorganized gathering, to an open, irregular but public meeting" (p. 2). The second period extended from the end of the Revolution to the "establishment of the present government in 1787" and "marks the appearance of local conventions of irregularly elected delegates, as supplementary to the caucuses, and like them, without continued life from year to year." Meyer's third phase "embraces about thirty-five years and ends in 1824." This time frame was characterized by a "rapid extension and further development of the local nominating institutions" of the second period and "also by the rise of central nominating bodies both state and national, the former being known as the legislative caucuses, and the latter as the congressional caucus." Meyer's final period involves the introduction of "a pure delegate convention system thoroughly representative in theory" and "possessing continuity of existence and unity of action" (p. 3).

The Founding Fathers' assumptive world was predicated on the belief that a "natural aristocracy of men imbued with such qualities as virtue, talent, wealth, distinguished decent learning, and even physical strength" existed; therefore, their charge was "to devise a method for selecting 'the best' from among this natural aristocracy to serve as chief executive of the United States" (David, Goldman, and Bain, 1960a, p. 9). Various methods of selection were rejected for a variety of reasons. The Virginia Plan, based on a congressional decision, was rejected owing to its obvious threat to separation of powers. A suggestion to have the state governors decide was also rejected, as was a plan for direct election by "the people" since, it was feared, they lacked the tools necessary for such an important decision. Consequently, an "ad hoc electoral college" was introduced: each state would convene its "most capable individuals to serve briefly as presidential electors." While the electoral college persists today, many facets of that original conception were short-lived. The lack of representation in the nomination process and—quite simply—the increasing size of the electorate combined with growing doubts about the Founding Fathers' "natural aristocracy" to create decision points that slowly changed the process.

One turning point was the emergence of state governments on the East Coast spawning state conventions of the type Meyer described. Chase (1973) advances four reasons why the convention prospered in the mid-Atlantic states: (1) The division of state government into progressively smaller units of activity (e.g., towns, counties); (2) the increasingly dense population created a situation where some method of representation was necessary since everybody cannot be directly involved in the nomination process; (3) the growing number of elective offices that naturally accompanied item 1; and (4) the emergence of a competitive party system (pp. 277–78). Hence, as political leaders came to question the caucus as not representative, too centralized, lacking continuity, and reinforcing elitest fears, adaptation of a device already popular in several eastern states, the nominating convention, grew attractive as an alternative. The convention provided for a diversity of representation, possessed the capacity to "reconcile deep factional cleavages" within the party, produced a binding nomination, and selected nominees "with a strong likelihood of winning voter support" (Davis, 1983, pp. 3–4). And, perhaps most important, the assembly gave considerable power to party leaders. Once established, the nominating convention was occasionally challenged, but never replaced. The 1836 Whigs did not hold a convention in an effort to thwart the process with three legislative nominations, but they failed. Every ticket since that time has been ratified via national convention.

From these beginnings, various convention functions emerged in a little over twenty years.[1] Without question, the principal order of business for a convention involves its *nomination function*. As noted in our Prelude, this function seldom matches the romantic fantasies of multiple-ballot, heart-wrenching nomination battles. The orchestration of party unity behind a predetermined nominee is, and virtually always has been, the prime activity associated with the nomination function and provides the umbrella under which other functions operate.

The *platform function*—originally termed the "Address to the People" and adopted "after the nomination of candidates" (Pomper, 1963, p. 23)—is also widely misunderstood. The platform represents "a process of psychological value" as it offers "a release for opinions and scope for the interplay of personalities" and, in turn, constitutes "one more step in the process of working out some kind of synthesis" (Herring, 1940, p. 234). V. O. Key (1964) argues that platforms are often mistaken for "blueprints for action" when, in fact, they are "electioneering documents" (p. 421). In that capacity, Key claims, they "mirror the characteristics of the party system itself" since "the platforms are as they are because the party system is as it is." The platforms—the two parties' only institutionally ratified statement of resolve—are indeed central to the orchestration of cordial concurrence.

The indigenous nature of the American convention is never more evident than in terms of its *campaign-rally function*. These acts of jubilation (and, occasionally, anger) are fundamental to the spectacle's emotional qualities. That many observers have misunderstood the conventions because they were distracted by the enactment of campaign-rally rituals says something about the color and enthusiasm of convention demonstrations.

Lastly, the *governing-body function* creates and promotes the continuity of the national party myth. Beginning with the caucus's "committee of correspondence" (Pomper, 1963, p. 17; David, Goldman, and Bain, 1960a; Marshall, 1981) and solidified by the 1848 Democrats' introduction of the "Democratic National Committee" (Davis, 1983, p. 30), this aspect of the process oversees the operations of the various convention committees and manages the party's business between events.[2] Over the years the national committee's influence has grown well beyond convention-related business to an extent that it is now a central force in party campaigns of all levels and types.

As we shall see, these four functions are the raw materials of orchestration. The governing-body operation oversees site selection and supervises logistics while party leaders, consultants, and campaign operatives coordinate the enactment of nomination, platform drafting, and campaign-rally rituals. For insight into the evolution of that orchestration process, we turn to convention history.

THE ERA OF GROUP MEDIATION: 1840–1920

Group mediation consists of the face-to-face, interpersonal encounters that constituted politics in the era before independent mass media. During this phase of American history political communication was primarily an interpersonal affair; opinion leaders, often the infamous political boss, controlled the content and flow of political information. Hence, the convention provided a forum for these leaders, of various levels and/or orientations, to assemble, energize themselves, and return home to spread the word to their respective constituencies under the banner of party unity. All of this had a significant impact on the orchestration of cordial concurrence. In order to facilitate group mediation, convention planners devised ways to involve multitudes of state and local party leaders in the proceedings. To provide the quadrennial renewal essential to the locally inspired party mobilization that followed, the parties allocated large amounts of podium time, platform space, and demonstration energy to scores of party faithful.

The orchestration of early party conventions—much like its sister spectacle, the opera—was an impresario-dominated process. Both shows were controlled by the impresario or party boss who decided who would appear when. Once the cast was introduced, however, improvisation was the order of the day. Martorella (1982) tells us how "singers ruled the stage" during opera's first two centuries in a fashion that "made both composers and librettists subservient to their wishes" (p. 20). Moreover, during opera's second century "not only was music written for a particular singer and his/her vocal technique, but singers often changed the scores at their whim." During this age of the "concert hall," the impresario provided a cast that would, in some respects, do what what they wished once upon the stage. Conventions, too, experienced an era of improvisation. Though the requirements of group mediation inspired party leaders to construct the cast carefully, once introduced these loyalists sang their own songs. Therefore, let us see how the bosses, our political impresarios, controlled the show; the level of improvisation inspired by the convention's format; the party-news media (i.e., performer-critic) relationship; and the various means of expression employed during this era.

We begin with the bosses. Revolutionary leaders dominated presidential campaigns until James K. Polk in 1844. Polk's nomination constitutes the first "original synthesis" produced by a convention and "marked the coming of age of the convention as an institution capable of creating as well as ratifying consensus within the party" (Key, 1964, p. 398). After three consecutive first-ballot decisions, the Polk nomination took nine ballots to achieve and, as a result, introduced the give-and-take of the boss-dominated age. From there state party leaders "took over control of the conventions and forced the various aspirants to bargain with them over matters of cabinent posts, patronage, or major issues facing various regions of the country before putting their stamp of approval on the favorite" (Davis, 1983, p. 31).

Impresarios controlled the concert hall, knew their talent, and carefully selected singers to do their bidding on stage. The bosses became "the most prominent figures" in the convention setting and "at whose beck and call subalterns" were "ever present" (Bruce, 1927, p. 244). The interpersonal emphasis that accompanies group mediation was evident: bosses knew "every personal detail, whim, and interest of their own delegates" and could "usually 'deliver the votes' when the proper time is deemed to have arrived" (Bruce, p. 244). As expected, this distribution of power among a select few created an aura of pomp and circumstance for elites. Henry Stoddard (1948) recounts some of this glamour: "No party leader or party boss of consequence enters the hall until the delegates from his state are seated and prepared to give him a hand and a cheer. Then, head up, he walks, sometimes serious, sometimes smiling, down the aisle. The galleries, if they recognize him, join in the acclaim—to keep busy if for no other reason" (p. 31).

Though the impresario-ruled stage featured improvisation, it also introduced institutional performances, notably the *keynote* and *nomination* speeches. Bruce describes the early keynote as an honor extended to the convention chairman who used that occasion to "express his gratitude for the honor bestowed upon him in a long speech which he has carefully prepared in advance" (pp. 246–47). Stoddard (1938) assures us the keynoter was "dolled up meticulously" for the speech, and he would "prance around the platform and gesticulate as wildly and furiously as he chose" (p. 320). Yet, after all that effort, if the convention should elect a new chairman upon the acceptance of the permanent roll, a second keynote speech would follow. Another institutional performance involved the nominating speech's arrival in 1876. Stoddard maintains prior to the "long nominating speech" the convention entertained "only brief formal announcements or none at all" (p. 320). With time, these institutional performances became a framework for the convention to orchestrate cordial concurrence.

During the age of group mediation the nomination, platform, and campaign-rally functions were protracted, delegate-centered, activities. Multiple nominating and seconding speeches, their corresponding demonstrations, and lengthy debates over credentials and/or platform planks allowed the respective delegations to offer their spokesperson to express that group's sentiments on a candidate and/or issue. Through these actions factions were able to articulate their constructions of political reality which, if nothing else, provided a starting point for the negotiation of a party reality suitable to the majority of the delegates. Of course, these practices added significantly to the assembly's length. Marathon sessions produced opportunities for virtually all groups to express themselves—acts essential to the group-mediated mobilization. A prime means of expression was the *favorite-son* nomination. This allowed the respective factions to extoll the virtues of their own stalwarts in a manner that facilitated rival claims yet contributed to face-saving, compromise, concurrence, and the emergence of a common party identity. Although such activities consumed considerable time, their symbolic value should not be minimized; they promoted involvement in group mediation by leaders and followers alike. During this phase of the convention's development, the opportunity for direct participation was central to the coalition formation process.

Multiple ballots for the presidential nomination contributed to a seemingly never-ending string of speeches, especially when Democrats adhered to the rule that a nominee must secure two-thirds of the delegates' votes. Of the 24 Democratic conventions of the group-mediated era, 13 extended to extra ballots—4 of the 13 ending on the second ballot. By contrast there were only 3 multiple-ballot assemblies of the 15 mass-mediated Democratic conventions (1952 was the last multiple-ballot gathering for both parties). Turning to the other side of the aisle, the 17 group-mediated Republican conventions contained 8 multiple-ballot affairs (with but one second-ballot decision), whereas only 1 of the 15 mass-mediated conclaves went beyond a first ballot (a third ballot settled that dispute).

A notable example of an extra-ballot convention was the 1880 GOP gathering in Chicago. After 36 ballots (the longest in Republican history), the party nominated James A. Garfield. Originally, Garfield placed John Sherman's name in nomination alongside candidates James G. Blaine, William Windom, U. S. Grant, George F. Edmunds, and Elihu B. Washburne (*Chicago Tribune*, 1892). Each nomination speech was seconded by one, and occasionally two, speakers. This long-windedness consumed the fourth day's evening session and required Republicans to assemble for two more days of voting. With time, Garfield's candidacy gained momentum and he was nominated on the 36th ballot (later made unanimous after 11 speeches endorsing the motion).

Aside from the number of speeches common to this era, an intense level of emotion typically accompanied their delivery. That this intensity added to the amount of improvisation is beyond question. Witness Robert Ingersoll's creation of the "Plumed Knight" in his 1876 nomination of Maine's James G. Blaine. In an effort to prevent a roll call, and in turn kill the emotion generated by Ingersoll's inspiring oratory, Stoddard (1938) reports, partisans entered the convention hall's basement and broke the gas pipes that fed the gaslights in the hall. Without lighting, the convention had to adjourn and, with that move, retired Blaine's 1876 candidacy (pp. 323–24). There are countless examples (such as William Jennings Bryan's powerful "Cross of Gold" oration) of emotionally charged convention speaking from this era of improvisation.

Ostrogorski (1902) asserts that the intensity of audience responses was not so much a product of oratorical excellence or diversity as the strategic use of an operatic devise, the claque. Ostrogorski claims "the campaign mangers of each aspirant . . . procure" the tempestuous audience reactions "by means of the paid claque, judiciously distributed over the enormous hall" so that as soon as the candidate's name is mentioned claques and supporters "jump on their seats and break into cheers and other less artic- ulate . . . convulsions" (pp. 267–68). The speeches sounded the same; only a rigged audience provided an illusion of diversity. Credentials disputes also allowed oratory to reach a fever pitch, only to be resolved in the smoke-filled rooms of late-night compromise. The famous Taft-Roosevelt "steamroller" credentials fight of 1912 is a prime case in point. Eaton (1964), Martin (1964), and Stoddard (1938) all report how "the galleries would make a shuffling, 'choo-choo' noise like a locomotive getting under way" (Stoddard, p. 313) as each Roosevelt delegate was "ousted" during the intense credentials fight.

Bosses controlled the stage, but they did allow for spontaneity. Hence, this era witnessed long, at times arduous, sessions in which improvisa- tion—from both the floor and the stage—was the order of the day. In many respects, political impresarios encouraged delegates within the con- vention hall to venture into flights of idiosyncratic arational fancy as the bosses negotiated party business in the infamous smoke-filled room. Af- terward, the impresarios emerged and seized the stage to generate the con- currence necessary to ratify what had become foregone conclusions.

In order to communicate verdicts to constituencies the bosses turned to their respective "house organs," the partisan press. An excellent example of the partisan press of this era is found in Eaton's description of New York governor Samuel J. Tilden's 1876 campaign. Eaton (1964) writes how Til- den conducted the first "modern" presidential campaign when he "set up a Newspaper Popularity Bureau" that "placed advertisements in over 1,200 newspapers throughout the country and supplied them with a steady stream of interesting and well-written stories about himself" (p. 61). Tilden also created a "Literary Bureau" that wrote "news articles, pamphlets, and speeches advocating his candidacy" in a manner that "went considerably beyond the usual run of campaign literature" since these publications "dealt with governmental expenditure, reform of the civil service, the tax structure" and more.

These tactics reflect the essential qualities of the partisan news media in the group-mediated era. Candidates operated their own newspapers, publishers and editors maintained a partisan presence at the conventions (a presence culminating in the 1920 nomination of two newspaper publishers as the respective party nominees, Warren Harding and James Cox), and reporters advocated partisan stands. There was nothing devious about the reporter-politician relationship; everyone realized the partisanship of newspapers and, as a result, construed news articles accordingly. In fact, during this phase of the convention's development (with its emphasis on "printed" mass mediation), the congressional press galleries came into being as an attempt to keep reporters (then called "claims agents") from lobbying legislators on the House and Senate floors.

And what of the means of expression the parties employed to orchestrate cordial concurrence? As we have seen, impresarios controlled what talent performed on the convention stage and, to a lesser extent, how. For the "how" there were limited production alternatives available to convention orchestrators: podium oratory, the platforms, demonstrations, roll calls, music, and entertainment. Extensive debates over credentials and platform planks inspired emotion-laden improvisations from the rostrum as speakers labored over extended periods; a never-ending series of candidates prompted interminable rounds of nomination-related speeches.

With these multiple nomination speeches and credentials or platform victories (and defeats) came innumerable demonstrations. As speakers appeared on the podium, prepared to leave, or simply said something clever, the orchestra played strategically selected music designed to complement the efforts of claques, supporters, and other easily excitable persons. Though these displays continued into the age of mass mediation, they, without question, enjoyed their finest hours during the group-mediation era.

Ostrogorski (1902), who had never before witnessed an event quite like an American convention, expressed disbelief when he observed that "God takes care of drunkards, of little children, and of the United States" (p. 279). Pendleton Herring (1940), some time later, responded: "Our conventions are a romantic and flamboyant attempt to get a high degree of popular participation in the high drama of democracy. It is not an institution to be dismissed contemptuously because of its noise and apparent confusion. It is characteristic of our free political system; the Nazi's have a pageantry of a different sort. Those who prefer order will find it in Nuremburg" (p. 237).

The conventions of the group-mediated era were "romantic and flamboyant" spectacles quite unlike anything before or after. In some respects, they were oxymorons. That is, while they were the tightly controlled pawns of bosses, they also featured countless improvisational performances by an endless array of speakers. Moreover, as these orators whipped their audiences into fits of emotion (contrived and spontaneous), the convention hall frequently erupted into demonstration upon demonstration. An in-house press operated by the very same impresarios who controlled the concert hall then reported to those outside what had happened within.

The group mediation and orchestration of partisan concert slowly gave way to a new convention, a convention that would move away from the attending delegations as the principal purveyors of the party message toward a spiraling network of independently operated media outlets. No longer would speakers be allowed to strut about the rostrum exhorting their audience by yelling and screaming. No longer could party bosses wink at reporters who would run off and dutifully record that which they had been told to write. No longer would the assembled delegates and galleries be allowed to erupt into hour-long celebrations thereby stonewalling the momentum generated on some candidate's behalf. Slowly but surely, a new audience would capture the attentions of convention planners—an audience who could experience the convention from the comfort of living rooms, meeting halls, and bars. To enthrall these audiences, a new breed of talent emerged. Singers who usurped the bosses' power and, through the use of musical standards, changed the orchestration of cordial concurrence forever.

THE ERA OF MASS MEDIATION: 1924–1980

With the rise of an increasingly independent news media and the emergence of radio and television, we observe major shifts of emphasis by convention orchestrators. The group-mediated era's reliance on the attending delegations' abilities to rally the troops was soon supplemented by other mobilization tactics. During this phase of the convention's development, the parties learned how to use the electronic media to communicate with their new "national" audience.

The gradual shift toward mass mediation had direct implications for the orchestration of cordial concurrence. The potential for multiple ballots slowly disappeared as the movement toward state primaries and caucuses spread. The long, protracted sessions traditionally associated with Monday's credentials and Tuesday's platform business were streamlined with public hearings occurring weeks preceding the show. And the nature of the production itself evolved with an expanding concern for set design, acoustics and lighting, program length, and timing. As we moved closer to the telepolitical age, preproduction demands expanded.

Once more we find interesting parallels between our two spectacles, the convention and the opera. At this juncture in their developments, both shows were moving away from Mencken's "concert hall" toward the more elaborate and technically sophisticated "opera house." With this increased concern for staging came additional attention to the show's script. Although the political impresario or boss lingered, politicians began to acquire celebrity status (and independence) and eschewed improvisation for scripted, rehearsed star-quality performances. Hence, a new player emerges: the conductor. Just as the rise of music publication elevated the conductor's status, created requests for "old standards," and facilitated the movement from private music societies to publically sponsored opera, the convention's newfound opportunities to communicate through network radio and television inspired similar changes. A few of the performances from the group-mediated era, the keynote and nomination speeches for example, were further institutionalized which, in turn, led to more standardized renditions. If Ostrogorski thought all the speeches sounded alike during an age of improvisation, he should have hung around another 80 years.

Joining the conductor's new status were additional demands on the composer and librettist. As noted in our Prelude, the order of emphasis began to change during this period in that the show's content (i.e., the "intelligibility of the words") became more and more important. Therefore, speechwriting grew in significance—in particular, in terms of the message's continuity. This dimension expanded when the show moved from one wherein the leading character is *in absentia* to one that builds toward the climatic capstone performance that is the central character's (presidential nominee's) acceptance speech.

With regard to orchestral criteria, we note the following changes: (1) the rise of the star-dominated production (and a corresponding decline in the impresario or boss); (2) an increasing trend toward standardization of roles and script; (3) a period of reportorial cooperation between the parties and the news media; and (4) a move toward both a diversity of expression (via film, celebrities, etc.) and a time-conscious show that, eventually, led to the demise of lengthy platform debates, multiple nomination speeches, spontaneous demonstrations, and favorite-son nominations.

It is ironic, however, that the first conventions of the mass-mediated era both foreshadowed the tightly scripted assemblies of the future and revisited the never-ending conclaves of the past. The 1924 GOP gathering in Cleveland was so uneventful it inspired humorist Will Rogers to comment that the ticket "could have been nominated by postcard" (Stout & Rollins, 1976, p. 33). On the other hand, the New York Democrats took all of 103 ballots (the most ever) to settle upon J. W. Davis as their candidate. The 1924 assemblies were the first to be nationally broadcast on radio. This innovation offered the general public its initial exposure to the convention process and provided the nation's political elite their inaugural national audience. We return to some of the specifics of the 1924 broadcasts in a moment, but it suffices to say at this point that the conventions would never be the same again—and the Democrats said good-bye in a grand fashion.

First, consider the rise of party "stars." The presence of exceptional stage talent often sets the scene for emulation and, eventually, changes in production styles. This is especially true during the introduction of a new form of artistic expression. In the case of the American politician's adjustment to radio, that star talent appeared in the form of Franklin Delano Roosevelt. Roosevelt's 1928 "Happy Warrior" nomination of Al Smith both inspired *and* instructed a generation of political orators. Moreover, his unprecedented appearance before the 1932 Democratic convention created a new ritual performance for presidential nominees: the acceptance speech. J. Leonard Reinsch (1988) explains that the radio speaker must command an ability to talk to the "members of a small family in their living room . . . sitting by their radio console, listening to you talk to *them*" (p. 13). For Roosevelt, Reinsch recalls, "the microphone personified a single American listener"; FDR "never forgot that radio listening was done by individuals and family groups, not by hordes who filled auditoriums" (p. xiii).

This approach to public speaking was a substantial departure from the days of fire and brimstone that inspired Ostrogorski's inarticulate "convulsions." The art of oratory now required the show's talented performers to maintain presence with a microphone, reduce body movements, and concentrate on that "single American listener." For many established politicians, this transition was too great. Others, such as Harry Truman, secured the assistance of professional consultants, like Leonard Reinsch, to learn the proper stylistic adjustments. H. L. Mencken (1956) captured the spirit of the moment. Speaking of politicians he noted that "they seldom if ever get there by merit alone, at least in democratic states." No, and this was becoming all too apparent in 1940 when he wrote these words: "They are chosen normally for quite different reasons, the chief of which is simply their power to impress and enchant." It is, he continued, "a talent like any other, and when it is exercised by a radio crooner or a movie actor or a bishop, it even takes on a certain austere and sorry respectability." But, he warned, "it is obviously not identical with a capacity for the intricate problems of statecraft" (pp. 148–49).

Yet stardom need not be restricted to those seeking success through the ballot box. The radio and television age introduced a whole new set of talent: those seeking the approval of readers, listeners, and viewers—the news correspondents. With the print media's increased independence, the news media slowly became one of the party's primary audiences. The 1908 Democrats and 1912 Republicans turned to Washington's congressional press galleries to credential correspondents attending the convention and to assist their needs. Over time the size of press stands grew and so too did the prestige of those writing the "convention story" for millions of readers. Famous columnists (Mencken among them) joined prominent reporters to form a cadre of star journalistic talent.

As radio and television slowly found their way into every home, celebrities switched to the new media. Some electronic talent came from other fields of entertainment (such as Graham McNamee, star of the 1924 Democratic broadcast) and others grew up with radio or TV. In either case, they represented a force for the parties to reckon with as politicians sought access to audiences controlled by broadcast executives and advertisers, and, as a result, the content and style of the mass-mediated convention emerged. In 1938, when Stoddard wrote about the convention's posh "boxes" that inspired "the same interests as upon the famous 'diamond horseshoe' in the Metropolitan Opera House . . . or in the Auditorium in Chicago" (p. 308), he could have hardly realized that his words would one day describe ABC, CBS, CNN, and NBC's anchor booths. Without question, the rise of party and news-media stars played a vital role in the orchestration process as they emerged as the show's organizing entities—all of which slowly drained the power traditionally reserved for party bosses.

This leads to a second consideration: the increased tendency toward standardization. The convention's move to reduce the number of speaking opportunities combined with the standardization of keynote and platform presentations to create a packaged repertoire for manipulation by conductors. This era also witnessed changes in voting rules (the end of the Democrats two-thirds rule in 1936 stands out); the advent of preconvention platform hearings and credentials meetings; and rules that ended favorite sons and limited nomination speeches—all *institutional* adjustments in the production's format. These changes standardized performances that, again, gradually introduced the scripted convention.

Thomson's (1956) excellent treatment of the 1952 convention telecasts describes how the parties learned from one another's experiences and led to scripting. The 1952 Democrats noted a flaw in the GOP convention telecast days earlier. Democrats corrected the Republican failure to provide a center camera stand (and, thus, the head-on camera shot) and "asked their delegates to watch Republican behavior" on television and "be guided accordingly" (p. 33). During the Democrats' convention, chair Sam Rayburn instructed delegates to keep their balloons out of the camera shots, and the party issued a leaflet warning delegates they could be on television any moment. In fact, the Democrats "gave each network a complete 'shooting script' each day in advance . . . and efforts were made to rehearse and time speakers and performers to match the scripts" (p. 34).

All of these developments set the scene for the level of staging essential to the orchestration of cordial concurrence in our telepolitical age. From the party perspective, the scripting of delegate activities, podium speeches, and media encounters is a good and proper thing. But from the news media's perspective, such attention to orchestral detail produces hurdles to be overcome. This, however, was not the news media's original position. Although moving a long way from the partisan press of the group-mediated era, the print and broadcast media were also far from adversarial in their logistical and journalistic practices. It required several years for the editorial policies of media organizations to free themselves from the shackles of partisanship.

Assuredly, the broadcast of the 1924 Democratic marathon displayed some unusual journalistic practices by today's standards. In case a fistfight erupted during the 1924 radio coverage, the Democrats instructed an employee stationed near the radio facilities to "pull the plug" on the broadcast. Further proof of censorship may be found in Democratic directives for announcers to ignore any "scuffles" among the delegates. There were quite a few "scuffles" and the announcers ignored most of them, but a few did get reported—much to the Democrats' chagrin (see Becker & Lower, 1977; McNamee, 1926).

There were a few threats to "pull the plug" as television entered the scene, but there was an intense level of cooperation among the networks and the two parties as TV made its debut. Television's limited coverage of the 1948 Philadelphia conventions did not reach many viewers (it was confined to a few East Coast cities), but it did establish an important precedent: network input into the selection of the convention site. Reinsch (1988) writes that the 1948 Democrats, Progressives, and Republicans "settled on Philadelphia because of television—and television alone" (p. 46). The parties also paid for the installation of the networks' equipment in the City of Brotherly Love (Thomson, 1956).

Thomson's and Waltzer's (1966) recollections of the 1952 party-network logistical arrangements are, once again, strange by modern standards. Debate occurred over sponsorship (there were no sponsors in 1948 since the parties paid), who would pay for the necessary lighting, where cameras could be stationed, and access to the convention floor. For instance, consider these compromises reached over commercial sponsorship: (1) the type of sponsor was subject to party approval; (2) commercials could only be aired during recesses or long pauses; (3) commercial messages had to reflect the highest standards of dignity, good taste, and length; (4) no commercial could originate from the convention floor; and (5) the networks had to run disclaimers with regard to their sponsorship at the opening and close of the show (Thomson, pp. 15–16). Both parties also agreed to meet in Chicago, which allowed the networks to operate from the much desired central time zone and to set up their equipment for both conventions simultaneously since they paid the installation costs.

From these initial telecasts, in which the networks actually provided *more* airtime than the period the conventions were in session, we move to 1956, when the parties announced their independence from television control by meeting in different cities and when CBS refused to air the first party-supplied film (entitled *The Pursuit of Happiness*, narrated by John Kennedy). In a fascinating display, the delegates were so upset with CBS's decision that they shook the central camera stand in protest.

Though the give-and-take of party–news media relations was maturing, this was still the age of party-network cooperation. Fant (1980) writes about the 24 meetings of the 1964 Television Advisory Committee during which "convention sites, facilities and schedules, sponsors, and network space, location, credentials, access, and coverage were discussed" (p. 133). On one level of analysis (i.e., the administrative), this interinstitutional cooperation exists in the contemporary telepolitical environment; on others (i.e., the reportorial), it does not.

Before turning from the matter of party-media cooperation, we must mention one extraordinary development: the appearance of "the boss in the anchor booth." While party leaders were constantly interviewed by network personnel during the conventions, in 1964 ABC *hired* former president Dwight Eisenhower for its GOP coverage. Harry Truman turned down a similar post with ABC's Democratic convention telecasts; instead, Democratic U. S. senators Sam Ervin and Hubert Humphrey acted as "special on-the-air consultants" (Waltzer, 1966, p. 45). After receiving his party's nomination as vice-president, Humphrey stepped out of the anchor booth and onto the podium while ABC featured an "engagement cancelled" graphic. With the rise of talent-based productions, the lines between party stars and media stars blurred.

An operatic view of the convention's format reveals a meaningful shift from the continuous stream of recitative associated with the group-mediated period toward the star-studded arias that eventually dominated the mass-mediated convention.[3] The steady harmony that constitutes recitative supplies continuity to opera but it simultaneously induces boredom. With time (and the rise of stardom), performers turned to the aria as a means to contribute emotion to the story line (the recitative) and show off their vocal talents.

The same principle emerged in opera's sister spectacle as the convention institutionalized certain moments in the show for star-oriented arias. Keynotes, nomination speeches, the roll call, and—most of all—the acceptance speeches allowed a new generation of performers to show off their abilities (or kill their careers). These prime-time performances were the natural consequences of the impresario or boss's decline, the rise of standardization, and the introduction of radio and television. The parties now turned toward party-supplied films that added a new telegenic flair to the show, and away from the "interminable demonstrations or harmonica solos by sons of important local politicians [that] make so little sense on national television" (Thomson, p. 145).

This era introduced structural changes in format that both provided opportunities for diverse constituencies to address the convention (the recitative) and elevated star performances (the aria). Moreover, the use of popular celebrities, films, and tighter production schedules combined with the appearance of political celebrities in the network anchor booths to create a different type of musical spectacle. These talent-based shows represented a marked departure from the days of boss-dominated group mediation and set the scene for a new approach to conventioning.

THE TELEPOLITICAL ERA: 1984-?

With 1984 the age of telepolitical conventions arrived to stay, but for how long no one knows. To this point we have omitted many fascinating events, such as the 1964 GOP's internal fighting, the tumultuous 1968 Chicago Democrats, the ultrascripted 1972 Miami Republicans, the chaos of the 1972 Democrats, and the network-inspired Republican "co-presidency" of 1980. Our interest, however, lies not in recounting the sensational stories of recent conventions; to the contrary, our emphasis is on orchestration—particularly as harmonic vibrations are created in a telepolitical age.

In the telepolitical era the operation of communication technologies are no longer restricted to such organizations as TV networks, but are available to any organization, group, or faction with the knowledge and resources to use them. Unlike the group-mediated era's reliance on state delegations, or the mass-mediated period's emphasis on news media coverage to shape the party spectacle, the telepolitical convention not only caters to delegates and media needs but exploits satellite technology, professional television producers, computers, and other means to create, coordinate, and disseminate the show.

Today the orchestration of cordial concurrence takes on several new dimensions. In part telepolitical conventions are a synthesis of group and mass mobilization techniques. However, the intense focus of convention planners on preproduction operations is distinctive. For example, convention sites, selected two or more years in advance, qualify only if capable of housing thousands of delegates, media, and party personnel; possess the transportation requirements of all these groups; are amenable to creating telegenic convention halls; and, most important, satisfy the political requirements of site-selection committees, party officials, and financial contributors.

Once again, there are several similarities between opera and conventions. As opera settled into the opera house, the production company displaced the impresario. The concert hall's impresario was no longer able to manage the complexities of the show's preproduction publicity, technical arrangements, and union negotiations, as well as its directorial and musical needs. The show grew into an immense bureaucratic production that consumed the talent and managerial personnel of specialists and professionals.

Return for a final time to the orchestral criteria manifested in earlier convention eras. In the telepolitical age we have: (1) the rise of the production company–dominated event with an attendant increased attention to pre-production logistical planning; (2) a growing emphasis on the spectacle's visual qualities in staging and content; (3) a move toward an adversarial party-reporter relationship; and (4) the creation of party-controlled mass-media formats. Let us examine each of these four aspects here merely to suggest what is involved. In Chapter 3 we will then describe the production phases in orchestrating cordial concurrence in detail. Ranging from the intricacies of site selection through the demands of postproduction breakdown and evaluation, the production company required for staging a national party convention has evolved into a vast bureaucracy. Consider three areas of this managerial emphasis: the growth of preproduction logistics, management input into the show's content, and the attention extended to the show's visual qualities.

The two political parties select the host city for their quadrennial gatherings in strikingly different ways; nonetheless, both devote considerable time and energy to this preproduction activity. Cities spend huge sums on visits by site-selection committees; professional consultants work on behalf of cities, the parties, the news media, and other groups; TV networks meet with party officials and select pool producers; congressional gallery personnel visit sites and confer with party and media representatives; conflicts arise; decisions are made. Aside from political considerations (the foremost criterion), preproduction planners must determine if the proposed site can house, transport, feed, entertain, protect, and pamper thousands of delegates, party and media VIPs, reporters, and support personnel. Deception abounds during this phase—nonexistent first-class hotel rooms are fabricated, transportation times and abilities misrepresented, and fictitious plans for seating and work space concocted.

With the site determined, preproduction operations move to a second step: the media *walk-throughs*. At this point the cities and parties conduct a two-day briefing of the news media regarding convention plans. These plans cover space allocations, construction of hall and adjunct facilities, technological requirements, schedules, and deadlines. Media representatives also advise convention officials of their needs. The walk-through serves not only to brief the news media but to warn convention officials of potential problems. In 1988, for example, Democrats replaced their communications director after problems surfaced with a second Atlanta site visit.

Once site selection is complete and walk-throughs either completed or underway, professional management teams take over. Management teams have numerous tasks—ensure equal opportunity hiring, raise and allocate funds, work with local host committees, coordinate union relations, and solicit bids from or make offers to construction, insurance, and communications companies (to name only a few contractors). Convention management also negotiates with network pool producers and congressional gal-

lery staffs over media work space inside and outside the hall, their technological and security needs, and related matters. Clearly, many of these
items are practices inherited from past conventions (remember the television advisory committee?). Yet, as the orchestration of conventions has become increasingly complex, the proliferation of professionals and specialists to cope with that complexity has rendered the telepolitical convention
almost as much of a showcase for managerial as for partisan political skill.
Thus, another level of production company operations involves the coordination of the show's content. Among the technicians hired are film producers, directors, and editors. "Message committees" (Democrats) and
"program groups" (Republicans) conduct polls, plan strategies, and chart
goals for the convention and for any given session or segment thereof. The
politics of who gets to speak and when produces negotiated choices—a
hallmark of cordial concurrence. And the content and form of the
party-operated satellite networks take shape through the efforts of party
TV producers. Each of these preproduction matters maintains its own intricate bureaucracy, which, in turn, requires exceptional levels of intrainstitutional cooperation.

A key consideration of such interinstitutional cooperation is the coordination of the convention hall's visual appearance and content. To achieve
the best possible visuals, for example, both parties retained professional
television producers in 1988. The Democrats hired Hollywood-based
Smith-Hemion Productions (Gary Smith and Dwight Hemion) and the
GOP turned to Washington-based Mark Goode Enterprises. When asked
why his party turned to professional television producers for assistance,
the Democrats' chief executive officer, Don Fowler, said: "What Smith-
Hemion did was to take what was decided upon politically and help us
to craft it into a good TV package. They did not tell us what to do . . . they
helped us shape [the show] and make it look as good as it possibly could."
In orchestrating the visual qualities of staging and content, the Democrats'
Smith-Hemion initially hoped to provide an innovative, entertaining convention format of "Barbra Streisand and Barry Manilow and Bill Cosby
and Aretha Franklin performing and introducing people and taking a very
active role in the show" (Bark, 1988a, p. 2F). As DNC communications director Mike McCurry pointed out, Smith-Hemion had to adjust its original
concept after a meeting with network executives. Nonetheless, it did produce a "more visually attractive" convention through its set design and
program direction.

Mark Goode supervised a staff of "at least 200" (in his words) while he
coordinated the preparation of the GOP convention hall, the activities on
the podium, and the production's dissemination. A veteran of 28 years of
convention television, Goode viewed his goal as not one of "glitz and
glamour" but of "substance" as he endeavored to "recapture that audience" lost by cutbacks in the TV entertainment networks' convention cov-

erage. Chapters 2 and 3 explore in greater detail the work of Gary Smith, Dwight Hemion, and Mark Goode in 1988 convention orchestration.

A specific recent innovation that contributes to the convention spectacle's visual content merits mention: the video introduction. Traditionally, one means of promoting the involvement of party members in convention proceedings was through speaker introductions—the parties' favorite sons and daughters inspired constituencies from the rostrum. In 1984, the Republicans virtually dismissed the practice of using partisans to introduce speakers. Instead, they employed a series of video introductions that were concise, revealed a wide range of party support, and were artistically suited for television. The use of video as a transitional device clearly streamlined the 1984 Dallas GOP convention. Whereas an orator might consume huge (and often unpredictable) blocks of time in an introduction, the video required but a few seconds, provided telegenic detail, restricted audience interruptions, allowed for strategically selected associations, and facilitated thematic continuity within the session. Such artistic creations of professional television producers contribute not only to the visual qualities of the convention hall's appearance, but add to the telegenic nature of the show's overall content. Video profiles of individual delegates, House and Senate candidates, and party history merge group-mediated references to party faithful with the technologies of the day to create a telepolitical production.

Another distinguishing aspect of the telepolitical convention is a pronounced emphasis on the production's thematic continuity. Today the political prima donna appears on a visually inspiring stage for a tightly scripted, prime-time aria and quickly exits once the roses (more accurately, balloons) are tossed on stage. Unlike the practices in group or mass mediation, however, these solos are products of message committees who work diligently to score continuity between standardized recitative performances. An example of the state of the art in thematic conventions was the Monday evening session of the 1984 Republican convention. The GOP presented a "ladies night" program that featured Margaret Heckler, Jeane Kirkpatrick, and Katherine Ortega (the keynoter) as principal speakers. All speakers pursued an "our house is your house" invitation for Democrats to join the Republican cause. The session was confined to two hours, used video introductions and brief speeches to maintain pace, and focused on a specific story line.

As the technology changes the parties' communication strategies, there are shifts in other areas as well. One such domain involves what Republican media director Mike Miller, Democratic counterpart Mike McCurry, Senate press gallery superintendent Robert Petersen, and House radio/TV gallery superintendent Tina Tate all considered to be the major innovation in the convention process: the dramatic increase in local television. McCurry claimed the parties are "reaching an extraordinarily large audience that's not reflected in the Nielsen ratings and nightly network broadcasts" since "people are getting their news in different ways." For McCurry, "all the basic themes and news" of the 1988 convention were communicated via local news outlets that produced stories in which "your own local people connect that news somehow or another to the local area."

The parties have discovered how local news personalities perform a function similar to that of the favorite sons and daughters of the group-mediated era. Instead of allocating unrestricted podium time for local politicians to address the hall, the telepolitical convention caters to local news outlets who "connect" with the people "back home." WTHR's (Indianapolis) Bruce Kopp described the situation in this manner: "With satellite technology, local stations can come here and cover their own delegations. Before, there was no way to get our video back . . . now we're able to tell the folks back home during our local evening news . . . here's what your representatives are doing down here."

Thus, the parties now treat independent and group broadcasters "almost on a par with networks" (according to McCurry), since they see these operations as an effective avenue for their messages.[4] Jane Hansen, reporter for the *Atlanta Journal and Constitution*, supported McCurry's point when she reported that "of the 13,500 journalists covering the [Atlanta] convention" the number of local broadcasters was "25 percent higher than in 1984, up almost 1,000 from the 3,390 who went to San Francisco" (1988h, p. 19C). These numbers inspired one commentator to remark: "They're growing like rabbits. . . . Four years ago, 50 percent of them weren't there. Eight years ago, 80 percent of them weren't there" (Dowd, 1988, p. 11). With these numbers, it comes as little surprise that McCurry's "overall philosophy . . . was oriented towards the grass roots, toward local stations" as the party wondered "how can we best serve the needs . . . of the local affiliates who aren't here" (the goal of the satellite operation) and "how do we take care of some of these local guys who are actually going to get more on the air than the networks" (in McCurry's words).

Not surprisingly, with more players in the production there are other changes. One major shift has been the steady move toward an adversarial network news and print press vs. party relationship. Cooperation in logistical matters—camera pools, camera placement, work space, and so forth—is still the norm. But the parties' efforts to control the networks' access to party "newsmakers," attempts to govern network choices by dimming the lights during certain speeches (an act that limits floor reporting and impacts the network choices of reaction shots), the on-going struggle over airing party-supplied films, coordination of press conference topics, and other actions perceived by media representatives as manipulative, contribute to adversarial bickering, charges, and counter-charges. For example, ABC producer Justin Friedland described how the Democrats and Republicans established "central booking units" in an attempt to coordinate network interviews. Friedland argued "we will get who we want" and rejected the idea that the parties can dictate "who is available and who isn't . . . and what subjects they are great on and what subject they are lousy on."

An adversarial tone also appears in party vs. print media relations. Former Senate press gallery superintendent Don Womack stated how the print press "went from being top dog [in 1952] to low man on the totem pole in the next convention" and, as a result, has to fight for work space, press stands, floor passes, and more. Though the two parties still pay for the press stand's construction, the attention extended to the once all-powerful print journalists dwindles with each convention. CBS radio's John Madigan remembered the conventions of the mass-mediated era (his first was in 1940) and how in those assemblies "proximity was close between the candidate, the platform and those covering it." Madigan told our interviewers: "There wasn't the distance. . . . The reporter and the big-name writers . . . would be right up sitting in the first few rows. . . . There was more romance to it because you didn't have the structured finesse demanded by television."

This "structured finesse" has generated animosity toward the parties and the conventions in general by some reporters. A National Public Radio producer asserted "I think we ought to skip this foolishness. . . . We're spending every nickle we got on this. . . . I'm sending people to briefings that don't matter and to press conferences that don't matter." A Texas newspaper's media critic took these sentiments a bit further:

I think they're [the conventions] a waste of everybody's time. I think a law ought to be passed that conventions should only be covered by the networks and wire services and that nobody else should be allowed. . . . What are they for? It is show business. Millions and millions of dollars are spent on something that doesn't mean anything. . . . I think maybe they ought to have conventions by satellite.

And the parties, though not completely in concurrence with these observations, have followed that suggestion. The telepolitical era's defining characteristic, the use of communications technology, not only created local stations' interest in the conventions (a situation that complicates matters for the entertainment networks and print press), but it also inspired the two political parties to build their own broadcasting entities—a major shift in the means by which convention orchestrators disseminate the show and the party message. Of the production innovations discussed thus far none is as sophisticated as the party-operated satellite networks. Beginning in 1984 with the Republicans' RNC Network (RNCN), the two parties now use satellite technology in a manner similar to that of local and group broadcasters. In 1984 the RNCN provided a telecast much like the C-SPAN production in that it presented the events inside the convention hall without interruption. Mark Goode (the 1984 and 1988 RNCN producer) described the network's purpose as threefold: (1) to facilitate "more extended coverage" for independent stations; (2) to "recapture" those audiences lost by the commercial networks' cutbacks; and (3) to appeal to certain ethnic groups. Goode claimed that prior to the 1984 conventions the nonnetwork stations and/or groups had to rely on the "very costly" satellite feeds provided by the commercial networks' pool cameras. The Republicans argued this arrangement hurt the distribution of their convention message and, in response, created the RNCN in an attempt to maximize cable television's potential to reach certain audiences.

The 1988 RNCN was an impressive operation that involved ten cameras (seven stationary, three mobile units) directed through a state-of-the-art production facility. The RNCN also expanded its 1984 offerings via its satellite distribution and the availabilty of a simultaneous Spanish translation. In addition, between sessions the RNCN made its facilities available to local stations or groups wishing to conduct two-way satellite interviews with party figures and the like—again, free of charge. The 1988 GOP convention manager, Bill Phillips, expressed reservations about the 1984 operation, yet after his 1988 experience he remarked how "someday the pool camera will be the party camera." A few broadcasters, however, question the RNCN's usefulness to local TV stations by noting that independents and locals may legally take as much as three minutes of C-SPAN's feed and meet virtually any video need.

A satellite option did not exist for Democrats in 1984. The Democratic National Committee offered only a closed-circuit talk show to delegation hotels. That operation, along with DNC news and information director Terry Michael's set-up video packages for media organizations, provided the genesis for a much larger 1988 operation. Former DNC communications director Bob Ferrante decided to "mimic" the 1984 GOP (according to Michael) and persuaded the Democratic National Committee's Harriman Communications Center to pursue the idea. In response, the Harriman Center retained Paul Byers (a former network producer) and created the Convention Satellite News Service (CSNS).

For Byers, the CSNS was a "way to facilitate the journalistic process . . . for those who could not be . . . in Atlanta" in a manner that was "apolitical." The CSNS, according to Byers, labored to "supplement" the networks by way of two-way satellite interviews, convention summaries, and prepackaged video reports. The CSNS maintained two television studios (one inside the Omni and another in the adjoining Georgia World Congress Center, the media work area) with a staff of 30 people (many were former network employees). The staff featured four field crews, two complete editing facilities, a control room, as well as former CBS correspondent Ike Pappas for stations in need of on-air talent. The CSNS also received the five-camera feed from the Smith-Hemion operation (which was shown throughout the Georgia World Congress Center) and used it in a variety of ways (highlight packages and the like).

The CSNS did not provide the live convention feed available on the RNCN. They were simply two different types of telepolitical operations. The RNCN wanted to disseminate the "business of the convention" (in Goode's words) via satellite technology whereas the CSNS viewed that approach as redundant and, instead, concentrated on highlight packages and interviews. Both networks did expand the potential for political favorite sons and daughters to be interviewed from the conventions by local news outlets (still more favorites). These entities operated under the direction of the respective national committees and convention management and, in every respect, constitute the epitome of the telepolitical convention.

The telepolitical age offers an interesting blend of past and present as mobilization tactics from days gone by reappear in new electronic formats. Though the show itself is streamlined for telegenic purposes, the rise of local media coverage joins party-based innovations to add a local spin on a national event—a characteristic reminiscent of the locally based strategies of group mediation. These strategies are not without consequences. Reductions in entertainment network coverage, the increasingly adversarial politician-reporter relationship, and added preproduction pressures accompany the move to telepolitics. Our subsequent chapters explore the intricacies of these interinstitutional dynamics in far greater detail.

FROM CONCERT HALL TO OPERA HOUSE: A SUMMARY

The national nominating convention is a dynamic field of action. Its principal purpose—the orchestration of cordial concurrence in support of the party's standard-bearer—has remained constant across the years. The means for achieving that end, however, have evolved through adjustments to emerging technologies. A convention labors to communicate with a nation of continental proportions. The mediation of the convention's message to those audiences is a fundamental part of what the message is intended to be, what it is, and how ever larger audiences perceive it. The conventions exist today because they are capable of change—and changed they have. We now turn to an account of telepolitical conventions of 1984 and 1988. True, if history tells us anything, it suggests the current practices of convention orchestration will not long remain as they were in the 1980s. Yet a detailed examination of convention orchestration in the 1980s is appropriate. As David, Goldman, and Bain (1960a) contend, "as further evolution continues and the attendant problems arise, it is well to recall the origins of this country's political customs" since that foundation "should be understood before changes are contemplated that might produce unanticipated effects" (p. 31). We consider in Chapter 2 the "political customs" of orchestration in the 1980s that most certainly constitute the origins of shaping cordial concurrence in the conventions of the remainder of this century.

NOTES

1. For further details on the convention's four functions consult the following source material. On the nomination function, see: Bain, 1960, pp. 2–7; Byrne and Marx, 1976, pp. 16–25; Key, 1964, p. 431; and Schattschneider, 1942, p. 101. For more on party platforms: Herring, 1940, p. 234; Pomper and Lederman, 1980, p. 173. With regard to the campaign-rally function: Bain, pp. 4–8; Chase, 1973, p. 284; David, Goldman, and Bain, 1960a, pp. 29–31; Davis, 1983, p. 84; and Herring, p. 229. Lastly, for more on the assembly's governing-body function see: David, Goldman, and Bain, p. 30; Davis, p. 42; and Marshall, 1981.

2. The two parties maintain different convention committee structures although they pursue similar tasks. The GOP's committees are: (1) the committee on credentials, (2) the committee on resolutions (the platform), (3) the committee on rules and order of business, and (4) the committee on permanent organization. For Democrats, the committees are: the standing committees on (1) platform, (2) rules, and (3) credentials.

3. Knapp (1972) offers precise definitions of recitative and aria that need some mention here. A recitative "attempts to imitate and emphasize the natural inflections of speech" and is essentially the "musical name given to the narrative" (p. 48). Knapp reports the "recitative is the part of the opera people are bored with most easily" since "singers often take less trouble . . . singing it badly, while waiting to do the aria or ensemble that shows off their vocal talents" (p. 51). Aria, on the other hand, is "an elaborate song" that may "be complicated, simple, long, or short" and reflects upon or expresses an emotional response to the story line established through recitative (p. 57). In all cases, the aria is an intensely emotional expression or, as Knapp states, "the recitative 'loaded the gun' and the aria 'fired it.' "

4. One way the parties reach out to the local and group broadcasters is through the provision of *skyboxes* and *stand-up* locations. These facilities were introduced by C-SPAN's Mike Michaelson (then superintendent of the House radio/TV gallery) in 1976. The skyboxes provide mini-anchor booths for network owned and operated stations, broadcasting groups (it is popular to share a skybox within a group), and independent stations who can afford them. The stand-up locations exist for broadcasters who cannot afford a skybox, but wish to report from inside the convention hall and consist of nothing more than a stool on a platform (often, if possible, with a view of the hall in the background).

The 1988 Democrats had 38 skyboxes in the Omni and the GOP had 40 in the Superdome. The RNC's Mike Miller told us his party's skyboxes cost about $5,000 before modifications (which can be considerable) and the stand-ups were around $3,000 each. The Republicans had to build but 7 of their 40 skyboxes owing to the presence of the New Orleans Saints' facilities that could be adapted to their ends. The Democrats had to build all of their skyboxes—a major construction task, indeed. The Democrats were proud of their stand-up facilities in the Omni (although their location was no place for someone afraid of heights!).

Chapter Two

Political Impresarios: Parties, Media, and Galleries as Orchestrators

A complex series of inter- and intrainstitutional interactions constitute convention orchestration. Key to those interactions are the modern-day political impresarios who design and implement the four-day spectacle. Unlike the impresarios of the group-mediated era, however, today's orchestrators are not political bosses in control of blocs of voters and campaign resources; instead, these impresarios are masters of managerial theory, media logistics, television production, and special-event coordination. In telepolitical conventions, these individuals work under the direction of partisan, media, and official production companies that retain and direct their technical expertise.

The two parties, like opera companies, choose from a host of management philosophies to implement their orchestration strategies. For instance, one opera house may employ certain stage designers who apply their talents to any artistic work scheduled for performance while another company may change personnel with each production. In the case of party conventions this administrative decision may be the product of "conscious action" or of "unrecognized pressures" (David, Goldman, & Bain, 1960a, p. 1). Either way, the choice has major implications for the spectacle's orchestration.

The 1988 Democrat and Republican parties undertook orchestration of their respective conventions in markedly different ways. The Democrats, as convention general manager Arleigh Greenblat observed, typically lack continuity in managerial philosophy and talent from one convention to the next. Their personnel have "a tendency to just do the [one] project and then they leave." The Republicans, on the other hand, have an established team with an accomplished institutional memory that carries on from one convention to another. Jim Baker, Josephine Goode, Mark Goode, Bill Harris, Mike Miller, and Bill Phillips have worked with GOP conventions for decades and, as a result, approach their orchestral tasks with considerable experience and relish. TV network executive producers, congressional gallery officials, working reporters, and TV pool producers refer to the Republicans' "institutional memory" as a positive attribute.

We open our account with the *ancillary personnel* as we explore the roles played by convention managers and their operations coordinators, host committees, congressional gallery superintendents and pool producers, and television network producers. Afterward, we turn to *nonperforming artists* and the activities of composers, stage directors, and set designers. Lastly, we consider the *performing artists* and the conductors, singers, and critics associated with the show. Our review of convention impresarios employs examples primarily from the 1988 national party conventions with references to the 1984 gatherings as appropriate.

THE ANCILLARY PERSONNEL

Ancillary personnel are busy during production and postproduction operations, but are most active during the preproduction period. Party management teams supervise site selection, administrative operations, and convention hall preparations while the congressional galleries, network pool producers, host committees, and media executives work with party management, and one another, to address their particular logistical needs.

It is at this point that the convention overwhelms its sister spectacle, the opera. Though several ancillary roles exist in opera companies, the extravagant bureaucracies that accompany them in convention orchestration do not. Although opera companies have local sponsors, few are welcomed by host committees on behalf of cities catering lavishly to their demands as well as to the wishes of patrons and music journalists. Even fewer operatic performances involve a five-to-one reporter-to-artist ratio. The presidential nominating convention is an orchestrated spectacle without peer. Consider, for example, the convention's ancillary personnel.

The Production Company Management

A cursory review of the parties' organizational configurations for convention orchestration reveals two distinct management strategies. Whereas the 1988 Democrats (which we refer to as the DNC as it pertains to convention-related entities) had a general manager (Greenblat) to oversee logistical operations and a chief executive officer (Don Fowler) to supervise the show's content and delivery, the 1988 Republicans (RNC) used a convention manager (Bill Phillips) to preside over all organization and planning. Likewise, the DNC employed one production team to design the hall and choreograph the show (Smith-Hemion) and another to operate its satellite network (Paul Byers). In contrast, the RNC retained one veteran operative to supervise both operations (Mark Goode). In each case, the Republicans hired people who had served in those management (or similar) capacities previously; only Fowler had convention experience with the Democrats. Although the Democrats' Arleigh Greenblat and the Republicans' Bill Phillips held similar titles, their respective activities personified two distinct administrative orientations. Greenblat was a logistics coordinator who organized the complexities of convention management in a manner not only for coordination of the 1988 DNC but for conventions to follow in the 1990s and beyond. Phillips, by contrast, inherited an orchestral scheme and plan assembled by a long line of experienced GOP convention impresarios dating back over two decades.

Most of the convention impresarios for both parties in 1988 possessed political and/or news media experience, but the Democrats' general manager did not. Arleigh Greenblat, president of Second Executive (a Washington-based consulting firm) and manager for many National Education Association national meetings, approached his job as a professional convention *manager*, not a politician or administrator. He envisioned his task as the installation of "a series of management systems" that would introduce the same type of continuity common to recurring conventions of educators to the quadrennial Democratic gathering of politicians and news people. Consequently, Greenblat applied computerized managerial principles in an apolitical manner. As he told *Meetings and Conventions* magazine, "if we're going to sink to political decisions—which generally mean whoever yells the loudest ends up getting something—we're going to end up with a lot of confusion on our hands" (Quinn, 1988, p. 50).

Yet Greenblat recognized that politics is what the 1988 Democratic assembly was all about and, as he predicted, confusion occurred. To cope with anticipated (and realized) chaos, Greenblat employed site-selection data to construct an infrastructure for convention management. A comprehensive yet feasible plan could, he thought, avoid political complications and introduce managerial continuity to convention orchestration. During site selection, Greenblat related, he "had technical advisors that were good at understanding things like traffic, hotel capacities and capabilities, [and] security." Therefore, he "floated information to each of the technical advisors before the site inspection" and, afterward, "recapped everything and quoted it to them" for confirmation. All such data were computerized (he created programs to manipulate his findings) and used for what Greenblat called the "management operation of the convention." Exemplifying Greenblat's managerial style was his "program budget" for the convention. Traditionally, Democrats used an administrative budget for each convention that accounted for the expenditures associated with that particular assembly. Greenblat reasoned "if you said, well, the Democrats have a project every four years, then it's . . . continual"; the best way to institute a game plan for subsequent conventions is to develop a program budget that charts the growth of expenditures across the various areas. With that goal in mind, in February and March 1987 he devised a 22-area program budget that tracked expenditures on security, housing, transportation, food service, telecommunications, and so on that allowed him to create a foundation for administrative continuity.

Greenblat also directly supervised the hiring process, and with a strong emphasis on minorities: "We're the party of the people you know." He coordinated food services, hotel assignments, and security arrangements and participated in contract negotiations for construction, insurance, and other required activities. Along with these logistical responsibilities, Greenblat worked with the television networks and the Atlanta host committees on a variety of construction, work space, and hospitality matters. In short, Arleigh Greenblat was directly involved in virtually every facet of the Atlanta convention's logistical planning.

Several seasoned convention impresarios interviewed for this study and/or quoted in press reports cited Greenblat's lack of political-convention experience as a serious liability for the 1988 Democrats. Since many of these veterans were unaware of Greenblat's long-range personal managerial objectives, they may have underestimated the extent of his success. Whether or not Greenblat suffered from political inexperience, nevertheless, he computerized the entire management process for his employers. Greenblat's "color-coded files"—provided to the Democratic National Committee for future convention planning—contain the orchestral plan for managerial continuity in subsequent party conventions. That party leaders will turn to those records in 1992 remains to be seen. If not, the long-term goal of Greenblat's 1988 efforts will remain unrealized.

Greenblat's *individual* concerns for continuity, technical advice, and fiscal accountability provide a stark contrast to the *institutional* framework under the management of the GOP's Bill Phillips. The Republican National Committee's Committee on Arrangements maintains five subcommittees (housing, news media, security, tickets and badges, and transportation) consisting of representatives from every state. Thus, Phillips's job involved the oversight of a series of established operations with access to detailed technical expertise—not the solicitation of advice from a variety of independent technical sources. Phillips described his role: "It is my job to make sure that every delegate has what he or she needs, that the program is in place, that the lights are on, and that the air conditioning is running, because if any of that goes wrong, there'll be a disruption of what we're down there to do" (Levin, 1988, p. 38). Notice the contrasting images the two managers hold about their positions: Greenblat expresses concerns for continuity and *management* principles; Phillips takes these matters for granted and, in turn, speaks to the event's *political* objectives.

Merri Jo Cleair, one of Phillips's principal assistants, called Phillips a "great detail person" and a "hands-on manager" who benefited from the experience of a cadre of Republican logistics personnel ("we don't have to start from ground one" for each event). According to Cleair, Phillips began with a small staff and added to that group when, and only when, it was necessary. Though she viewed logistical planning to be the key to all conventions, Cleair felt "the fact that this was the first political convention to be held in a dome facility . . . a larger facility than has ever been used" elevated the significance of Phillips's administrative duties.

To meet those challenges Phillips turned to his party's strength: its institutional memory. A telling example of the GOP's institutional memory involves the 1988 tickets-and-badges operative, Josephine L. Goode. Goode has worked with Republican National Conventions since 1956, and between 1956 and 1960 devised the first "blueprint for staging a national convention" (Cotter & Hennessy, 1964, p. 108). In 1988 Goode had the unenviable task of assigning seats for the thousands of party officials, family, and guests attending the convention. The subcommittee on tickets and badges maintains a formula for credentials distribution, but the experience of over 30 years of national conventions probably served the *political aspects* of that distribution process well (owing to the Superdome's size, Goode modified the distribution formula to include groups such as the GOP's honorary delegates).

For convention hall preparations the GOP relied on Jim Baker—a man who has worked with national conventions since 1952. Levin (1988) observed how "an American political convention" is often characterized as a "circus" and the Republicans have "gotten themselves a real ringmaster" in Baker (p. 43). Baker, who once moved the Ringling Brothers Circus from city to city, has a background that prepared him for the Greatest Political Show on Earth. He supervised the installation of chairs, microphones, telephones, banners and decorations, carpeting, office furniture and supplies, wiring and cabling, balloons, and camera stands for the New Orleans convention. In 1988, once each evening's session was over, it was not unusual to find Baker lining up delegation seats and checking banners and signs.

Goode and Baker were joined by veterans Mark Goode, Bill Harris (whom Phillips described as his "principal deputy" and "man of the year"), and Mike Miller to form an operations team of several years' accumulated experience. ABC News's Justin Friedland related how it was difficult to fool the experienced Republican communications director: "The problem with dealing with Mike [Miller] is when you come in and say Mike we've got to have this . . . he's got you because he knows that you don't really have to have it, he knows it would be nice if you did, but he knows it really [does not] affect your ability to cover the story." Similarly, Senate press gallery superintendent Bob Petersen recalled how he could go to Democrats and say "you guys gave us the sun, stars, and our own personal limousines . . . and they don't know the difference." But "the Republicans, you can't fool" since they have the "continuity" that comes with seasoned personnel. And the CNN Special Events crew told us that they would occasionally go ahead and do things without the Democrats' permission. Often, this was because they did not know *who* to ask *for* that permission. In contrast, the RNC displayed an operations structure that, while restrictive, left little doubt about who ran what operation.

The Democrat operations, perhaps because of a relative absence of orchestral experience, were more fragmented than the GOP's. One prime example of the DNC's complicated organizational structure was their communications operation. Since the director of communications was dismissed some six weeks prior to the convention, the presence of any administrative structure was, indeed, a credit to those involved. Former Bruce Babbitt press secretary Mike McCurry, the party's new director of communications, was assisted by manager of operations Terry Michael in the oversight of a 13-division convention communications staff (the Democrats' communications structure requires an 11-page program to list its personnel). McCurry, needing help in establishing the complex press operation in a limited amount of time, turned to "the guy with the most experience around" (Terry Michael) and said "help bail me out on this." Michael's first convention was in 1984.

Thus, two very different managerial philosophies guided the 1988 conventions. One party, the Republicans, maintained a rigid, seasoned, administrative structure that not only understood the intricacies of convention orchestration but provided focal points of information for other orchestrators. The other party, the Democrats, retained a convention manager interested in *introducing* logistical continuity between events, and featured an inexperienced, fragmented, operations staff. Greenblat claimed the Democrats suffered from "management in isolation" (hence our references to fragmentation) that detracted from a sense of "team spirit." Republicans, on the other hand, possessed an experienced "team" with an established method of operation. Phillips, aware of his team's procedural continuity, tried both to keep his players "out of a rut" and to promote continuity by gradually incorporating new personalities into the management team (e.g., transportation impresario Jeff Means was a new player in 1988). These two managerial frameworks set the pace for two equally different approaches to convention orchestration.

The Host Committees

One set of ancillary personnel that transcends party lines consists of each convention city's host committee. The *Atlanta '88* and the *Louisiana Host Committee* operations played vital roles in the coordination of entertainment, housing, security, and transportation in 1988. Both convention managers praised the assistance they received from their respective host committees. A brief review of host operations reveals why.

The Louisiana Host Committee had "Mae the Baby Elephant on standby at the Audubon Park and Zoological Gardens," made arrangements for restaurants to stay open later than normal after Superdome sessions, had volunteer drivers on call to carry reporters and others to and from the airport, and provided a variety of other service activities (Levin, 1988, pp. 38–39). Correspondingly, the Atlanta '88 group coordinated a luncheon during the December media walk-through, supervised housing arrangements, and hosted an extravagant closing party after Thursday night's final session. The host committees are a focal point of activity and, therefore, work closely with other ancillary personnel. These special-events coordinators reach out to virtually every facet of convention planning to ensure the host city both provides for convention-related needs and garners positive publicity in return for those services.

The respective cities stand to earn considerable profit from the party conventions. The exact amounts to be gained are hard to ascertain, yet the cities' profits are potentially substantial. For instance, Kosterlitz (1988) projected that New Orleans expected "$140 million worth of economic activity" (p. 8) from the GOP conclave. More specifically, that figure involved "about $55 million in direct spending and another $85 million in economic activity," including visitors spending "$12 million on hotels" and another "$15 million on construction—most of it by the television networks." Little wonder so much competition emerges in site visitation and selection. The convention cities experience an economic boom from hosting a party gathering.

Not all host committees operate in the same fashion. Greenblat felt the Atlanta '88 entity was a far more focused group than the "more generic" San Francisco operation from 1984. Atlanta '88 contributed "millions of dollars to the administrative and managerial side" of the convention (in Greenblat's words). Laura Broadwell (1988) wrote that "city officials passed a three-year hotel bed tax that provided the Atlanta '88 host committee with $13.5 million" (p. 96). For Greenblat, a host committee and their legal staff can "make or break" convention planning and, fortunately for Democrats, Atlanta '88 was "just fantastic." Merri Jo Cleair cited the "bipartisan" qualities of the Louisiana Host Committee as well as the different entities operating under that banner. Both the Superdome and the city of New Orleans maintained its own host-committee operation, which in turn required considerable coordination. For instance, since the city was responsible for certain security, transportation, and construction arrangements, it entertained bids for those services independently of the party and the Louisiana Host entity. The city retained media and party work space in the Hyatt (the host hotel) and negotiated reduced hotel rates in the city—all either paid for (in the Hyatt's case) or coordinated by city planners.

Although receiving little attention and, perhaps, being taken for granted by some orchestrators, a convention city's host committee is an invaluable element in convention orchestration. To make money for their city, host impresarios are willing to spend money. It comes as no surprise that the existence of a well-coordinated host committee is both a persuasive force in site selection and that host operations are so extensive and expensive that only a few cities are able to provide such services.

The Congressional Press Galleries and Pool Producers

One of the more intriguing ancillary relationships in the orchestration process involves public officials acting as impresarios on behalf of political journalists. The congressional galleries and TV network pool producers are mediators between the political parties and the news media. That mediation occurs by negotiation—for work space, over operations logistics (camera locations, press stand dimensions, and so on), and the allocation of press credentials for the convention. What makes all this intriguing is that these negotiations may be congenial at one point, acrimonious at another. Intense battles over press-stand dimensions, floor access by reporters, sight lines, security arrangements, hotel assignments, and finances frequently occur between these impresarios. Yet without exception, the political parties and news media appreciate how the galleries and pool producers make everyone's convention labors much easier; as a result, party and media operatives applaud the participation of gallery and pool producers.

Consider these ticklish, prestige-laden questions. How could the Democrats decide whether to give the *New York Times* or the *Washington Post* the better press-stand seats, and how many should each publication receive? How could the Republicans inform CBS that NBC's camera will be awarded the best shot in the nominee's hotel suite? And, more important, how could the parties make certain that a newspaper with a small circulation receives the same access and privileges as *USA Today*? Such questions are nothing but political dynamite for the two political parties—on the order of telling either of two opera stars who gets the more lavish dressing room. Both parties avoid the pitfalls (and pratfalls) of such choices by allowing the press galleries and pool producers to play Solomon. The Senate Ethics Committee has ruled it appropriate for the congressional galleries (the Senate and House press, periodical, photographers, and radio/TV galleries) to serve as the credentialing agents for the two national conventions. The TV networks do not work with the galleries; instead, they work directly with the political parties or through the pool producers in credentialing.

Although gallery personnel are involved throughout all phases of the orchestration process, they are most active with preproduction arrangements. They participate in site selection, make presentations before the convention hierarchy during the media walk-throughs, and announce the credentialing procedures for their particular medium. During the convention they disseminate press credentials and coordinate the distribution of floor passes (the print and electronic media perform these tasks differently—a point we discuss in Chapter 3). After the convention each gallery prepares a report for its Standing Committee of Correspondents, the governing bodies of the various galleries.

Tina Tate, superintendent of the House radio/TV gallery, described her role as a "nonpartisan effort . . . to handle the needs of the broadcasters. . . . We are advocates to the parties for the broadcasters and a point of information." Tate's role, in particular, has enlarged substantially in the age of telepolitical conventions. This is due to the marked increase in convention coverage by local and group broadcasters mentioned in Chapter 1. She works with the political parties to coordinate credentials distribution, the allocation of work space, the assignment of coveted skybox and stand-up locations, the parking of satellite trucks, and other technical aspects of on-location convention coverage by local broadcasters. Tate notes that her job is made easier by the fact that her constituents pay for their technical needs. She observed "we pay for anything we get so [the parties] are responsive to try to provide what we need . . . there is nothing given to us by the parties." This is not the case with the print press. The Democrats and Republicans pay for the construction of the press stands that are so prominent to the right and left of the podium at each party's convention. For the parties to charge newspaper or magazine organizations for this space—as they charge broadcasters for skyboxes and stand-up locations—would significantly alter the party–gallery–print press relationship. If the political parties were to charge for press-stand seats, the galleries would immediately withdraw from convention orchestration—at least if one gallery impresario's view prevails. Bob Petersen, superintendent of the Senate press gallery, firmly asserted "we would not act as agents to collect funds for construction of stands" owing, primarily, to a fear that charges would hurt the smaller circulation publications.

The television networks are not active in the congressional gallery-party process and, in effect, have created their own "gallery" in the form of the pool system. Here, necessity is the mother of invention: there can only be one head-on camera shot, one microphone on the rostrum, one camera in the candidate's hotel suite, and so on. The necessity to consolidate broadcast resources owing to technical restrictions produced the adoption of the network pool system in the convention context. As both TV network pool producers confirmed in separate interviews, there are two main reasons for the pool: limited access (as with the head-on shot) and the magnitude

of the event. (Space shots, inaugurals, and state visits are other prime examples of pooling operations.)

The TV networks draw straws to determine which organizations will coordinate the pool for each convention. In 1988, NBC opted out of the responsibility for pool operations owing to commitments for Olympic coverage in Seoul, Korea. Therefore, ABC, CBS, and CNN drew lots. ABC and
CBS were the winners (or perhaps losers from the producers' perspective).
The two networks selected Charles Frey (ABC) and John Reade (CBS) as
the respective pool producers for the Atlanta and New Orleans conventions. Frey has been involved with convention coverage since 1960, Reade
since 1972. Neither had been the pool producer before, though both had
been associated in one capacity or another with pool coverage.

The TV networks make serious logistical commitments to the pool process through the assignment of technical assistance. In 1988, because of
its union contract, ABC was unable to join CBS's use of a local affiliate
(CBS used the technical staff of New Orleans WWL-TV), which contributed even more to ABC's pool costs. Pool producers are involved in convention hall preparations (camera location construction and distribution,
cabling, etc.), work space acquisition and allocation (both inside the hall
and outside in the so-called trailer farms), lighting and audio (for both inside the hall and remotes), as well as their directorial responsibilities during the actual show. Pool duties are wide ranging and their impact on the
orchestration process is beyond measure.

The touch that pool producers must exert in working with the parties
and with the networks simultaneously is as delicate as that of a maestro
conducting a duet of prima donnas. Reade confided "you have to be very
careful when you pool . . . it's a very fine line" and, at times, the "hardest
network to work with . . . is your own." Once more, the respective political
parties' administrative structures are key to the orchestration. Reade referred to the GOP's Mike Miller in glowing terms ("Mike Miller is just fan-
tastic!"), whereas Frey seldom mentioned contacts with DNC-TV Network
liasons at all. Miller and Reade developed a close relationship, even traveled together to the Democratic convention in Atlanta where they carefully studied the camera shots and logistics in preparation for pool coverage of the GOP a month later. Frey did not have this type of relationship
with Democrats owing, in part, to the recency of McCurry's appointment
and to the structure underlying DNC orchestration. Frey viewed this lack
of continuity as "a disadvantage" for the Democrats; on occasion, he said
he had to "steer them" through decisions. Unlike the GOP's Miller, who
"is aware of all the problems and knows them better than anybody," the
Democrats "deferred" and asked "what do you think we ought to do
about it?" Interestingly, when asked who he worked with among Democrats, Frey replied: "That's hard to characterize. In many ways, I don't feel
I was working with anybody. That was the unique thing. There was no

Mike Miller . . . McCurry was not a Mike Miller, he came in so late." Thus, Frey worked directly with the architects on the Omni's internal construction—an unlikely undertaking for a pool producer dealing with the GOP administrative structure. Frey, an experienced pool operative, not only served the TV networks well, he undertook orchestration responsibilities more normally and appropriately performed by party designers.

The gallery superintendents and pool producers are impresarios with considerable influence in the orchestration process. As the Democratic convention's CEO Fowler declared, "I shudder to think of what would have happened without those people."

The Network Producers

Any discussion of the network producers must necessarily stress their involvement in such key preproduction activities as housing acquisition, meetings with party officials, and (in NBC's Joe Angotti's words) "physical" concerns. That emphasis, however, is not to imply that impresarios from other than network organizations are not involved as well. For example, nonnetwork, smaller news organizations work with the host committees to secure housing, they obtain work space and credentials from the congressional galleries, and—in general—they negotiate preproduction logistics through established channels. Larger media companies, on occasion, do not. Consider the *Washington Post*. Our interviews revealed that in 1988 the *Post*'s Bob Longstreet purchased airlines tickets to each of the cities selected as convention site finalists; then, immediately upon the national committees' announcement of the winning city, Longstreet flew to that site and acquired hotel accommodations for his organization. Longstreet, armed with a blank check signed by Post Company CEO Katharine Graham, gained prime housing for his company and frustrated host committees and hotels alike through this clever maneuver—what Don Fowler termed "Lone Ranger" tactics.

Other organizations play roles in convention orchestration, but they, in no way, enjoy the television networks' status. Justin Friedland (ABC), Joe Angotti and Lloyd Siegel (NBC), the CNN Special Events team of Jane Maxwell, John Towriss, and Alec Miran, and C-SPAN's Mike Michaelson all described the details of site visitations, party-network production meetings, and convention hall and work space construction operations. A measure of how seriously cities competing for the privilege of hosting party conventions take the presence of the TV networks is that the city of Houston made its "convention site pitch" before the *networks* in New York, not in Houston!

Network producers vary in their perceptions of their relationships to the political parties, but there is little disagreement that their commitment is to *their* networks and not to the party spectacle. NBC's Angotti captured the situation when he observed: "The relationship between the network and party kind of reminds me of a mating dance. You kind of circle each other and you make your needs and desires known, and they make their needs and desires known, and you are always kind of circling and always looking for an opening." The constant search for an "opening" is what the networks producers are all about. Mike Michaelson, for example, wants respect and choice camera locations for his network, C-SPAN; ABC, CBS, CNN, and NBC want prime access to political notables without party interference.

The basic services provided the TV networks depend partly on the administrative structures of the two parties described earlier. Justin Friedland of ABC recalled the frustrations of dealing with the inexperienced Democratic Atlanta production team: "You keep discovering things. Oh, you need telephones? Well, yes we do, we need telephones. Oh, well I hadn't figured on that and you say you want air-conditioning? Well, yes . . . we use a lot of fancy equipment and it doesn't like the heat." These "oh-by-the-ways" (in Friedland's terms) are a constant source of frustration for the networks. Networks encounter them in dealings with both parties. But, as Friedland acknowledged, the situation in 1988 was eased by working with experienced GOP personnel: "You deal with a bunch of professionals and so it went much easier, the camera selection went easier, the access went easier, you're dealing with a professional team right from the beginning. . . . That makes a big difference."

The entertainment network producers begin convention preparations with plans to meet housing, utilities, construction, communications, and other logistical needs. As a commercial, yet all-news network, the CNN production team also addressed these fundamentals, but pursued other avenues as well. Jane Maxwell told us that as a CNN convention producer she distributed an in-house survey to all CNN show producers in order to determine the individual requirements of CNN personnel and plans. Unlike the purely entertainment networks who preempt prime-time programming to cover the conventions, CNN regards network prime time as coverage of the event itself. In preparation, the Special Events team sought input from each normally scheduled news program and attempted to "marry" its "blue sky" requests with the network's convention coverage. Productions such as "Sonya Live," "Crossfire," and the "Larry King Show" traveled next door to the Omni or to New Orleans for live broadcasts. Thus, the Special Events staff had to devise ways to accommodate a variety of production needs. In contrast, the entertainment networks do not turn to content matters until much later, as we shall see in Chapter 3.

The fifth network, the nonprofit C-SPAN, was also involved in the logistical arrangements for the conventions, but on a much smaller scale. Hotel accommodations and electronic logistics are as important to its operation as any other; still, it clearly does not demand the attention the other networks require. C-SPAN covered its first convention in 1984 because the company's executives could not afford the "over $60,000" in pool feed costs (remember the pool feed costs inspired the RNCN's creation) and believed money could be better spent on C-SPAN's own production. The network traveled to San Francisco and Dallas and covered the two events for *less* than the cost of the pool feed. Mike Michaelson affectionately recounted taking his group to California and watching them enter the Moscone Center for the first time: "These kids walked into that room and their eyes lit up like pinball machines. It was like Christmas in July and they couldn't believe that they were going to be a part of this great spectacle alongside the networks." C-SPAN obtained free studio space just three blocks from the Moscone Center and covered the Democrats gavel-to-gavel. Though they remain a relatively low-budget operation with restrictive funding levels, C-SPAN programming is an important part of the convention process.

Owing to the huge sums of money spent on their convention coverage, the various over-the-air and cable networks exercise great care in their logistic arrangements. Other media entities spend money during the conventions, but none endure the construction, support staff, and operations costs the networks encounter. The network impresarios responsible for these tasks play essential roles in the orchestration process. They may no longer dominate orchestration as in the mass-mediated era, but continue to be major concert masters in the telepolitical age.

THE NONPERFORMING ARTISTS

Our review of the administrative duties associated with ancillary operations sets the scene for an examination of the nonperforming impresarios who function within those organizational structures. We now move away from the never-ending list of logistical details toward a consideration of the personnel responsible for the convention spectacle's content and delivery. Unlike the behind-the-scenes arrangements for housing, work space, security, and hospitality, these nonperforming artists produce the program to be witnessed by millions of people.

Just as an opera's appearance on television provokes producers' concerns regarding the telegenic qualities of set design, stage direction, and show content, a telepolitical convention centers on these features as well. The telepolitical assembly's emphasis on tightly scripted program copy delivered through a series of institutionalized performances places intense demands on the show's composing operations. Moreover, its reliance on telegenic stage direction requires the parties to enlist production teams who create sets and choreograph character movement in a fashion that effectively conveys their carefully crafted content. Two such teams are especially noteworthy: the composing operations and the set design and stage direction teams. Both 1988 conventions enlisted seasoned composers who used polling data and political savvy to plan their assembly's content. Our set design, stage direction, and spin operations teams, however, reflect the different administrative styles we observed in preceding sections.

The Composers

Quinn (1988) observed that "one of the reasons" the Democrats hired Arleigh Greenblat "as general manager was to free up the DNCC's CEO, Don Fowler, a communications company president and former South Carolina Democratic party chairman, to concentrate on program planning" (p. 50). Subsequently, Fowler was responsible for the party's message committee as well as the retention of the Smith-Hemion production company (he was also involved in logistic matters). Fowler's experience on two Democratic site-selection committees (he was chair of the 1980 committee) prepared him for his role as chief executive officer.

Fowler's *message committee* consisted of national committee chair Paul Kirk, pollster Peter Hart, media consultant Bob Squire, political strategist Kirk O'Donnell, and himself. According to Fowler, the group concentrated on "what are we going to tell these people [convention audiences] about the Democratic Party" through this "four-night mini-series." To devise that strategy, the group met "around May or June of 1987" and "almost every month for a year." Hart conducted "two or three national polls, two or three focus group sessions" and "some other research trying to define the message of the Democratic party." The CEO described the message committee's plans in this manner: "Our message was that the Democratic party is a political organization capable of solving the real problems of the average American in the 1990s." The strategy, then, was to focus on the future: "We tried not to talk as much about Harry Truman, Jack Kennedy, [and] Franklin Roosevelt as we had in previous conventions" and, instead, featured talent that was "younger, less well known and less encumbered with the perceived difficulties of the Democratic party" (in Fowler's words). The party turned to the Chris Dodds, Bill Bradleys, and Bill Clintons to convey this youthful message since, as Fowler suggested, "in the media age the messenger is more important than the message." We consider the success of this strategy and the message committee's efforts to coordinate the continuity of the script's enactment later; however, at this point notice the sophistication of the Democrats' composing operation— *an activity essential to a telepolitical convention's success.*

The second Democratic composing entity, the *spin operation*, illustrates the party's attempts to control the mediation of convention realities for external audiences and, once more, the influence of Democratic administrative structure. Communications operative Terry Michael was precise in his review of how the DNC used "technology and technique" to influence convention coverage (provide a strategic "spin"). Yet, when he related efforts to implement those plans he described a multitude of people. The number of people involved with the DNC's communications operation could not help but inspire the confusion described by pool producer Charles Frey and by the CNN Special Events squad. Structure aside, the DNC's spin operation contained computer-transmitted speech texts; the designation of party "newsmakers" for media interviews who were skillful in handling those encounters; and the use of the "party line" that facilitated the media's access to demographic information, schedules, and party newsletters. In virtually every respect, the DNC spin-control operation, though administratively diverse, represented a major move into the age of telepolitical orchestration.

The GOP's *program group* functioned much like the DNC's message committee with the exception of Mark Goode's involvement. The starting point for the program group, as Merri Jo Cleair observed, involved the "basic shell" that is the convention's order of business. Simply, delegates have to be officially seated, platforms ratified, people nominated, roll calls conducted, and acceptance speeches delivered. From there the program group filled in "the entertainment or speeches and the special effects and the things you do for television."

Convention manager Bill Phillips, consistent with his managerial philosophy of undertaking tasks as the process unfolds, made clear that the program committee started "very small by design" owing to the number of candidates in the GOP race. Once Bush "nailed it down" Phillips asked Bush convention coordinator Fred Malek to serve as the group's chair and, afterward, enlisted media consultant Roger Ailes, pollster Bob Teeter, 1984 convention manager Ron Walker, and Mark Goode to "start talking about speakers and themes and mix of speakers." Much like the DNC's Smith-Hemion team, Phillips and Goode agreed that Goode would operate from "the technical standpoint" since "he sat in the trailer" (the RNC's state-of-the-art television control room) and functioned as "a TV producer or director" (in Phillips's words). Unlike the DNC's Smith-Hemion, however, Goode was an active participant in the script-preparation process.

The program group designed and implemented a "politics of inclusion" theme that, in contrast with the streamlined Dallas convention (with its emphasis on video introductions and telegenic pacing), stressed podium oratory as the principal means of expression. Hence, over 150 Republicans addressed the convention and invited audiences to join the GOP's "patriotic cause." Phillips proudly acknowledged his convention was one "of inclusion instead of exclusion" in both the number and diversity of speakers as well as the number of delegates, alternates, and guests seated inside their huge facility (a clear reference to the Atlanta convention's tendency to lock the Omni's doors because of overcrowding).

Republicans also maintained an active spin operation albeit in terms distinct from their Democratic counterparts. The RNC's spin mechanism focused more on message control than information dissemination. Delegates received the daily *hymnals* we mentioned in our Prelude and the party used daily press conferences to emphasize predetermined themes. The hymnals were a device used to assist delegates with media interviews. Each morning the GOP devised a "line of the day" and distributed that information under the doors of delegate hotel rooms. These thematic messages, it was hoped, would help Republicans offer a single message via a variety of voices: a harmony of political sentiment.

Correspondingly, a daily GOP two o'clock press conference addressed a series of strategic themes. Unlike Democrats, the 1984 and 1988 Republican conventions established a press conference facility that encouraged the news media to set up video, audio, and lighting equipment for the convention's duration. Instead of holding one press conference in one location and another somewhere else, the GOP created a stage and score that facilitated party influence of media coverage; thus, the two o'clock hour was a well-timed opportunity for assuring widespread coverage on local and national TV news shows. There were, of course, other news conferences held by the GOP in New Orleans, but this daily, regularly scheduled event directed delegates to their hymnals and, in turn, reinforced the "line of the day."

Other composing operations in 1988 transcended party lines. Both national parties maintained television network liaisons, had central speech units, and featured scripted roll calls of the states. One Democratic offical told the *Los Angeles Times*'s Thomas Rosenstiel (1988a) that the DNC's central speech unit was an attempt "to make sure all the notes are sounded in this symphony" (p. 6)—a clear reference to the party's pursuit of harmony. The various GOP delegations also "cleared" their roll-call announcements with the party in order to ensure the harmonius qualities of their individual performances (this inspired one writer to lament the passing of the "last bastion of spontaneity" from the conventions ["Roll Call," 1988]). Though network producers dislike attempts to control interviews, the parties' efforts demonstrate unrelenting orchestration strategies to promote harmony from the rostrum, the anchor booth, and/or the convention floor.

Telepolitical conventions have most certainly institutionalized specific performances to be added to official party business to constitute a "shell" completed by the parties' composing operations. Both parties, therefore, assembled 1988 teams composed of media advisers, pollsters, and political strategists who provided copy to be shaped by in-house television producers. For these composers, improvisation is a ticket for disaster; as a result, they prepare strategically conceived scripts tailored for podium speeches, roll calls, media interviews, and press conferences. Yet the telepolitical composer still faces the unfortunate reality that talent is talent and, as we shall observe in Chapter 4, once upon the stage anything can happen.

Stage Directors and Set Designers

This group of nonperforming personnel is difficult to construe in terms of individuals, but rather must be considered as teams. The *team* is a nonperforming entity even though some team *members* have other—administrative, nonperforming, and/or performing—roles as well. For instance, the show's conductor—the Democrats' dual operation of Smith-Hemion and Paul Byers, and the GOP's Mark Goode—played performing roles during the production, but in the preproduction phase they worked with composers and operations impresarios to design the set and choreograph the program (nonperforming activities).

Knapp (1972) describes the complexities of operatic stage direction and sets the scene for a consideration of this role in the convention context. He writes that the "stage director is generally in charge of the purely theatrical elements of the opera: acting, movement on stage, and the entire *mise-en-scène* (settings, lights, costumes, and properties)" (p. 110). Moreover, the stage director "generally has a vocal score of the music prepared with blank pages inserted opposite each page of music (the production book)," which assures "that there is no doubt about what is to occur on stage at any time with the music."

The stage director's principal problem involves "making actors out of singers, yet not allowing their vocal performances to suffer" (p. 110). Since "gestures and movements" have "to be adapted accordingly," the stage director must "determine how musical introductions and interludes are to be filled onstage and how much freedom can be allowed without detracting from the music." As with its sister spectacle, the convention, this role did not exist in opera's early development. But, in "an intensely visual age of television" (p. 111), Knapp contends, the role is crucial. In our television era, "appearance has become the catchword, and music has suffered accordingly" (recall Fowler's remarks about the messenger's importance?); "well-known directors from the spoken stage have been brought to opera and have imposed their personal vision upon the spectacle without knowing much about music." Knapp concludes "in many instances, this new approach has helped to let fresh air into the stultifying atmosphere of opera."

The political parties, too, have endeavored to let some "fresh air" into the convention production. Like opera companies, the Democrats turned to a well-known production team "from the spoken stage" (in this case, television) via the Smith-Hemion company. Though the "political" may suffer when given a lower priority than "appearance," and, in turn, confound the political music emanating from the show, the coordination of set design and program continuity contributes to the production's visual qualities. By contrast the Republicans relied on an established political operative, Mark Goode, to oversee stage direction and set design, but scarcely sacrificed "appearance" in so doing.

The DNC team consisted of Fowler, Smith-Hemion, McCurry's operation, and Byers. As noted earlier, the DNC separated the Smith-Hemion operation from the party's Convention Satellite News Service (Byers's duties). This two-tier style of coordination created a situation where Smith-Hemion designed the set, choreographed the show, and directed the party's cameras within the Omni. Byers, on the other hand, received the Smith-Hemion feed, molded highlight packages from that video, and occasionally featured prominent convention speeches in the production but emphasized primarily two-way satellite interviews and other locally oriented performances. For Democrats, there were two stage sets serving two separate functions, each with its own director.

The RNC team involved Mark Goode, Mike Miller, and, to a lesser extent, Phillips. In contrast to the DNC's approach, Goode was in charge of set design, stage direction, *and* the RNC Network. In this particular instance, this arrangement probably says more about the two parties' communications operations than their administrative styles. The CSNS and the RNCN stressed two different orientations: the former focused on locally oriented interviews with party newsmakers while the latter aired the "convention's business" (in Goode's words) and did not maintain a separate studio for interviews. According to Goode, between or before sessions, satellite interviews were transmitted from the Superdome floor.

THE PERFORMING ARTISTS

The joint activities of party administrative structures and their hired consultants, network executives, host committees, and congressional gallery staffs display a remarkable spirit of cooperation throughout the show's production. Though there is occasional strife, the ancillary and nonperforming personnel professionally cope with these problems and, somehow, produce this grand spectacle that is an American nominating convention. Still, what the world sees of these operations is not the off-stage efforts of ancillary and nonperforming performances but comes down to an unpredictable phenomenon: the performing talent. Here enter the production the political party and television network conductors and the highly visible performers who *enact* the carefully prepared scripts of message committees, program groups, and network executive producers. Here, too, are the sources for two separate productions that emanate from the same convention setting, two sets of performances that create the adversarial relationships that so characterize the telepolitical convention. Party conductors and pool producers occasionally argue, reporters and politicians confront one another, and high-priced anchors compete with party celebrities and filmed entertainment for air time.

No opera experiences anything like the level of scrutiny afforded a national party convention. Opera certainly maintains an in-house television operation and nurtures its critics, but it seldom has a critic sitting in a glass booth perched over the stage offering analysis of the unfolding show below, and—in the process—occupies center stage or sings the lead. Never do opera critics interrupt the recitative for commentary or commercial advertising. Convention spectacles, however, abound with political reporters and critics—not to mention the network executives and directors or the publishers and editors who *critique* their performances.

The Conductors

Chapter 1 described the conductor's emergence during the age of mass mediation. We noted how standardization required coordination and, as a result, the conductor's direction. A telepolitical convention's emphasis on telegenic detail demands even more from this crucial role. Knapp (1972) observes how operatic conductors must concentrate on both the music and the show's dramatic elements; therefore, "some conductors have become so involved in stagecraft that they insist on being both stage and musical director" (p. 109). Knapp's remarks directly capture Republican convention orchestration. Mark Goode worked with the GOP's program group and shaped that content according to group wishes. The Democrats, on the other hand, retained Smith-Hemion for set design, stage direction, and conducting, and their message committee provided the "music" to be choreographed (there were a few exceptions, such as the production's entertainment segments). Consider, therefore, four sets of conducting impresarios: the Democrats' Smith-Hemion and Paul Byers, the GOP's Goode, and the network pool producers. During a performance each controls the production's delivery from the conductor's pit and functions thereby as a performing artist.

Smith-Hemion. Don Fowler decided to hire professional television producers to choreograph the Atlanta convention, thus it was his job to go out and interview production companies. Fowler interviewed at least five production groups ranging from Dick Clark, to "the people who produce 'Saturday Night Live,' " to a sports production entity. The decision came down to Universal Studios and Smith-Hemion. Based upon input from a client, Fowler hired Smith-Hemion.

Known for its work with the "Liberty Weekend" extravaganza and the Academy Awards, Smith-Hemion has a strong reputation in the television industry. According to Paul Byers, "Don Fowler has certain skills, strengths, and advantages, but he is not a television producer" and, Byers argued, "the more complex and videogenic these [events] become, you need expertise of that sort." The use of Hollywood producers did attract attention. Mike McCurry described the Smith-Hemion–national committee relationship as "tempestuous." The party continuously had to stress that "this is a political convention which is by definition a serious event

. . . it's a news event." McCurry related that Smith-Hemion had to be convinced that the networks "were here covering this thing because it was news, not because it was going to be entertaining."

Chapter 3 describes Smith-Hemion's efforts to determine what the networks would and would not cover and how Democrats and Hollywood reached compromises. We should note here, however, that this "tempestuous" relationship between Smith-Hemion and the Democrats also extended to the networks. For example, ABC's Friedland did not hide his feelings about Smith-Hemion: "These guys . . . were playing in the wrong league. They were playing hockey in a sandlot baseball game. They are real good at what they do, you can't take that away from them, but this is news and news isn't what they do." Friedland echoed other network producers' sentiments when he declared "nobody cares how many tap dancers are coming out on stage before the convention begins and what city they are from and what patriotic number they are doing."

The decision to hire Smith-Hemion was controversial not only with the networks but, as Fowler acknowledged, with the Dukakis campaign itself. From the networks' viewpoint efforts to determine what journalists would or should cover were inappropriate. CNN's Jane Maxwell, for instance, said "you stage your thing, we'll stage ours." Dwight Hemion's attempt to supply pool producer Charles Frey with a "hotline" was also rejected as Frey "gave it back to them, politely" (in his words). Eventually, the controversy subsided and the personality conflicts mellowed. When all was said and done, Dukakis communications director Leslie Dach concluded, people probably did not confuse the Democratic convention with the Academy Awards since "the Academy Awards are covered gavel to gavel and the convention [wasn't]" (Grove, 1988, p. 13).

In any event, ranging from the Omni's color scheme, to the podium's form, to entertainment and opening and closing segments, Smith-Hemion designed the Atlanta Democrats' show. In Gary Smith's preconvention words, he tried "to inject the right look and a certain amount of pacing . . . I'm talking about a look that shows we are taking advantage of the most up-to-date technology—lighting, sound, computer involvement, video production" (Grove, 1988, p. 13).

Paul Byers. Paul Byers, yet another professional television producer, did not experience the controversy associated with the Smith-Hemion operation for a variety of reasons. The principal one was the nature of his Convention Satellite News Service. Originally conceived as an imitation of the GOP's RNC Network, the CSNS actually proved to be a distinctive approach to convention mediation. The CSNS focus on two-way satellite interviews, highlights packages, and to a far lesser extent, the events from the podium constituted an "apolitical" orientation less concerned with the dissemination of events inside the Omni than with the facilitation of locally based interviews with party newsmakers. Byers said "it was not our aim to control what was said in the interview. All we did was provide an environment where the interview could take place." He argued that his operation did not compete "with anybody"; it supplemented "what everybody else [was] doing and if we could be helpful and facilitate the communication process that's why we [were there], no more glorious ambition than that."

Among the CSNS sponsors were the Association of State Democratic Chairs, the Democratic Congressional Campaign Committee, the Democratic Governors Association, the Democratic National Committee, the Democratic Senatorial Committee, and the National Conference of Democratic Mayors. Byers said "all those entities were represented in the planning and in the divvying up of the time and the setting up of funding" and all of them "made contributions into a kitty to support the budget." The CSNS joined the increased number of group and local broadcasters as 1988 convention orchestrators. The size of audiences reached through these operations is difficult to measure (although Byers has some statistics on station use), but the party's dedication to the idea is not. CEO Fowler concluded: "I think [the CSNS] was . . . well worth the time and money that went into it and I'm sure it will be done . . . in '92." With the mix of groups using the CSNS, the Democrats may have truly "rehung the moon" (as Byers quoted one CSNS patron) in terms of telepolitical communications strategies.

Mark Goode. As already noted, the Republicans consolidated production and broadcast operations under Mark Goode's guidance. Goode claimed the conventions are so "sophisticated in the media and staging sense" that the party needs "a producer who is not a political person. Period." Goode argued "it is wise to have a producer who has that background and some political sensitivity." For Goode the expertise required to conduct the telepolitical convention is a unique blend of the political and the technical. Goode's role reached its current key status in 1984, with the Dallas GOP convention's increased attention to telegenic style. There he produced virtually all of the party videos (the film introducing Ronald Reagan was a major exception), coordinated the RNC Network, and supervised other elements of the show's production (entertainment, etc.). In 1988 he led a staff of "at least 200" that included volunteers, college students, and paid personnel. Goode was responsible for the RNC Network technical crew, the lighting crews, the "rigging crews that hung the big speakers," the sound crew, the orchestra, "the balloon designers and riggers," and "anything that was involved with technical or production" operations. During the 1988 production, Goode had a two-tier style of conducting. He both directed the flow of events on stage and was in constant communication with the RNC Network director. Furthermore, he was in contact with the pool producer and the individual network producers (if necessary) as he sat in front of a bank of television monitors and supervised the unfolding show. From his place in the conductor's pit, Mark Goode thus controlled the convention's flow just as Dwight Hemion did in Atlanta. Yet Goode's responsibilities extended much further, since he had input into the script and the show's dissemination on the party's in-house network.

The Pool Producers. Unlike the *nonperforming* duties of party-oriented conductors (Smith-Hemion, Byers, and Goode), pool producers Charles Frey and John Reade wore *ancillary* hats when they left their conductor's pits. In pre- and postproduction phases these two men supervised a wide range of logistical operations. During the show, however, they directed the pool camera feed—the most important camera shots of the entire production.

Frey, and later Reade, introduced a completely new directorial system during the 1988 conventions that merits attention. Traditionally, the pool producer directs camera shots just as any other TV director: exercising his or her judgment as to which head-on shot is most appropriate (the tight or long-range shot) and selecting from the two side shots that are treasured by their network counterparts. Unfortunately for network directors, once they subscribe to the pool feed the pool director may change shots, thereby leaving the network with an undesirable or uneven cut or a change of pacing. In 1988 Frey initiated the practice of supplying independent feeds for each of his four cameras. Though this placed an additional burden on the pool director, it allowed the network directors the comfort of knowing that the selected shot would not be radically changed or subjected to different pacing. According to Frey, "we got the pool camera probably to more air time this time than ever [before] because it was in four unique feeds and the directors felt they were in control of the cameras themselves and didn't have to worry about another camera undercutting." Reade, giving full credit to Frey for this innovation, followed the same strategy in New Orleans. Although the pool producers play powerful roles in preproduction activities such as camera assignments, work space distribution, and more, their supervision of the pool cameras is just as important. Reade and Frey not only directed the head-on shots but were responsible for the now-traditional hotel-room shot from the nominee's suite as well as remote lighting and audio (these activities are referred to as the "external pool" since they occur outside the convention hall).

The Talent

The most visible of all convention personnel are the men and women who perform from the rostrum and convention floor. This is the most conspicuous, and least complicated, set of performing artists. Their task is simple, yet crucial. It takes but one failure to destroy completely the entire evening's program. Their roles may be straightforward, but party talent must be judiciously selected lest years of planning be jeopardized. Here, then, are the principal types of talent available to convention orchestrators.

The Podium Cast. As Merri Jo Cleair observed, a convention maintains a program "shell" and the convention spectacle's specifics must be shaped around that framework. From the official business of the convention's initial moments (credentials and other committee business) and the opening-day aria that is the keynote speech, through the capstone event that is the presidential acceptance speech, the party *composing operations* create a show that features a steady recitative, prime-time arias, state-of-the-art films, and vainglorious displays of convention demonstrations (postnomination and roll-call demonstrations combine with postacceptance speech displays as the principal demonstrations).

The two parties' composing operations vary with respect to both organizations and events regarding the assembly of a cast. For example, in 1988 the Republicans provided opportunities for all candidates who had competed for the GOP nomination to address the convention (in either morning or evening sessions). By contrast, the Democrats' Don Fowler felt no need to award "the losers" precious podium time. Moreover, in 1984 the GOP had used video introductions of speakers, but returned to oratory in introducing podium performers in 1988. Entertainment celebrities were also cast members (Dollar, 1988). The Democrats turned to Garrison Keillor, Ally Sheedy, Casey Kasem, and others; the GOP featured Tom Selleck, Helen Hayes, and Joe Paterno in various roles.

In all cases, the convention displays its institutional heritage through the "shell" that is the show's order of business. The implementation of this shell, however, is a strategic enterprise. Which partisan will be selected to enact the convention's theme on Monday evening via the prime-time aria that is the keynote speech? Who will lead the platform discussions and nominate the respective candidates? One may disagree with Don Fowler's view that the messenger is more important than the message, yet there is credibility in the remark. In any case, former candidates and presidents, prominent leaders, ecclesiastics, celebrities, family members, and future stars are strategically placed to implement the composing teams' plans—if the party is lucky.

The Delegates. The delegations attending a national political convention are a widely misunderstood part of the orchestration process. Their central convention orchestration role has, to be sure, changed since the origins of cordial concurrence in American presidential politics. Certainly, as Arleigh Greenblat surmised, there are "two conventions," one staged for television and the other for the delegates. Yet the delegates' significance has in no way disappeared. The value of gathering political leaders from all parts of the nation for a one-week extravaganza has meaningful impact on the parties' abilities to sustain winning coalitions. Chapter 4 describes the character of 1988 party delegates in some detail. Here we focus on their roles in the orchestration process.

The *New York Times* reported "the real truth of modern political conventions" is that "the prime, and sometimes the only, purpose of what happens on the floor is to serve as a backdrop for television" such that the "delegates, who once were the central players at these conventions, are now the extras" (Oreskes, 1988a, p. 13). Technically, convention delegates are hardly "extras" solicited from some streetcorner to fill space in the convention hall for television producers. From an operatic view, they represent the party chorus called upon from time to time to perform in the show (both individually and collectively). They are, indeed, one of the largest choruses to be found in any production—so large that they are often difficult to manage by stage directors. Still, they are vital to the show's success, both theatrically and politically. Certainly, they may occasionally function as extras, but to limit their role to that part exclusively is virtually to trivialize all of American politics.

Delegate performances are contingent upon the convention in question. How they appear on TV in nominations, roll calls, platform debates, and the like are orchestration decisions made by that year's production teams. The GOP's Bill Phillips, for example, concluded: "Because of the communications system today and because of the VIPs and stars and that type of thing, it would be easy to forget that the reason you're there is so the 5,000 delegates and alternates [can] be placed. So we kept emphasizing that we wanted to take care of the delegates and build around them." And that is exactly what the 1988 RNC did.

Film Producers. Our final party-controlled performing artists are the film producers. As we have observed, the parties' reliance on telegenic devices has varied in recent conventions. After the 1984 GOP Dallas convention one could have argued that film would soon be a driving force in convention orchestration. But the New Orleans Republicans in 1988 reversed the course and used films in only a minimal way. Again, a great deal depends upon who is producing the spectacle. For example, Mark Goode's perspective as a television producer emerged in discussions of the film producer's role. Goode clearly prefers film introductions to podium oratory for that role. With each speaker comes time-consuming applause before and after, as well as uncertainty that the selected speaker will confine remarks to the allotted time frame. Video segues avoid all of these problems and, perhaps most important, provide for a variety of strategic associations. For example, "Jan" introduces "Senator Sue" from Pennsylvania. As Jan undertakes this task she dutifully receives applause before, after, and if lucky, during her remarks; lengthy applause occurs between her departure and Senator Sue's arrival and opening lines. A video introduction of Senator Sue can picture the senator with Jan, prominent party leaders and office holders, foreign leaders, and a variety of strategically selected constituency groups and settings. All of this takes place in about 30 seconds and ends with Senator Sue's appearance before her adoring crowd. Little wonder the "television people" whole-heartedly endorse the use of video introductions.

As Chapter 4 reveals, the 1988 Democrats and Republicans exploited video for a variety of purposes. Both parties introduced their nominees with these devices, showed historical pieces about prominent individuals, and used video to exalt parting and former presidents and primary-season runners-up. Smith-Hemion, Byers, Goode, various campaign groups, and the national party committees produced these videos. The future level of film use is uncertain, but the film producers' role within a telepolitical production is an institutionalized one.

The Journalists and/or Critics

No stage production or sporting event experiences the level of scrutiny the conventions receive. News organizations dominate the housing situation; bask in the lavish hospitality of political parties, sponsors, host committees, politicians, and interest groups; and spend millions of dollars on production facilities and technical operations. We divide the news organizations into two groups: the print press and the electronic media. Our purpose is not to describe the processes through which reporters cover the convention or the content of their reviews (the subjects of future chapters), but to establish their role in the production. We begin with the "pencil press."

The Print Media. Some print organizations send reporters to cover national conventions with a little or no support staff. But a casual glance around a convention hall suggests this is probably the exception, not the rule. Blocks of hotel rooms and credentials are set aside for publishers and editors (and their families) as well as reporters and photographers. Katz (1988b) put it well in *USA Today*'s report on the "media Woodstock" that is a convention: "It is a game of see and be seen. Top editors and publishers want to be seen having cocktails with top politicians, and vice versa. Status counts. . . . Who's in the resplendent Ritz-Carlton and who's at the airport Days Inn? Who's so important they have absolutely nothing to do?" (p. 2). That reporters are pampered with "fresh-up lounges" with their electronic foot massages, hair stylists, check cashing, and restaurant reservation operations (Dart, 1988, p. 17) suggests that journalists are convention celebrities in their own right in the telepolitical era.

Terry Michael claimed that most reporters represent what he called the "tourist press" who "never even write a word." Instead, "they are really just there as spectators." Michael argued "if there are 12,000 to 13,000 people there I would say that 1,000 of those people would really need information quickly and during the course of the week." Katz (1988b) echoed Michael's view when he wrote that the " 'media village' adjacent to the convention hall is part office, part playpen, and part college reunion"

(p. 1). Katz went on: "The traditionally ink-stained wretches have a vested interest in justifying their presence, for seldom in their careers have they been as well fed and properly exercised . . . poached salmon, blackened redfish or filet mignon, please—and enough free drinks to make self-control a crucial work skill."

Many of Michael's 1,000 truly working journalists represent certain media groups who set the pace and tone of convention coverage for their peers. One such publication, the *National Journal Convention Daily*, has become, in essence, the conventions' sacred text. The *Journal* and the host city's papers are the prime sources of convention information for everybody. Daily schedules, political and media profiles, and feature columns occupy the *NJCD*'s and host city's paper pages. *NJCD* editor Richard Frank told us "there are 35,000 people [in New Orleans] who are very much interested in politics" and "what goes on at the convention . . . we're a part of it as reporters. It's sort of a little community here for a week and we're trying to serve other community newspapers" with information "about the politics of the convention." The importance of the host city's dailies is apparent in the convention specials produced each day. For example, the *New Orleans Times-Picayune* featured special coverage of the Atlanta Democrats as a "trial run" for its GOP coverage a month later.

So-called off-beat publications are also present in the convention setting and attract the attention of parties and media alike. Rauch (1988b) wrote "as conventions become less places where the major television networks provide definitive coverage, the little guys see their opening and grab it" (p. 12). Papers such as the *Atlanta Jewish Times, Muslim Journal, American Atheist Press*, and *Washington Blade* covered Democrats in Atlanta (Rauch, p. 12).

Dailies, weeklies, periodicals, and other publications invade the convention city, each following an agenda of its own. *Time* magazine's Jack White described his publication's role in this fashion: "Most of the events that happen this week will have been covered on television, the newspapers, and the wire services. We don't have that kind of space. We don't do this every day, so we look at things a little differently than the daily or hourly media. . . . We can provide a perspective where we can step back and try to sort out what was real and unreal in a way that maybe daily newspapers and television can't do it. That's our job."

Newsmagazines and newspapers also assign photographers to cover conventions in a manner distinct from reporters and columnists. *Time*'s Shelly Katz told our interviewers: "The photographers are unlike the writers. We don't usually go out to cover one segment. We're here to do the whole convention. Anything that appeals to us, anything that we see as relative through images to the story of the convention. Now that could mean that we're on the floor shooting funny hats, we're on the floor shooting people crying and dancing. . . . We could be on the streets shooting demonstrators. The other day I spent two hours walking backwards in a march. . . . It's not as if we treat this as 25 different stories. It's one story. It's the convention." These were the print media-related personnel from 1988.

The Electronic Media. Widely reported reductions in technical support by the entertainment networks may have had some impact on their convention budgets in 1988, but a quick review of the number of electronic media–related personnel in Atlanta and New Orleans makes one wonder how that group could possibly be any larger. The considerable increase in local and group television coverage no doubt contributed to the fact that electronic journalists constituted the largest single presence in the convention setting. Tina Tate told us that the number of television stations sending crews to the 1988 conventions did not increase that much from 1984; however, the size of those staffs and their commitment to "serious programming" did. For Tate, the "growth in satellite availability and satellite technology" was the "major consideration" in this increased presence. Since there is always "a local story" at the conventions, Tate maintained, local stations from across the nation band together, use the technology, and cover the conventions—many of them "live." Crews from local stations proudly wore tee-shirts proclaiming "we came, we edited, we up-linked" (Dowd, 1988, p. 11).

Tate, the definitive source on these trends, noted of the 350 or so local stations that traveled to Atlanta and New Orleans, "we had no more than 25 or 30 who came on their own." Instead, 90 percent of them were in groups. The House radio/TV superintendent said "you can't handle 350 individual stations with their own exact qualifications, but what you can do is handle a Potomac or CONUS who has been servicing 15 or 20 or 40 stations." For example, WNNE-TV of White River Junction, Vermont, purchased a "$400,000" satellite truck and shared it with Potomac Communications in exchange for "partial use of the news service's anchor booth in the Omni and work space in the World Congress Center" (Hansen, 1988h, p. 19C). Similarly, Diamond (1988b) described how "CONUS Communications" serviced "15 stations with 115 persons in Atlanta" and Potomac Communications "formed a consortium of 80 stations represented by 461 persons" (p. 18). The diversity of these operations produced problems for Terry Michael in his attempts to computerize the DNC media plans, since "trying to define the presence of station" was difficult when some stations sent crews and left talent at home, some sent talent, and some sent both.

Radio networks are present in force as well. CBS's Les Woodruff told our interviewers how the radio journalist's role has evolved owing to the technology: "I've got two computers. I've got one that accesses the information networks . . . [and] I've got a digital audio computer in which I do editing. . . . The technical revolution is making it easier to disseminate the news than ever before." Woodruff concluded, "It's not the old typewriter, razor blade and splicing tape kind of journalism that I cut my teeth on in the fifties."

Joining this vast array of independent stations, radio networks (such as National Public Radio), and groups were, of course, the TV network news organizations. Tate pointed out that CNN had affiliates for the first time in 1988 and, as a result, joined ABC, CBS, and NBC's owned and operated and affiliate stations to create a network newsgathering force of considerable size. Within these operations we have a wide range of support and technical staff that—like the independents and groups—occupy much space and require technical assistance. Cables must be run, work space negotiated and distributed, satellite trucks parked and much, much more.

Part of this array of electronic personnel, of course, is the highly visible network talent. Lorando (1988b) claimed the networks have "an ulterior concern" in their convention coverage in that it is "a prime promotional vehicle for their high-priced on-air talent" (p. B2). Hence, competition for air time may be intense. Sam Donaldson suggested some of these on-air roles are changing as "the floor correspondent is becoming the floor pundit" (Donlon & Katz, 1988c, p. 4A) which, in turn, fuels the battle for air time between the "high-priced" network talent and the carefully selected party talent (one of the prime sources of tension in convention orchestration). There is, finally, the politician-pundit. Jane Hansen (1988c) reported: "With political conventions come political commentators, but at this one, the line between politics and press has begun to blur. Like retired football players who analyze the play-by-play of Sunday afternoon football, a growing number of politicians are crossing the line as paid political commentators" (p. 17C).

The former campaign manager for Walter Mondale, Bob Beckel, led the way in such punditry through his 1988 "BeckelVision" (Guskind, 1988a, p. 15). Beckel worked for CONUS Communications and did interviews with some 35 stations in Atlanta from various skybooth locations. He was joined by former presidential candidate Bruce Babbit, Geraldine Ferraro, and Ed Rollins and Charles Manatt on local station coverage while Robert Squire and John Sears (NBC's "Today"), Mark Green and Robert Dornan (CNN), Pat Buchanan and Pat Schroeder (ABC's "Good Morning America"), and Christopher Matthews, John Buckley, and Thomas Donilon (CBS's "This Morning") worked the network morning shows. For the viewers at home, the variance between party and news media performing talent may, after all, be a distinction without a difference.

There is truly a wide range of performing talent present in the media coverage of a nominating convention. Television coverage—local, group, and network—demands a pool of talent, support staff, and administrative personnel who pursue fundamentally distinct agendas from their hosts, the two political parties. Though the parties conduct their own media operations, the primary force in convention mediation is still with the news organizations—a complex group of interrelated yet independent operations.

Whereas the political boss was once an impresario of vast influence, the technical boss eventually usurped that power and, in turn, negotiates with production-company management in the posh "smoke-filled offices" of television networks, publisher suites, and national committees. The complexity of this inter- and intrainstitutional operation is its most striking feature. In one field of action we witness both cooperative and adversarial relationships involving the *same* people. As they perform one role, they cooperate; when they turn to other responsibilities, they fight. Such is the life of the Greatest Political Show on Earth.

Chapter Three

Picturesque Stages and Patriotic Programs: Concurrence in Orchestrating Places, People, and Events

In 1927 Harold Bruce wrote that "the procedure followed by the two major parties in the arrangements for their conventions and the conduct of business at the gatherings is substantially the same, except for a few details" (p. 235). This may have been the case during the early stages of the mass-mediated convention, but it is hardly the case in the 1990s. As we have seen through our discussion of convention personnel, the two parties orchestrate their conventions in different ways. To demonstrate our point, consider the allocation of hotels among state delegations for each of the 1988 party conclaves.

In October 1987, the Democratic state chairs gathered in Washington, D.C., for a "baseball-draw lottery" to decide housing assignments (Quinn, 1988, p. 50). The state chairs drew "a numbered baseball out of a duffle bag" and, later, selected which hotel they preferred based on the order determined by the baseball draw (Louisiana, ironically, was number one and selected the Atlanta Hilton). The Republicans, on the other hand, assigned New Orleans hotel space based on *political* reasons. States who were considered to be close to Bush received priority (Texas and New England states) with other prominent partisans receiving preferential treatment (Nebraska's governor, Kay Orr, fared well for her delegation owing to her role as platform chair). Levin (1988) informs us: "One might expect that Minnesota, the only state . . . to support Walter Mondale in 1984, would be given rooms in Biloxi. But that's not the way it works . . . Evie Teegen, the housing committee chairwoman, is from Minnesota. That delegation will stay at the Holiday Inn Crowne Plaza, right down Poydras Street from the Superdome" (p. 41).

What a contrast! One party draws numbered baseballs, the other uses patronage. One relies on luck for one of the most important logistic deci-sions of the preproduction phase, the other rewards loyalty. While the pro-cedures for convention arrangements and the conduct of business may have been similar in 1927, they are dramatically different in a telepolitical age. For further proof of these contrasting styles, we turn to the production process itself and the details associated with the show's three production phases: first, the *preproduction* concerns that range from site selection through convention hall preparations; second, the *production* stage and the show's implementation, spin operations, and the reportorial practices through which critics mediate convention realities for their audiences; third, the *postproduction* phase of closing events, the convention hall tear-down, and evaluation procedures conducted by various impresarios. In these three phases two traits stand out. One, the characters and roles we introduced in Chapters 1 and 2 through descriptions of "who does what" assumes in the show's life cycle an aura of "who does what, *when*" (once again, we use the events of 1987–88 as our examples). Two, we emphasize preproduction because of that phase's importance in a *telepolitical* envi-ronment. For a modern convention, preproduction is crucial; in fact, many orchestration roles are fully enacted by the time the spectacle begins, hence they virtually disappear afterward. What takes months to plan and build requires only hours to perform, mere minutes to dismantle.

THE PREPRODUCTION PHASE

From the beginning of the site-selection process through the Sunday af-ternoon "security sweep" before the opening session, the preconvention phase covers well over two years of planning; actually, planning begins when the curtain falls on the previous convention. In many respects, the show's implementation and postproduction operations are minor when compared to preproduction activities. The intricacies of preproduction or-chestration will no doubt excite Adorno's expert listener, but they are es-sential for other music lovers' understanding of orchestral politics as well.

Site Selection

Site selection begins with a series of public hearings. Cities interested in hosting the conventions make presentations before the two national parties' site-selection committees. The extent and style of these hearings, of course, is contingent upon the year in question; some national commit-tees spend more time on hearings than others. For example, in 1984 the coterie gathered to reelect Ronald Reagan decided very early that Dallas was the preferred site for the 1984 GOP national convention. Once that choice was apparent the phases of site selection—hearings, visitations, and so on—were mere formalities. Normally, however, following hearings the committees narrow the list of potential sites and undertake "site visitations" to gather pertinent information via direct observation.

The 1988 Republicans considered such cities as New Orleans, Los Angeles, St. Louis, and Kansas City; Democrats' entries included Atlanta, Houston, New Orleans, St. Louis, and Washington, D.C. Once the GOP decided on New Orleans, it insisted on a contract that gave the party exclusive rights to the Superdome for the six weeks prior to the event. When the city agreed, it simultaneously eliminated the Democrats. (Ironically, the Democrats were in New Orleans on a site visitation the day the GOP announced its decision.) Several sources felt Houston should and would be the Democrats' final choice. Atlanta's Omni was viewed as a technical impossibility, hence when the DNC settled on Atlanta anyway, the choice was puzzling.

The superintendent of the Senate press gallery, Bob Petersen, contrasted the two parties' site-visitation strategies. He noted that the Republicans maintain a 9-member committee; the Democrats have a committee of 50 people. Petersen surmised that the Democrats "don't want to leave anybody out" and, as a result, go from city to city with this substantial entourage. If a city can afford to wine and dine the Democrats' site-visitation team, it is deemed capable of handling the convention. For some cities competing to be host sites, the size of the Democratic site-visitation entourage does not set well. In fact, what some cities were willing to endure in 1988 they no longer found acceptable in competing for the 1992 conventions. A case in point was the city of New Orleans in 1990. In April of that year 75 members of the DNC site-selection group—including staff and technical advisers—visited New Orleans. They were given free room and board at four of the city's leading hotels for the three-day inspection visit. When several members of the site-selection committee asked for two days' extra lodging in order to attend the New Orleans Jazz Festival, city officials drew the line. "We're trying to discourage them from staying over. This is a site visit, not a . . . whatever," said one official. New Orleans was not the only city to complain: New York and Cleveland each spent more than $300,000 for Democratic visitations, Houston paid $100,000 ("New Orleans," 1990, p. 20A). Apparently for the Big Apple it was a sound investment; the DNC will be in New York in 1992. Houston paid the price for the Democrats' visitation only to lose out to another city, as it had to Atlanta in 1988. But all was not lost. The GOP chose Houston for 1992. Such are the risks and rewards of site selection.

Of the criteria uppermost in selecting a site—housing, transportation, work space both inside and outside the hall, communications, sight lines, and the like—Petersen argued persuasively that the principal criterion is politics. Technical consultants appear before the national committees and state their particular needs, the committee considers them, and it renders a decision. Yet that decision may counter all the technical advice. Atlanta is a prime case. RNC media operative Mike Miller told us he gave a "pretty scathing report" on Atlanta and that the city "didn't make any sense" from a technical perspective; nevertheless, the Democrats decided to go to the Omni despite technical reservations. Sources for this study who declined to be identified reported that a political dispute between the Texas state chair, Bob Slagle, and the national committee chair, Paul Kirk, played a central role in the decision to go to Georgia. With a committee of 50 and a host of technical experts on hand, Kirk made the call! Thus, political factors figure prominently in who receives the economic boom that results from hosting a presidential nominating convention.

One main concern in site selection—transportation—serves as an example of how complicated the overall process is. Arleigh Greenblat, 1988 DNC manager, stated that "bus transportation, airport, limousines, rent-a-cars . . . it's all under one roof." The roof covers several criteria in site selection:

1. holding the event in one of the major airline's hubs for more reasonable airfare;
2. convenient and inexpensive travel to and from the airport (buses, taxis, rentals, and limousines);
3. convenient and inexpensive travel in the city (taxies, subways, buses, limos, and parking);
4. ability and willingness to undertake highway construction (if relevant); and
5. adequate security measures.

These factors are even more key for a city (Atlanta) with "more than 60 percent of your people outside the downtown area" and with major highways under construction. In hopes of coping with potential problems posed for transportation in Atlanta, Greenblat computerized key transportation variables to generate solutions and provide a foundation for his overall management system. One such solution, as it turned out, was in two-party cooperation. Both parties accepted "loan cars" from General Motors and worked together (on a staff level) to "get about the same kind of contract" (in Greenblat's words) from the automaker.

Convention hosts are contractually obligated for the transportation system, communications, a substantial amount of construction, security, hospitality, and other items. Each such item figures into site selection and acts as a basis for the "master contract" between the host city and the political party. Party and host-city lawyers negotiate to ensure the agreement's legality—adding yet another set of orchestrators. Most site-selection details can be verified with certainty while others are difficult to confirm. Security, transportation, construction, and communications can be negotiated and validated, but housing provokes controversy. Hotel and motel promoters occasionally misrepresent the availability of the number of affordable, quality rooms. Therefore, during and following national conventions many horror stories invariably circulate. People are no doubt upset when buses fail to run on time, or when the convention hall doors are shut owing to overcrowding or for security reasons (the building is *sealed* when the president of the United States enters). Such things happen. But when hotels are roach-infested, burglarized, or located in inconvenient places, the party's image suffers. This happens to both parties (housing difficulties are bipartisan). Hence, housing facilities are always a pivotal consideration in site selection.

Convention manager Bill Phillips and the Republicans in 1988 faced similar tasks in site selection as did the Democrats, but handled them differently. The GOP's site-selection committee structure (consisting of a nine-person visitation team and the institutional "committees on arrangements") streamlined the process considerably. In fact, according to GOP officials, things ran so smoothly with the Republican operation that only an item that might otherwise seem superficial, the Superdome's curtain, figured in a major way in the GOP decision to go to the Big Easy. The Louisiana Superdome has one of the world's largest curtains used to divide the facility in half. Phillips explained when he first saw that curtain and how it could transform the dome, he was sold on the facility. For instance, the option of having ample party work space immediately behind the podium and curtained off from TV cameras was very attractive to Phillips. Since transportation and housing are no problem in New Orleans, the GOP decided to hold the country's first "domed convention."

Several impresarios are involved in varying ways in site selection. Bob Petersen attends as many site visitations as possible; his counterpart in the House radio/TV gallery, Tina Tate does not. Tate argued "the party is going to choose what they want, which state they want and which cities they want" and since "both Mikes" (the RNC's Miller and the DNC's McCurry) know what she thinks anyway, she feels no need to travel for site visits. Similarly, network producers (the pool producers at this time are not yet selected) differ over how much of a role to play in site visitations. In 1988 NBC's Joe Angotti attended some visits, ABC's Friedland did not, CNN's team did. All of the producers refrain from offering technical advice to the parties (primarily it is the Democrats who ask; the Republicans do not!). Friedland maintained "television is always accused of . . . [using] its weight to affect things . . . and the last thing we want to do is to be seen [as] influencing decisions for purely technical reasons." Yet privately, technical matters are important to the networks. The CNN production team used site visitations to conduct technical research, examining potential cities for possible microwave transmission points and from other technical perspectives. A first-come, first-served method for obtaining remote work space and working facilities prompts early, and intense, interest in opportunities for each network posed by each alternative site.

An example of the struggle over technical facilities involved an Atlanta hotel with a roof conducive to microwave transmission within the city. CNN had used this hotel's roof on several occasions and paid $125 for the privilege. During the Democratic convention, this same hotel wanted $10,000 per day, per unit, for access to the roof. Such is the price-gouging associated with conventions. CNN finessed the $10,000 charge through clever engineering that reduced the network's need to have the roof.

Administrative Logistics

With the announcement of the convention site a plethora of logistical activities follow: hotel space must be allocated between the political parties and news media; the credentialing procedures for news organizations must be announced; construction, food service, computer service, communications, and insurance bids must be solicited, and contracts must be negotiated and approved by legal staffs; and consultants must be retained for set design, technical assistance, script preparation, and so on.

The detail involved is exemplified in the time Arleigh Greenblat devoted to matters of insurance in 1988. He spent over 150 hours going through details of insurance policies alone. So much time, in fact, that he suggested in the future that the two parties work together and save considerable money and effort, as in the case of contracting for automobiles. In addition, Greenblat interviewed (and kept records on) approximately 30 different contractors for communications, construction, and the like to ensure fairness in the bidding process. He created "interview teams" to include minorities—again, to ensure equity. The Republicans' convention-planning structure produced a situation in 1988 that burdened Bill Phillips with fewer details than Greenblat had to confront. Merri Jo Cleair noted that Phillips reduced the number of convention-planning committees from the dozen in 1984 to five. The availabilty to Phillips of experienced personnel made hotel assignments, credentials distribution, food service acquisition, and all other planning chores less cumbersome than it was for the Democrats.

The congressional galleries undertake their first official order of business, the announcement of credentialing procedures, once a convention site is known. For the print media, this consists of a series of wire-service notices to news organizations; for the electronic media, it involves a major mass-mailing to broadcast and related organizations. The Senate press gallery's use of the Associated Press and United Press International wire services was a convenient notification tool. By contrast, Tina Tate and her staff at the House radio/TV gallery conducted a major mailing effort while continuing the daily operations of the gallery. Once the announcements are out, the print press galleries use a formula for credentials distribution that is based on the circulation of the publication making the request. If the publication happens to be from one of the convention sites, they are eligible for additional credentials. Terry Michael and Mike McCurry of the DNC made special efforts to contact the "between-the-cracks press" (their way of describing organizations that do not maintain an active presence in Washington or that fall outside the purview of the galleries).

Along with the credentials announcements, the galleries and, eventually, the pool producers begin to negotiate technical arrangements with the parties. This involves, among other matters, discussions of construction schedules and work-space requests. In working with Republicans, gallery officials turn to experiences at previous conventions as a basis for negotiation; with Democrats, gallery personnel start anew every four years. In 1988, the Democrats produced no models of their Omni construction plans—an act that created rancor among impresarios trying to deal with party officials. Greenblat expressed dismay: "When you're involved in a meeting this big you almost have a responsibility to build a model of your facility and of our parking lot and of your traffic." For Greenblat, the "ten, fifteen thousand dollars" for a model is not much money out of a "$23 million" project. When, in the absence of a model, media operatives could not read their skybox blueprints, they inevitably complained about sight lines once they saw the completed structure. Greenblat argued that precise models would remedy these problems. The GOP by contrast had these models in 1988. The CNN team improvised a way around the problems posed for TV networks by Democrat orchestrators; the network obtained a copy of the construction plans *from the architect*, even duplicated those drawings and gave them to the pool producer. In an ironic twist CNN thereby served the telegenic aims of the Democrats in spite of the party's flawed preconvention orchestration.

The networks turn over much logistical planning to their functional equivalent of a press gallery: the pool producers. The pool producers act as on-site negotiators for trailer space, anchor booth locations and dimensions, camera placement, and other essential technical details. Just as Bob Petersen and his colleague, Thayer Illsley from the House press gallery, negotiate over press stands and work space for their print press constituents, the pool producers handle these negotiations for the TV networks. In addition, Tina Tate represents local and group broadcasters in hammering out essentials over work space, skyboxes, and stand-up locations. The crucial and central role of the galleries and pool producers to the orchestration of teleconventions is never more evident than in these vital preproduction negotiations. The networks are scarcely inactive during this period. NBC's Joseph Angotti pointed to the many "physical" arrangements that occupy preproduction schedules of TV executives including, if necessary, building anchor booths. Moreover, network officials are involved with convention managers—for example, Arleigh Greenblat's "outreach program" (personal meetings with network executives) in 1988. There is, indeed, much activity on a variety of fronts during this portion of the pre-production phase.

The Walk-Throughs

A major turning point in preconvention activities arrives between eight and six months prior to the opening of the telepolitical spectacle. Construction bids have been extended, transportation plans concocted, and the convention's internal design devised. The time arrives for the parties and host committees to invite the media to an on-site visitation. For many news organizations the media walk-throughs are the first opportunity to learn the party's plans for its nominating convention. In 1987, the Republicans held their site visit in late October with the Democrats following in mid-December. (The Democrats held a second walk-through in May.) As noted in Chapter 2, this event consists of:

1. a formal presentation by the parties;
2. a detailed tour through the facility;
3. a "hearing" where news organizations and others testify regarding their particular needs and plans (some more formal than others);
4. technical sessions where construction, communications, security, and other consultants make presentations and respond to questions; and
5. host-city hospitality via lunches and socials.

Finally, walk-throughs also provide the first detailed view of the convention's administrative structures.

The GOP session in 1987 was an orderly preview of what was to happen in August. The Republican walk-through began in the center of the Superdome's floor with a series of brief remarks by party representatives. The party disseminated precise drawings of how the 90-foot-high curtain would divide the dome to produce a TV studiolike hall. Orchestrators explained the allocation of skyboxes, stand-up locations, and work space. Afterward, a tour of the dome culminated in a Dixieland jazz band–accompanied parade back to the convention hotel. That evening the *New Orleans Times-Picayune* sponsored a reception. The event concluded the following morning with hearings featuring appearances by representatives of news organizations, congressional galleries, and so on.

The DNC walk-through in December 1987 was, by contrast, disorganized. The initial Atlanta debacle opened in a grand fashion as the Atlanta '88 host committee coordinated a luncheon (sponsored by Cox Enterprises, Inc.) to welcome participants. Mayor Andrew Young and others greeted the assembled media representatives and described Atlanta '88 plans for the following summer. After lunch, the DNC made a presentation in the Georgia World Congress Center (adjacent to the Omni) similar to the Republican version in the Superdome but with a major exception: there were no drawings of the Omni's construction plans. In response, media personnel attempted to construct their own drawings based on the generic maps of the Omni provided by the Democrats. Errors, inaccuracies, and gross misrepresentations of space dimensions, sight lines, and projected facilities rendered the jerry-built drawings useless. Following the party's formal presentation, there was a tour of the Omni. The evening closed with more Atlanta '88 hospitality. The walk-through concluded with a series of "technical sessions" the following morning (involving descriptions of projected transportation, housing, and construction plans). Throughout this December gathering many media representatives grew increasingly frustrated at the absence of floor plans and definitive responses to questions directed at convention officials.

What special event holds a gathering of 400 to 700 media representatives some six months prior to the production in order to unveil plans for that show? The television networks and broadcasting groups spend millions of dollars on convention hall construction and, as Arleigh Greenblat noted, deserve a formal presentation of the party's logistical plans. Other news organizations may not spend vast sums of money, but they too are interested in the convention hall's preparation and host-city accommodations. The significance of these walk-throughs, and the desire of the political party to assure its success in the eyes of news media representatives, was emphasized by the Democrats' perceived need to hold another session some six weeks prior to the 1988 convention in order to sooth ruffled feelings and to reassure news organizations that all would go well.

Convention Hall Preparations

Our review of convention hall preparations centers on three points: the difference in facilities and schedules, the ever-present distinction in administrative style, and technical and structural refinements. Both 1988 convention sites had strengths and weaknesses that manifested themselves in the convention-hall preparation process. The Omni's restrictive size placed pressure on the construction crews' abilities to devise mini–anchor booths for the networks, stand-up broadcasting locations for independents and groups, skyboxes with adequate sight lines, and sturdy camera stands (especially the central camera platform). The Superdome's size created lighting and audio problems, increased attention to VIP sight lines, and offered the challenge of building a "GOP village" (the previously mentioned series of trailers behind the curtain) to house official party operations.

The possibility that the Omni might not be *available* until a month before the show exacerbated the DNC's problems. The Atlanta Hawks, the city's professional basketball franchise, was involved in the NBA playoffs that could have extended until mid-June. Fortunately for Democrats, the Hawks were true to form and eliminated; the Omni was available earlier. The Republicans' contractual commitment to have the dome six weeks in advance of their convention was a wise precaution to avoid a problem in New Orleans.

This phase of preproduction involves protracted debate over work space, press-stand size and sight lines, camera location (for both still photographers and video), skybox specifications, trailer space for the television networks, and places for satellite truck parking. Several news organizations expressed dissatisfaction with the Omni, but they did enjoy optimal working facilities in the adjoining Georgia World Congress Center centered on one floor in areas curtained off to form a "media village." On the other hand, the work space in New Orleans was more dispersed, with news organizations assigned locations in the adjoining Hyatt Hotel and in the Superdome.

Interviews with pool producers Charles Frey and John Reade revealed that camera-location allocations produced few disputes. If two organizations desired the same spot, they would draw straws to decide. Frey told us "there was very little conflict in camera positions and as it turned out each of the networks took different approaches . . . on how to shoot" the Atlanta convention. Interestingly, Frey did not remember ever receiving official approval for camera placement; in his view, "things just sort of evolve."

As "things evolve," the still photographers often must fight for their positions. In Atlanta the central camera platform was originally to be placed 125 feet from the podium—a distance that presents no problems for television cameras, but major difficulties for the still photographers. Eventually, the central camera stand was moved to within 70 feet in order to accommodate the stills, but on TV yielded the appearance of a gigantic obstacle. There were other problems with both central camera platforms. The Atlanta platform was fortified to meet safety and production standards; in New Orleans the Republicans never fully corrected a similar problem. Some TV producers claim the GOP central-stand cameras occasionally vibrated from the still photographers' movements and the activities in the hall. Security guards were placed around the structure during the sessions to minimize inadvertent, and deliberate, shaking. It would not do well to appear to have an earthquake during a prima donna's performance!

Central to the resolution of these and other problems are each party's managerial schemes. An example of the GOP managerial style was the daily 3:00 P.M. meetings conducted by Bill Phillips's chief deputy, Bill Harris. CNN's John Towriss and Alec Miran recalled these sessions as orderly, often brief, reviews of the day's events and next day's schedule. Towriss remembered that these sessions sometimes addressed such mundane matters as the speed with which drivers operated their golf carts (those working in the dome had golf carts assigned for transportation). Nonetheless, he also realized who to ask questions of and when it was appropriate to do so. Miran said the local sheriff was present during these sessions, hence it was convenient to inquire about New Orleans road problems and traffic patterns. Working from Harris's "master list" (which he distributed to everyone at the outset), the 3:00 P.M. meetings and the weekly Friday "big picture" meeting (as the CNN team called it) kept all involved parties abreast of the schedule. According to ABC's Justin Friedland, "everybody had their marching lists," and Mike Miller and Bill Harris "made the trains run on time." As the skyboxes neared completion, the network trailers moved into place, and camera stands appeared, these daily afternoon meetings proved less and less tedious, more and more valuable.

Previously, we mentioned that those representatives of news organizations working to cover the Democrats in Atlanta did things without permission simply because they did not know whom to ask. Democrats did not hold daily briefings, although Greenblat remembered weekly internal meetings. During this portion of the convention hall's preparation Friedland's "oh-by-the-ways" described in Chapter 2 popped up more and more frequently. Central coordination is crucial. Basic needs that have, somehow, been overlooked must be met. Camera locations that have been ignored are sought and, perhaps, assigned. Tina Tate kept busy accommodating local and group broadcasters and trying to save them money whenever possible. (Shortcuts in running cable lines can save *a lot* of money.) Skyboxes that were supposedly assigned are suddenly available, reassigned, and modified. And potential snafus, such as the parking of satellite trucks, are the bane of planners.

Tina Tate, Mike McCurry, and Mike Miller—a gallery, DNC, and RNC orchestrator, respectively—all laughed about what could have been a major problem overlooked at first by everybody in convention planning. It became apparent with the arrival of satellite trucks that no one had parking plans for them. Unless those vehicles are properly arranged, no signals can be transmitted. Remarkably, not one person with either political party at either convention site had the expertise to park the trucks. To the rescue came Skip Erickson (of station WCPO, Minneapolis), who successfully parked the trucks. He was motivated by the desire to send *his* signal, which, again, he could not unless *all* were properly deployed. Satellite trucks are not "bread trucks," as Tina Tate noted, but state-of-the-art electronic devices that require expertise in management. For want of a nail, a shoe, and a horse a kingdom was lost—so said Ben Franklin. For want of Skip Erickson the orchestration of both national party conventions might have been lost!

After the walk-throughs, the parties—primarily the Democrats in 1988—grow interested in the networks' convention-coverage plans.

Greenblat's "outreach program" was designed to create a positive relationship between the party and the TV networks, and did in some respects. Other meetings and consultations occurred as well. One such involved Smith-Hemion's attempt to discover just what the networks would and would not carry. Here the Hollywood team called for convention appearances by Barbra Streisand and Barry Manilow. The networks rebelled.

Ed Bark (1988a) quoted former CBS News vice-president David Buksbaum's response to Smith-Hemion's inquiry about the network's coverage plans: "The clear sentiment on [Gary Smith's] part was that this was what we were going to carry. And we told him, flat out, this is *not* what we're going to carry. It was not acrimonious. There wasn't any venal attitude on his part. He was just unaware" (p. 2F). The DNC's CEO Don Fowler characterized the networks' responses more colorfully, and bluntly: he said the networks "told us to go to hell." NBC's Lloyd Siegel summed the situation well when he concluded: "But the fact of the matter is that they have a function and we have a function and we really need to work to a great degree independently of one another." It comes down to a point made by CNN's Jane Maxwell: "You stage your thing, we'll stage ours." The parties and networks cooperate on logistic matters, but their relationship is pointedly adversarial on editorial concerns.

Once the podium is up, the cameras in place, the lighting racks hung, the script prepared, and the press stands, stand-up locations, and skyboxes completed, damage control begins. In 1984, Bob Petersen of the Senate press gallery entered the Moscone Center only to find that the press stand failed to meet the standards described on the blueprints. He insisted that the Democrats correct the problem, which they did. In 1988, news organizations that purchased skyboxes from the Republicans grew incensed over the placement of a lighting grid that directly blocked their view of the podium. Occasionally, a problem erupts and good old-fashioned horse trading takes over. An example was the location of the TV network podium correspondents—ABC's Jim Wooten, CBS's Diane Sawyer, CNN's Charles Bierbauer, and NBC's Connie Chung—on the Omni's press stand. In exchange for a better location for the podium reporters, the networks gave the Smith-Hemion team a free head-on camera feed (remember, the pool controls the two head-on shots and nonsubscribers must pay for that video). Indeed, the politics of national party conventions extends well beyond the staging of dramatic *partisan* relations to that of negotiations of *institutional* boundries and turf.

Preproduction Publicity

As the convention's premier approaches the pundits begin to play the "expectation" game of preconvention publicity. Reporters and columnists argue about the convention's purpose, describe the convention hall's preparations (Hulbert, 1988a), discuss party strategies (Apple, 1988; Elving, 1988), and project what the convention means to the fall election.

A prime example is Germond and Witcover's (1988) pre-Atlanta remarks in the *National Journal*. The writers observed "public opinion surveys suggest most voters don't pay much attention to presidential campaigns before the nominating conventions" and that many viewers "form lasting impressions" from the show. They went on with conventional wisdom: "Voters want to know if this potential President is competent to manage a national Administration and lead the country and the free world. A successful convention doesn't necessarily answer those questions, but the last thing Dukakis needs right now is a televised brouhaha that would make them seem even more pertinent" (p. 1886). Germond and Witcover emphasized what hundreds of other observers have stressed: the *nominee's activities* during this four-night mini-series. As we have seen, however, what the nominee and other high-profile politicians do and how they look are the products of convention impresarios. It is doubtful that Michael Dukakis sent out one credentialing announcement or that George Bush had anything to do with camera assignments. Yet without the orchestration of these and thousands of other seemingly minute and trivial tasks, the cordial concurrence that showcased both might have been a flight of fantasy akin to a high school senior prom.

THE PRODUCTION PHASE

The stakes are now set, the stage is ready, the security in place, and, as Joe Gideon says in the movie *All That Jazz*, "It's show time, folks." Years of planning now make way for party and journalistic talent. For some impresarios, it's time to sit back and enjoy the show; for others, it's time to get nervous. Anything can happen during the four days of a national party convention, and with 15,000 journalists present, things may go ugly early.

Show Time is always the most exciting portion of any stage production. Ancillary personnel nervously guard against trouble. Nonperforming artists pore over scripts. Performing artists eagerly await the spot light. In 1988, Bill Phillips sat on the GOP podium in front of a bank of five television monitors, smiling and seemingly untroubled. A month earlier in Atlanta his Democratic counterpart, Don Fowler, joined national committee chair Paul Kirk on the rostrum and maintained contact with the Smith-Hemion team, the party's central speech unit, Paul Byers, and other key nonperforming artists. And Arleigh Greenblat was nowhere to be seen. Instead of gathering in the Omni with his employers, Greenblat was in the Atlanta '88 suite dealing with a variety of logistic problems ranging from souvenir and trinket vendors' complaints about their assigned sales locations to housing and transportation problems to fire-marshall lockouts.

As an example of housing difficulties, consider Michael Adams's report about a GOP housing problem in the Big Easy. Adams (1988) cited the New York delegation's displeasure over its assignment (the Pallas Suite Hotel): "One delegate I spoke to reported falling ceilings, no hot water, and unflushable toilets. . . . As for the Pallas Suite, it responded in a well-publicized riposte, 'We're not the best hotel in town. If we were, we'd be hosting the California or Texas delegation' " (p. 98). These instances happened in both convention cities, thereby solidifying the bipartisan nature of housing difficulties.

Once the curtain rises many convention impresarios shift to other roles or monitor the production's progress. Pool producers assume directorial responsibilities within the hall and deal with remote production logistics (e.g., press conferences and hotel suite telecasts). Gallery superintendents are supervising floor-pass distribution or enjoying the benefits (and occasionally disappointments) of their preproduction labors. Network producers refine their editorial plans once production facilities have been tested. Host-city entities deal with damage control in transportation, security, and housing, and simultaneously enact their entertainment and celebration plans to please delegates, the press, and visitors.

Months of negotiations and problem solving now crystallize in one fast-paced week of special events and partisan politics. The 1988 political spectacles actually opened on Saturday night in advance of Monday's convention sessions with gala parties hosted by prominent citizens, party patrons, celebrities, and/or host-city entities. Media personalities (both news and entertainment), technicians, and administrators gathered with party operatives, VIPs, and visitors to enjoy carefully planned entertainment and hospitality, rub elbows with the mighty, and *be seen*. Sunday, too, was a busy day as the TV networks assembled inside the convention hall to check equipment. Owing to the concentration of so much sophisticated electronic equipment, audio frequencies must be thoroughly checked to ensure their clarity. TV producers go over plans. Party officials and network producers conduct pep rallies for volunteers and employees. Jane Hansen (1988a) quoted NBC president Larry Grossman's preconvention pep rally comments in Atlanta: "Give 'em hell, report the news as the greatest news organization there ever was" (p. 19C). Afterward, Grossman distributed tee-shirts to the motivated stagehands. Similarly, the various campaign organizations discussed their strategies with floor whips, tested communications equipment, and learned the way about the Omni or Superdome. Print reporters picked up credentials. Security arrangements were finalized and a final preconvention security sweep was conducted once all the equipment was in place. By Sunday evening the scene was set for *the greatest concentrated, live, continuing spectacle in American politics*.

Three sets of production-phase activities are key: the show's implementation, spin operations, and the reportorial processes the news media use to cover the show. Let us examine each with a focus on the production's *plan* rather than each 1988 convention's specifics.

Show Time and Spin Control

Since the introduction of telepolitical conventions, the two political parties have adopted differing scheduling formats. The Republicans have a six-session format with Monday and Tuesday morning sessions set aside for credentials, rules, and platform business. During the four evenings the GOP implements a series of two- to three-hour sessions tailored for television. The Democrats through 1988 employed a four-session format with marathonlike schedules that may extend from 3:00 or 4:00 in the afternoon to well past midnight.

The consequences of differing scheduling tactics are noteworthy. Both Democrats and Republicans are visibly exhausted by the end of the week, but the split-session format offers the GOP faithful much-needed breaks. Morning sessions are relaxing pep rallies the delegates find nontaxing (and GOP delegates profess to *hate* taxes). In addition, between sessions the RNC Network conducts two-way satellite interviews, Republican notables hold press conferences, and the GOP host committee coordinates special events designed to entertain delegates and to facilitate spin operations. The split-session plan ran like clockwork in Dallas in 1984; buses brought the delegates to and from the hall efficiently. However, in New Orleans in 1988 the morning sessions extended well beyond the scheduled two-hour time frame owing to the number of speeches. As a result, many delegates left the hall long before the session was over, often, to attend other scheduled events.

In both San Fransciso in 1984 and Atlanta in 1988 the Democrats' marathons took a toll on party faithful. The Omni's size especially contributed to the problem, since delegates wishing to leave the hall for a break would return only to find the doors locked because of overcrowding. This meant "arrive early, remain seated, stay late." Moreover, Democratic party platforms sometimes arouse the emotions of delegates and/or advocates. The conduct of platform business in the late afternoon or early evening often means that partisan animosities either drift into prime time or throw the evening's schedule off target (the former happened in San Francisco, the latter in Atlanta). With considerations in mind such as fatigue, the telegenic qualities of the spectacle's prime-time portions, and likely airing of potential disputes always possible, convention orchestrators are wise to attend closely to the subtleties of convention schedules. As Bill Phillips said, "if you're going to have a fight over a plank in the platform, I would rather have it be [Tuesday] morning than [Tuesday] night because there are fewer people to see you fighting."

Although scripts and schedules are in place and actors are prepared to deliver their lines, party planners continue to hold meetings to assess the production's progress and make necessary adjustments. The CEO of the DNC, Don Fowler, and his message committee met every evening after the preceding session closed to "conduct a retrospective analysis of what happened and [make] some adjustments [for] the following day" (in the CEO's words). Republicans, too, held these meetings. Mark Goode lamented that he had difficulty attending the "postmortems after each session" where the GOP's program group reviewed that session and discussed plans for the following one. Goode was too busy directing the production to attend these meetings!

Also, both parties busily orchestrated orchestral leitmotifs. The Republican "line of the day" strategy was in operation; the GOP distributed daily hymnals to delegates in 1988. For Democrats, Terry Michael put the "party line" in operation by entering speeches in computers for electronic dissemination and maintaining electronic billboards that were readily accessible. And both parties' paper factories churned out copies of biographies, demographics, speeches, platforms, platform analyses, press releases, press kits, schedules, announcements, and much, much more.

As a convention session unfolds, few orchestrators are more crucial to its success or failure than the stage director. RNC director Mark Goode sat "in a control room with a bank of monitors" that allowed him to "see what all the networks [were] carrying" as he directed the convention. From that location, he had contact with the RNC Network director, the pool producer (CBS's John Reade), and the "people on the floor." These floor directors choreographed demonstrations, balloon drops, music, entrances and exits of party celebrities in the hall, and "rolling films." Goode, like the DNC's Dwight Hemion, was the force behind the show's direction; however, unlike Hemion, Goode maintained contact with his RNC Network personnel at all times to ensure that RNCN cameras were sensitive to every production nuance. Some sources for the study suggested that there were occasions when the RNCN cameras knew *more* about what was developing than their pool and/or network counterparts.

In Atlanta at the Georgia World Congress Center, Paul Byers produced two-way satellite interviews, highlight packages, and other Convention Satellite News Service materials. During the convention sessions Byers maintained a schedule independent of gavel-to-gavel podium coverage responsibilities. Instead he produced interviews, covered remote events (demonstrations, etc.), and selected highlights from his Smith-Hemion feed for CSNS broadcast. All told, CSNS provided 46 hours of coverage: 11 hours and 51 minutes of live coverage; three convention highlight packages (totaling 32 minutes); 151 two-way satellite interviews; 15 in-studio interviews; 81 taped interviews; 11 prepackaged videotaped reports (on delegates, etc.); and 15 taped packages of related news events (press conferences and the like). These totals represent a marked contrast to the

RNCN and its emphasis on the "business of the convention" (i.e., podium coverage).

The gallery superintendents and pool producers engaged in various activities during convention week. The pool producers, of course, were busy directing the pool cameras. The new pool system required that Charles Frey in Atlanta and John Reade in New Orleans direct four separate camera feeds. They were busy conducting four individual versions of convention happenings. The gallery superintendents either slowed the pace of their labors (Tina Tate said she was basically finished by curtain call) or focused on giving out floor passes. Compared with the frenzy of the preproduction phase, gallery superintendents find the convention itself an anticlimax—barring the occasional crisis.

The print media used a rotating floor-pass system in 1988. Reporters were allowed on the floor for 20-minute intervals. Failure to comply with the time limit resulted in a blacklisting of the culprit's name to prevent future abuses. The electronic media, on the other hand, followed a two-tier strategy. Broadcasters operated a rotating system for independent stations *and* distributed a certain number of floor credentials to the broadcasting groups, who then rotated them among subscribers. Occasionally, a station would "fall between the cracks" (in Tate's words) and require her intervention.

Turmoil over floor-pass distribution does break out and, once in a while, a humorous story emerges. Don Womack, former superintendent of the Senate press gallery, described one convention when the party tried a credit-card system for floor access. Each reporter was issued a card—much like a credit card with its magnetic strip—that allowed access to the convention floor. During the convention, someone discovered how *any* credit card would open the door and, obviously, the system broke down completely. Womack gleefully told of a sign on the photographers' gallery door: *Photographers' gallery closed—to get on floor use your charge card.*

The Journalists and Critics

We have emphasized that there are "two conventions" during a national party conclave: one for the political party and one for the news media. Whether or not they *are* two conventions is really unimportant; what is significant is that there are separate productions of the same assembly. They may originate from the same site and share stages, but the TV networks and the parties work from two completely different scripts. In fact, as we shall see in Chapters 5 and 6, there are as many network scripts as their are TV organizations to cover the convention.

To capture the rich qualities of convention news operations, one must acknowledge the multiplicity of news activity. The host cities' local papers and the *National Journal Convention Daily* constitute the daily renditions of the working press along with 20 to 30 metropolitian newspapers that provide copies of their daily publications for distribution at the convention. Each day reporters in 1988 gathered in the Bell South Lounge—the replacement for the Railroad Lounge that served journalistic on-location hospitality needs by supplying free food and drink for over a century. There the working journalists ate, drank, and perused newspapers, watched TV, studied advance copies of speeches, and planned their day.

The print media work space in Atlanta's "media village" was a vital source of scheduling information, coverage coordination, and fraternization. Since the political parties now issue credentials for the entire week at the outset (the galleries used to issue credentials *each day*), print journalists concern themselves primarily with securing access to special events and, once the convention opens, floor passes. Feature stories are filed at a variety of times, and reporters responsible for accounts of a variety of convention hall proceedings operate under several constraints, some ideosyncratic. A Florida reporter covering the 1984 San Francisco convention went into instant depression when Florida "passed" during the roll call of the states; in passing the delegation made it impossible for the reporter to meet his deadline. Journalists' laptop computers remove some anxiety traditionally associated with meeting deadlines since editors and copyreaders may electronically edit their copy back home and save valuable time. Many reporters set their personal computers on the press stand and leave them throughout the week (others use portable computers or set up in their work space).

The electronic news media work under very different conditions. Newspaper editors gather their staffs, establish a coverage theme, and send reporters to cover events; the reporters are not burdened with the technical demands of television, or even radio. A reporter with tape recorder or a still photographer with camera is more mobile and flexible than a TV reporter, a videographer, a sound person (if necessary), and a producer. Much of the electronic media's coverage features remote or convention events scheduled during the day by producers for prime-time airing. The CNN Special Events crew interviewed for this study described their "rock and roll" operation (their coverage of remote events). John Towriss said "some remotes, obviously, we knew about [such as] the candidate hotels, and we knew enough to make sure that we had positions in their press briefing room, and we had some sort of transmission from there back to our main facility, be it microwave or local lines we ordered through the telephone company or even in some cases a satellite uplink and downlink again." There were times, such as George Bush's announcement of his running mate, when CNN did not know where that announcement would occur. In anticipation, Towriss covered "every event he [Bush] was doing; every small little handshaking event and little speech here and there, we were trying to figure out how we could do it live." Fortunately, CNN was there when Bush announced his decision and was the only network to cover it live. Towriss concluded: "A lot of that is just . . . what we call rock and roll, you just deal with it on location. That's where Alec and I spent a lot of time . . . during the convention. Where Jane spent most of her time actually in the control room watching the convention coverage, we were out in other areas . . . we just turned out lucky on the Quayle announcement." Since efforts to be present during arrivals and departures of newsworthy politicians, coverage of special events (such as the Carter Library luncheon in Atlanta or the Nancy Reagan birthday luncheon in New Orleans), and press conferences are just as much a part of on-location coverage as the events inside the hall, one can understand why the CNN Special Events and other network crews scout for microwave transmission points as early as site visitations.

When electronic newsgatherers are not scrambling about town on "rock and roll" missions, they are steadfastly following carefully prepared scripts of their own. These scripts have two dimensions: the newscast's subject matter and its production qualities. With regard to the content, NBC's Joe Angotti devised a "thematic" plan for his network's coverage that stressed predetermined topics for wrap-around floor reports (a series of reports with correspondents introducing one another without the anchor's intervention), his *convention-without-walls* remote interview segments, and anchor-controlled interviews (we return to these topics in Chapters 5 and 6). Angotti told us "instead of randomly going about covering various issues," NBC decided to "provide some structure to the editorial approach and . . . assign specific subjects to be addressed on any given night." The themes that emerged during NBC's coverage were several weeks in the making. Angotti said "we began thinking about certain times of the convention [and] what themes we might address and we kept refining that . . . to the point that the week before the convention, we had in mind specific things that we wanted to address" both inside and outside the hall.

During the show, NBC director George Paul used advance copies of speech texts to plan camera shots for each performance (Rosenstiel, 1988c; Minutaglio, 1988). He examined texts for references to women, minorities, certain state delegations, married couples, and so on and, as the speaker approached that topic, Paul set up camera shots that featured delegates or personalities who personified that remark. When we discuss the intricacies of the network coverage in Chapters 5 and 6, keep in mind that NBC's use of the tight facial camera shot was facilitated by Paul's close perusal of advanced speech texts.

ABC's plans for convention coverage differed from its rivals at NBC. Justin Friedland revealed that producers and correspondents met every afternoon to "discuss where we think the story is going." During those sessions ABC would "pick a couple of themes for the evening . . . or if something else presents itself, throw those three things away and . . . go with the news." Friedland said "we never try to make the convention fit in an arm-hole; we always try to stay with it, maybe a little bit ahead of it, if we could, but we try to figure out which way the wind was going instead of making it go a certain way." NBC planned its themes weeks in advance; ABC did so before each session—quite a contrast.

Occasionally, the pace of the convention slows (from the media's per-spective) and the networks go to prerecorded materials. The networks pre-pared segments on party history, demographics, and the party films (to name a few) for these situations. These segments were particularly useful for CNN with its extended gavel-to-gavel coverage. Along with a ten-dency to cut to live remotes, the "network of record" used a series of focus group interviews, commentary, "Larry King", or "Crossfire" segments, and preproduced videos during their broadcasts. John Towriss observed "as something developed or became more important" CNN would pull video reports "off the shelf" and air them.

Unlike the other network anchor booths, CNN's facility had two adjoin-ing sets. This allowed the network to use one set of cameras, lights, and teleprompters to create the impression the production originated from two separate studios. The main anchor set, of course, was designed to accom-modate CNN's dual-anchor format; the "interview set" was the home of "Larry King" or "Crossfire" segments. As we shall see in Chapters 5 and 6, the "network of record" turned to its second studio, videotaped seg-ments, and floor commentary or interviews as much—if not more than—it did to the Democrats and Republicans.

Another production concern that networks and pool producers consider involves camera assignments. Floor reporters, podium correspondents, and roll-call announcements all emanate from certain spots on the con-vention floor or podium; consequently, producers divide the hall into zones with certain cameras strategically placed to cover those areas. For instance, if CNN's Tom Mintier is reporting on the delegations in Zone A, designated cameras cover that zone and he is informed which camera(s) to work toward. Once in a while, a network will request the pool camera cover some floor happening and, if possible, the pool producer complies. (John Reade described this option as his "request line.") In both scripts and production plans, the networks travel to the conventions with specific strategies in mind.

Damage control occurs in this context as well. When the Democrats broke policy and dimmed their convention-hall lights during prominent speeches, the networks and pool producers had to adjust. NBC's Lloyd Siegel maintained the DNC lighting maneuvers "drove everybody crazy" and pool producer Reade argued that the Democrats were "killing their own story by dousing the lights." Dimming the lights, according to Reade, limits the camera's ability to show the "interaction" between "speaker and

audience." In effect, therefore, party orchestrators may work at cross purposes, for the parties also stack the audience with blacks when a black is
speaking, women when a woman is speaking, and so on to *heighten* a
sense of interaction. The networks also cope with two parties intent on
controlling access to certain party newsmakers. Siegel did not "remember
any sense of frustration" over obtaining interviews in that you just "had
to get your order in," whereas Friedland and the CNN crew found the process objectionable.

For close to a week, 15,000 journalists work with thousands of delegates, alternates, party officials, local personalities, and politicians in the
most concentrated newsgathering environment imaginable. Both the
newsmakers and the newsgatherers plan scenarios that reflect weeks and
months of preproduction efforts. Remarkably, one slip of the tongue or
controversial act can throw all those plans away and convention orchestration immediately becomes convention damage control.

THE POSTPRODUCTION PHASE

In the preproduction and production phases of convention orchestration
all manner of orchestrators are active in diverse ways—party, networks,
congressional galleries, host committees, and news organizations perform
in the spectacle's first two phases. This is not, however, the case in postproduction. For instance, NBC's Lloyd Siegel said his network did not undertake any postconvention evaluation of network coverage in 1988. Press
gallery personnel, on the other hand, prepare detailed reports of credentialing, expenditures, and other matters. Here we consider the activities of
those orchestrators who continue into the postproduction phase.

Closing Events and Tear-Down

When the balloons drop after the presidential nominee's acceptance
speech and there is final benediction, the participants of a national nominating convention are tired, relieved, and rewarded; yet there remain for
partisans and media personnel alike several postproduction chores. One
is to stage a round of celebration. Each host city goes about this final bash
in its own way. In San Francisco and Dallas in 1984, and New Orleans in
1988, the vogue was invitation-only parties—a press pass sufficed in some
instances—dispersed across the city. Atlanta '88, however, sponsored a
huge party in the Georgia World Congress Center, featuring music and
beverage with a special appearance by Michael Dukakis and Lloyd Bentsen. As with the opening party on Saturday, the Atlanta '88 committee
spared no expense.

In New Orleans, the broadcast networks held postconvention "wrap"
parties to celebrate the completion of the *two* 1988 conventions. CBS held

a party at J.B. River's on the Mississippi. Present were scores of CBS technicians, volunteers (many of whom were relatives of CBS employees), administrators, and on-air celebrities, all relishing the New Orleans hospitality. The sight of floor correspondent Bob Schieffer joyfully dancing with teenage girls (daughters of network executives) was an off-camera performance that might have livened up CBS's coverage had it been aired as part of the convention. The network, limited budget notwithstanding, provided ample food, drink, and entertainment for its weary employees.

Once the partying ceases and heads clear, impresarios turn to the task of the convention hall *tear-down*. Orchestrators of the two conventions go about this differently, owing to the order of the two assemblies and each political party's administrative style. With the Democrats meeting a month before the Republicans, media and gallery impresarios approached the Atlanta tear-down with an eye toward moving equipment to the Crescent City. The TV anchor booths and other equipment were sent to New Orleans to begin technical preparations for the GOP convention. The network technicians were pleased with the Republicans' insistence on a six-week exclusivity clause on the Superdome. It allowed them to move directly into the facility and set up. DNC efforts to coordinate the Omni's tear-down had only a marginal impact on the TV networks' moving chores. This was not the case in New Orleans. The CNN Special Events team pointed out that RNC chief deputy Bill Harris continued his daily meetings *after* the convention. His "master list" coordinated the means to get everybody out of the Superdome to accommodate preparations for a football game scheduled one week after the GOP convention. The Republicans' contract for the dome stipulated this requirement, but the GOP's hands-on administrative style involved plans for a coordinated tear-down anyway.

Meanwhile, the respective nominees of the two political parties prepare for the last "official" act of the nominating process: appearances before the party national committees on Friday. After four days of intense celebration, these appearances are a formal opportunity once every four years for candidates actually to meet the principal officials of what is the *national* party. There is little reason to expect trouble, yet a slip of the tongue during the national committee meeting can literally destroy four days of momentum. Consider the Democrats in 1984. Geraldine A. Ferraro, the first woman to appear on a major party's presidential ticket, responded to a question about financial disclosure, assuring the committee that she would not only comply with the law (which requires completing a generally superficial form about finances) but provide tax returns for both her husband and herself for the past ten years. The overzealous statement by an exuberant candidate produced a crescendo of journalistic inquiry. Ferraro's remark provoked controversy owing to her husband's (John Zaccaro of New York City) widespread real-estate dealings. Journalists examined Zaccaro-owned warehouses for their contents, reviewed leases and agreements for possible wrong-doings, and in general, subjected the Democrats' vice-presidential candidate's financial holdings to the sort of scrutiny that few of us could endure. These activities placed Ferraro—and the front end of the ticket, Walter Mondale—in the unenviable defensive position that all candidates seek to avoid. Instead of advancing the ticket's agenda for the general election, they constantly had to respond to "the latest rumor" regarding Ferraro-Zaccaro's finances. Republicans wisely refused to comment on the matter (again, who can endure such microscopic examinations?) that continued to dominate the news until the GOP's Dallas convention. Ferraro had handled her historic candidacy flawlessly, until that national committee meeting. Thus, orchestration of cordial concurrence is not over until everyone gets "out of Dodge City" before or after sundown!

Evaluation Procedures

The political parties must file financial statements with the Federal Election Commission. The parties do, after all, spend the People's Money (i.e., tax dollars) on their quadrennial extravaganzas. In addition to reports required by law there are other evaluations. For example, in 1988 Paul Byers filed a report with party chair Paul Kirk, describing the focus and use of the DNC's Convention Satellite News Service. Byers's report reviewed the CSNS budget, the nature of facilities, the content of productions, publicity received by the service, and storage of videotapes of CSNS and Smith-Hemion programming. The report concluded: "CSNS helped party leaders communicate with voters back home by means of news coverage and interviews from Atlanta. CSNS also provided broadcasters and cable systems with an alternative source of convention coverage for their newscasts. . . . With positive feedback from both users and participants, this experiment by the DNC in utilizing new electronic technologies seems to have been successful." Similarly, the congressional gallery superintendents filed detailed accounts of their activities with their respective Standing Committee of Correspondents. The reports contain precise records of credentials distributed. In 1984, former Senate press gallery superintendent Don Womack, hired as a gallery consultant, also filed a report for the Standing Committee summarizing his role.

After countless meetings involving convention preparations, an intense preproduction schedule, frantic activity during the convention, damage and spin control, the postproduction phase of conventions is anticlimactic by comparison. Partisan and news organizations turn to the general election; convention impresarios return to other duties, resurface four years later, or disappear forever; host committees count up their profits and/or losses; and gallery personnel return to the nation's capital. For many, it is time to move on; for others, it is time for a much-deserved vacation.

Chapter Four

Stages, Pits, Floors, Balconies, and Boxes: The Parties' Productions at National Political Conventions

As 1988 conventioneers arrived in Atlanta and New Orleans, they encountered renovated highways and refurbished airports; fleets of limos, cabs, and buses; typical midsummer Southern weather (hot and humid); and—as they entered the host hotels and/or adjacent media work areas in the Georgia World Congress Center or the Hyatt Regency New Orleans—stacks of newspapers, magazines, delegate and media packets, and local promotional materials. For the events' first two days, volunteers feverishly distributed media and delegate packets and host-city souvenirs (coffee mugs were popular); the newspapers and magazines remained available throughout the week.

Of the variety of convention "programs" available, the special convention editions of the nation's three leading newsmagazines, *Newsweek, Time,* and *U.S. News & World Report,* conveniently appeared in media lounges, hotel lobbies, and party press rooms of both conventions. Such editions were not only news organs but preproduction publicity. In Atlanta, *Newsweek* (1988a) offered a "special report" on Dukakis "by the people who know him best" (based on interviews with a childhood playmate, high school teacher, college roommate, a "law school friend," his wife and son, and others) along with pieces on "Atlanta's Odd Couple" (the Democratic ticket), Jesse Jackson, vice-presidential nominee designate Lloyd Bentsen's "record," Ann Richards, and a "Viewer's Guide to Atlanta Antics"(on "people to watch"). *Time's* (1988a) cover displayed Bentsen and Dukakis's photograph with a large "The Odd Couple" headline centered between them and carried stories on the Democrats' new "postliberal age"; the party ticket; Jesse Jackson; Lloyd Bentsen; a Hugh Sidey piece on the 1960 Boston-Austin ticket; a Garry Wills essay on Dukakis's background; and a closing article on the city of Atlanta. The *U.S. News* (1988a) cover asked "How Good a President?"and articles profiled Dukakis, his family, and Bentsen; the magazine also reviewed "Black Power in the Big Peach."

In New Orleans, the three newsweeklies followed a similar strategy. *Newsweek* (1988b) emphasized the "passing of the torch" from Reagan to Bush along with an article on speechwriter Peggy Noonan, a Bush interview, and a Richard Nixon commentary on the fall campaign. *Time* (1988b) headlined "The Torch is Passed" and included a Bush interview, another Garry Wills piece, and an article on Roger Ailes and the Bush team, and closed with an overview of New Orleans and a brief interview with Dukakis. And *U.S. News* (1988b) again posed a question ("What Does He Stand For?") and answered by describing Bush as a "good scout" with a second article discussing the "retooling of the right."

For two years the Arleigh Greenblats, Bill Phillips, Don Fowlers, and other convention impresarios labored to orchestrate national conventions that would be preludes to electoral victories. Yet no word appears about their efforts in these preconvention *Playbills.* Instead the focus was on "star talent," the prospects for the 1988 election, and commentary by star columnists. This chapter endeavors to go beyond that focus. As with musical drama, convention extravaganza depends upon— sometimes in concert, sometimes in conflict—efforts of personnel in the conductor's pit occupied by TV directors, the box seats of TV anchor booths, the press-stand seating political critics, floor and balconies packed with delegates and spectators, and the environs surrounding the opera house of a convention hall. Specifically we are concerned with how the efforts of these persons—the orchestrators and the orchestrated—are reflected and refracted by the flickerings of what happens on the convention stage.

Party composers and stage directors can carefully script a show's story lines, segues, balloon drops, film content, and timing—a scripting, barring breakdowns, reflected in the spotlight of the four-night spectacle witnessed in the hall and on TV. But no composer can know with certitude that star talents such as Jesse Jackson, Teddy Kennedy, Barbara Jordan, Gerald Ford, Elizabeth Dole, or even Ronald Reagan will sing the arias as scripted. Small wonder, then, that party librettists work carefully on star arias, bending and adjusting the scripted lines to meet the idiosyncrasies of each performer. Small wonder, also, that convention notables numbered among the memberships of message committees and program groups anxiously await the prime-time performances of their prima donnas. Will, they wonder, the show spotlighted on stage reflect their painstaking orchestral artistry in a warm and positive glow, or will the limelight be a distorted, horrifying refraction of their best-laid plans?

To explore how these orchestrators' wonderment was resolved in 1988 we examine the convention shows' plots (i.e., the recitative) and how each story line developed in the convention hall during individual sessions and across the entire four-day event. Consequently, we emphasize each night's on-stage "star performances" (the arias) and how those prime-time renditions fit within the recitative. As in opera, the convention must establish a story line for continuity, and strategically place virtuoso performances in the show to enliven the proceedings— for, as we have seen, the recitative "loads the gun" and the aria "fires it." Ideally, the opening-night aria, the keynote speech, introduces the national viewing audience to the story told across the following three nights for which the nominee's Thursday night aria provides a resolution.

The Atlanta Democrats staged an uneven tale of "competence and hope" by trying to merge the campaign themes of primary winner Michael Dukakis (competence) and runner-up Jesse L. Jackson (compassion and hope), respectively. This plot featured the heroic defenders of the American Dream in conflict with the evil elites who constitute the incumbent Republican party. To enact this drama, the Democrats depicted themselves as the "trustees of a dream" striving to maintain the sense of "fair play" necessary to sustain their Ellis Island fantasy. This master plot, the Ellis Island fantasy, was the central organizing feature of the DNC's 1988 message—an "immigrant's rise to freedom and prosperity" yarn that set up attacks on the GOP as a threat to the American Dream. Central to the recitative's development was the "unity" leitmotif as the leading motive—the operatic device identifying recurring characters, objects, moods, situations, and ideas. Meanwhile, the New Orleans Republicans used their "Party of Lincoln" history as a foundation for their "politics of inclusion" recitative. This plot stressed individual freedom over group affiliation. It invited all *Americans* to voice their patriotism (the GOP's leitmotif) and support America's party. For the 1988 RNC, ideological continuity asked Americans to stay the course, support the "mission" initiated by Ronald Reagan, and join together to fight the villain "big government" (the principal threat to the Reagan-Bush "mission"). A two-party system thrives on an "us. vs. them" melodramatic imperative, just as opera relies on melodramatic representation. Yet the GOP chose not to attack mainstream Democrats or their heroes, but to play "Happy Days Are Here Again." The domed convention invited Democrats to join the GOP by positioning Dukakis as a "liberal" (the tale's villain) who failed to espouse *mainstream* concerns. Let us explore each of these political recitatives in detail as they played themselves out in the respective conventions halls. In Chapters 5 and 6 we allude to the degree that they reached TV audiences via network coverage.

THE ATLANTA DEMOCRATS

When delegates, media, party officials, and guests walked into Atlanta's Omni Colisium, they entered what CBS's John Reade termed the "world's greatest television studio." With skyboxes dispersed around the hall's rim, network anchor booths perched on steel platforms over exits, camera terrets scattered about, and a huge podium dominating close to half the facility, one quickly gained the impression that delegate seating was a secondary consideration for DNC orchestrators. Newspapers reported of delegate complaints and made references to the "podium that ate the convention hall." Those comments aside, however, the Democrats got their wish: the Omni looked "wonderful" on television.

Pool producer Charles Frey compared the lighting tactics for the two conventions and provided insights into their respective strategies. Frey noted that the RNC placed its overhead lighting grid in such a manner to make the entire hall its "stage," whereas the DNC lit the podium and made it the stage by dimming the hall lights during prominent performances. This set design had both positive and negative aspects. On the positive side the podium (with its pastel color scheme and camera angles) looked attractive on television. Yet the facility's small size made crowd noise a genuine negative embarrassment. When the lights were not dimmed and the audience did not pay attention to speakers on stage, the crowd noise occasionally overwhelmed the show's audio, both inside the hall *and* on television.

As to the cast, the delegates in Atlanta were a less experienced chorus than their counterparts in the Crescent City. The CNN–*Los Angeles Times* preproduction poll (a survey of *all* delegates distributed at each convention) indicated that the Atlanta assembly was the first convention for 58 percent of the DNC's delegates, the second for 21 percent, and the third for 10 percent. The delegates were evenly divided in gender (51 percent female, 49 percent male) and more racially diverse than Republicans (68 percent white, 21 percent black, 8 percent Latino, 3 percent other). Twenty-six percent of the Democrats' families earned between $50,000 and $75,000 a year (16 percent over $100,000; 15 percent $40,000–$50,000; 15 percent $30,000–$40,000) and 56 percent of the assembled Democrats were Protestant (32 percent Catholic, 7 percent Jewish, 4 percent other, 1 percent atheist). Forty percent of the delegates had graduate degrees and 26 percent worked in government (14 percent in business, 13 percent law, 12 percent other professions, 11 percent teaching). Finally, 43 percent considered themselves to be "somewhat liberal" while 29 percent were "middle-of-the-road" (18 percent were "very liberal," 9 percent "somewhat conservative," and 1 percent "very conservative"). Interestingly, 58 percent of the Atlanta Democrats claimed they had *no connection* with labor or teacher organizations. The 1988 DNC delegates were thus an inexperienced chorus whose minorities would enjoy more prominence on stage than any place else.

Opening Night: E Pluribus Unum

During his evening appearance, party chair Paul Kirk told his audience "we gather in the *Omni*, the latin word for 'all.' " With that remark, Kirk invoked the *e pluribus unum* ("from many, one") theme that dominated this five-act show. The five acts were: (1) Welcome I, (2) Party Business, (3) Welcome II, (4) The Keynote, and (5) The Recitative Revisited. The two Welcome acts featured brief appearances by local politicians and members of the Atlanta '88 host committee separated by a long, officially required, Party Business segment dealing with credentials and rules, addresses by national committee vice-chairs in the noisy hall, and party and Dukakis fund-raisers' claims of financial success. The Keynote and Recitative Revisited acts involved Ann Richards's performance and postkeynote activities (a Garrison Keillor–led routine, a Jimmy Carter segment, and closing entertainment), respectively.

The unity leitmotif first appeared during the Welcome I opening following brief remarks by Kirk and Don Fowler (the time-conscious Fowler's speech lasted *seven seconds*). Michael Lomax (a Fulton County commissioner and one of the blacks mentioned in the *U.S. News* article) established the recurring tune after he welcomed his colleagues to the "reborn Atlanta." Lomax declared *e pluribus unum* to be the "motto" and urged Democrats to retain "their individuality" but set "aside our differences" on "behalf of a shared purpose." The "unity" leitmotif echoed throughout the required performances constituting party business. For example, the credentials segment contained "no minority reports" and allowed K. Leroy Irvis to proclaim the DNC to be "a united party without divisions." The rules report flowed just as smoothly with the unanimous approval of Texas's Jim Wright (the Speaker of the U.S. House of Representatives) as the show's permanent chair. Kathleen Vick sang of the "road of cooperation" and her rules committee's "rules of inclusion, not exclusion." With credentials and rules business completed, a series of Democratic fund-raisers sang to a very loud crowd: speakers gave their best lines, paused, and got virtually no response—unless, of course, they mentioned Jesse Jackson's name or yielded to the "Jesse, Jesse" chant that occasionally sounded for no apparent reason.

The DNC's Welcome II featured Detroit mayor Coleman Young's song of "unity" in which he harmonized "what we have in common, sure as hell, is a lot more than what we have as differences." As Young performed, the DNC prepared the stage for its opening ceremonies, as the Marine band filed around the podium, an activity that further distracted an already inattentive audience.

With the session well underway, convention impresarios undertook various activities. For instance, party ancillary personnel fretted over transportation snafus as the hall filled very slowly and even the orchestra arrived late. Meanwhile Bob Petersen demanded Don Fowler supply more seats for "pundit row" (the label Petersen gave an area reserved for columnists), since the party had failed to provide the adequate number. Damage control thus began early in this opening session.

Once the pundits were seated, floor-pass distribution was underway, the party contributors were gathered in the Georgia World Congress Center (GWCC, where they watched the Smith-Hemion feed and enjoyed local hospitality), and the network cameras were rolling, the show moved to its first prime-time aria: Texas treasurer Ann Richards's keynote. Following a brief video introduction, and with the lights dimmed, the colorful Richards began her much-heralded wit when she lampooned "after listening to George Bush all these years, I figured you needed to know what a real Texas accent sounds like." Not only did this quip reflect her sense of humor, but it also captured the thrust of her performance—a steady attack on Bush and the Republicans. Richards, in a mock sing-song, warbled "that in a little more that 100 days, the Reagan-Meese-Deaver-Nofziger-Poindexter-North-Weinberger-Watt-Gorsuch-Lavelle-Stockman-Haig-Bork-Noriega-George Bush [era] will be over." After several references to her Texas upbringing, Richards described her job: "Tonight, we're going to tell how the cow ate the cabbage."

To establish a context for the deficiencies the Republicans represent, Richards read a letter from a "young [Texas] mother." The letter, Richards said, characterized the "forgotten" people who have been victimized by a Republican "divide and conquer" strategy. The keynoter announced that Democrats, in contrast, stand for "fair play" for everyone. With remarks such as "poor George, he can't help it—he was born with a silver foot in his mouth," Richards issued a steady attack on the Republican nominee and GOP elitism. As a resolution to this desperate situation, Richards recalled Democratic leaders from the Depression and World War II and how they used "straight talk" to communicate with the American people. For Richards, that tradition was alive in Michael Dukakis. Richards closed with the American Dream story and how that aspiration can only be restored via policies that reflect the "fair play" Democrats practice.

Richards's aria, described by Ronald Brownstein (1988) as "light, chatty and approachable, a full-fledged, tough-as-nails female good ol' boy" (p. 12) performance, achieved the keynote's institutional function—namely, the creation of an "us vs. them" melodrama that emphasized orchestrated themes of elitist threats to "fair play," the American Dream, an Ellis Island portrayal of hope, compassion, and opportunity. Following such a tough-as-nails keynoter would, no doubt, be a hard act. Smith-Hemion chose instead a change of pace with a Garrison Keillor–led reading of letters written by children. Actors Ed Begley and Ally Sheddy joined Keillor (who had already appeared during the opening ceremonies when he led a group of small children through the Pledge of Allegiance and the national anthem) for this "entertainment" interlude that was largely ignored by delegates.

The Recitative Revisited featured Esteban Torres's (self-proclaimed first Hispanic to address a Democratic convention in prime time) introduction of Paul Kirk's remarks and a Jimmy Carter segment including a Brock Adams introduction of Edmund Muskie, a Muskie segue to a Carter film, and Carter's speech. Carter scarcely echoed the message committee's plans to speak of the "party of the nineties"; instead he recalled the by-gone days of Franklin Roosevelt, Harry Truman, and John Kennedy. When he made his plea for "party unity" ("one more time: unity"), the former president hummed melodies dear to Jesse Jackson supporters by urging Democrats to "keep your eyes on the prize." The curtain fell after a closing entertainment segment and the party adjourned until Tuesday afternoon. All in all, two welcoming acts wrapped around the obligatory party business before a very noisy audience immune to the entertainment interludes made for an opening session that at least introduced the unity theme and identified the party's enemy (the GOP). That coupling resulted in a unity not so much a product of what the DNC was *for*, but what it was *against*.

A Crowded Evening: "It's a Good Night to Be a Democrat"

After several hours of platform-related business and toward the end of the first half of the Democrats' five-act Tuesday show, Californian Tony Coelho proclaimed "it's a good night to be a Democrat" as he previewed upcoming events. The Democrats' second session focused on the party platform, congressional candidates, and star arias featuring two of the party's most prominent families: the Kennedys and the Jacksons. Indeed, it was a fine night to be a Democrat—unless, of course, you were a member of the now fully neglected message committee.

The show opened with the required platform business (Act 1), moved to a segment featuring U.S. House and Senate candidates (Act 2), to a Teddy Kennedy prime-time sing-along (Act 3), to a Platform Reprise (Act 4), and closed with Jesse Jackson and the Jacksons (Act 5). Throughout the day, the "Jesse, Jesse" chant could be heard (once again, many times for no apparent reason) and speakers shamelessly stole Jackson lines whenever they liked. Should a speaker feel the lack of karma that characterizes an inattentive crowd, he or she need only mention Jackson or quote one of his rhythmic lines to gain applause. To this point, there was very little evidence that this was Michael Dukakis's convention.

In a series of performances that constituted the first act, any overriding convention recitative was virtually muted. Aside from booing U. S. senators Alan Cranston (CA) and the much-respected Daniel Inouye (HW), the

Democrats assembled in the Omni paid very little attention. This provoked chair Jim Wright to urge the audience to quiet down and extend speakers the right to be heard. What looked good on television sounded otherwise; the loud audience was audible throughout the hall and on television. Moreover, the party's computerized voting system stymied the voting process on party platform planks. As debate would finish, for example, on the third minority plank, voting on the first was still underway. Therefore, DNC secretary Dorothy Bush and/or Wright repeatedly urged delegations to complete their voting, or embarassingly announced results of votes that occurred hours ago. The "party of the future" it appeared had difficulty harnessing contemporary computer technology.

The subject of Act 1, the platform, was a marked departure from past statements of Democratic resolve, if for no other reason than its brevity. Paul Kirk's description of the platform as a "letter to the American people" was testimony to the platform's length (Knight News Service, 1987, p. 5). The seven-page document was entitled the "Restoration of Competence and the Revival of Hope." It endeavored to strike a responsive chord between the Dukakis and Jackson forces (as indicated in the title). The Atlanta platform made nine references to the two parties' identities: one extolling the virtues of Democrat-controlled state and local governments and the other eight attacking the GOP. Nowhere were traditional Democratic constituency groups mentioned. Instead the document stressed the evil of Republican abuses and, in doing so, pointed to Republican elitism and/or incompetence.

For example, the platform introduced concerns for "economic justice" and briefly applied that notion to "good jobs at good raises," a "first-rate employment economy . . . that can help lift and keep families out of poverty," and "a safeguarded" social security system. References to GOP "voodoo economics" and "economic violence" underscored threats to those aspirations. Through this strategy the DNC characterized the Republicans as elites who favor "irresponsible corporate conduct" and "the repeated toleration . . . of unethical and unlawful greed." The GOP was "increasingly monolithic both racially and culturally" and, hence, represented an enemy of "the people." These excerpts reflect the DNC platform's strategy: far more space devoted to attacks than to discussions of party ideology. Since the Atlanta platform was only seven pages in length, as the long debates on its content dragged on, one gained the impression that never had so many commented so long on so little.

Once the party suspended the rules to include a series of Jackson "unity amendments," the Democrats engaged in a time-controlled "debate" on the platform. Suddenly, time ran out and the debate closed. Without segue, the show turned to a second act showcasing congressional personnel and a few party hopefuls. Nebraska senator Robert Kerry, Minnesota U.S. Senate candidate H. H. "Skip" Humphrey (whose mere presence violated the message committee's plans), and California representative Tony Coelho (who initiated the "Where was George Bush?" chant in his attack on the GOP) performed. Act 2 moved to Jim Wright's non-prime-time speech on the 100th Congress and closed with one of the 1988 assembly's most understated and unrecognized performances.

Following a video introduction, Senator Robert Byrd (WV) sang a reasoned, precise, aria of government's positive role in American society and contrasted that view with the Reagan administration's "mocking" of the lofty status government must maintain. Byrd stated "our party has a clear-cut task" to "restore America's confidence in government" so that "government can once again become a credible force for good." Byrd chastised "this [the Reagan] administration" for its "arrogance" and "dark dealings" and declared "national policy cannot be made by wisecrack and blunder." For Byrd, the "times have changed, but the truths haven't." The senator concluded: "The Bible teaches us that where there is no vision the people perish. Government can inspire and give vision—if it has the right leaders. For a nation as with individuals, in the chaos of events, it is character that endures."

Byrd's statement of party principle stood alone among the many performances in Atlanta. He did not practice the politics of personality that slowly captured this convention, much to the chagrin of party impresarios. Instead, he argued from principle, not personal experience. As the Ellis Island plot unfolded, singers turned more and more to songs of personal experience with little or no reference to political philosophy or ideology. Though the Republican-bashing melodramatic chanty was evident in Byrd's performance, he did not contrast that condition with personal matters, but used party philosophy and a belief in government institutions to make his point.

Meanwhile, outside the convention hall Kathleen Vick's party of inclusion had shut its doors. Delegates and media personalities were left outside the Omni and, on several occasions, were screaming at local police. Arleigh Greenblat revealed that it was generally expected that a shutout would occur since Atlanta fire marshals frequently voiced concerns over the crowd size inside the hall. The closing yielded an ironic moment witnessed by a co-author of this study. When Martin Luther King III pleaded with a black, plain-clothed Atlanta police officer for admission into the locked hall (asking "Do you know who I am?"), the officer responded "yes, and nobody wants to be in that hall more than I do." With that reply King disappeared. Others locked out sat on a curb and watched the show on a one-inch television. A strange sight indeed: a Democratic convention in Atlanta constantly paying homage to Martin Luther King, Jr., actually barred the son of the slain civil rights leader from its own proceedings—even if inadvertently.

Inside the hall, Act 4 began with opening ceremonies that provided both the segue to the Kennedy segment and the show's movement into prime time. In an incredibly nostalgic move for a convention whose theme was to be the "party of the nineties," the Kennedy sequence opened with John F. Kennedy, Jr.'s introduction of the "man we call Teddy." Though Edward Kennedy's address was to be heralded most for its "Where was George?" chant, the performance did recall party principles and contrast the GOP's Bush with the Democrat Dukakis. After calling Bush "a dead duck," Kennedy deemed his party "the diversity of America" and the "party of hope, the party of both competence and concern" (notice, once more, the presence of both the Dukakis competence and Jackson concern themes). He also declared his "faith" in Dukakis, Bentsen, and Jackson and proclaimed "we have a job to do together—and if all of us are together, we shall not fail." Kennedy reinforced the "us vs. them" strategy by urging with "them" would come "the permanent division of our nation into three societies—one doing well, a second barely holding on, the third trapped decade after decade in hopelessness, anger, and violence." The senator defined his party as "trustees" of the American Dream that his brothers and Martin Luther King, Jr., died for; "now is the time" to preserve their dreams, he concluded.

Between family arias, the party presented the night's fourth act: The Platform—A Reprise. The delegates in the hall witnessed a video on platform chair John Blanchard, and heard speeches from Blanchard, Jim Hightower, Barbara Milkulski, and Sam Nunn. Of these performances, Hightower's was the most animated. It was filled with witty one-liners: It's time to "get the fat hogs out of the creek" and put "a people's president" in the White House; Bush is a "toothache of a man" who "was born on third base and thinks he hit a triple." Hightower gleefully claimed that Bush's idea of a farm program was "Hee Haw." Following these Bush-bashing tunes, the DNC abruptly voted to ratify its platform and, with that, closed its fourth act.

Finally, with platform matters decided and the Kennedys now safely backstage, the scene was set for the long-awaited fifth and final act. It unfolded in six parts: Tony Anaya's introduction of Jesse Jackson's five children, their individual speeches, an introductory video, Jackson's speech, a demonstration, and Jackson's trip into his adoring crowd (with a stop off to chat with the TV networks). As music lovers everywhere expected, Jackson's performance was spectacular. This singer used his background in the ministry to re-create the bel canto style (singing that emphasizes beauty of tone and elegance of phrasing, virtuosity, and agility) of days gone by. Jackson is an extemporaneous speaker who occasionally interjects the text of his prepared remarks. Hence, his full text was not available until the next day! Jesse Jackson—like those of the group-mediated era—is a singer who varies his song at will.

Jackson's speech vigorously attacked the enemy; however, he did so only after identifying his party (via his rainbow-coalition metaphor) and applauding the efforts of Rosa Parks, his family, Andrew Young, Jimmy Carter, Fanny Lou Hamer, and others who worked and suffered so that this moment could occur. Jackson, too, invoked the unity leitmotif: "Shall we expand, be inclusive, find unity and power; or suffer division and impotence. . . . Common ground. . . . Left wing. Right wing. Progress will not come through boundless liberalism nor static conservatism, but at the critical mass of mutual survival. It takes two wings to fly." After a "salute to Michael Dukakis" and his "well-managed and dignified campaign" Jackson sang a greatest hits medley that included a boat metaphor (he argued Americans may have arrived in different boats, but "we're in the same boat tonight") and a quilt metaphor (he depicted the various facets of his party as patches on his grandmother's quilt that needed to expand their respective patches and, in turn, strengthen the coalition). Through these verses Jackson urged his party to unify and fight the "reverse Robin Hood" that characterizes Republican policies ("they" take from the "poor," give to the "rich," all of which is "paid for" by the "middle class").

Jackson closed with an intensely personal recollection of his childhood and how, because of those experiences, he identifies with the poor. "I was born in the slum, but the slum was not born in me," he declared. For Jackson, the disparities he described were taken personally; subsequently, he urged his party to join *his* crusade and overcome the abuses of eight years of Republican rule. From top to bottom, it was a memorable performance. Critic William Safire (1988) commented that Jackson's speech "was paced like a concerto: the first movement established the lead theme of party unity . . . the second movement changed the mood by dipping in the no-no's of this convention, mentioning certain tax hikes to come . . . the third movement was intensely personal, using his life experience to inspire all those who start with nearly nothing" (p. 25).

Clearly, there were several stellar virtuoso performances in the Atlanta Democrats' second session. Though the platform recitative was long and boring, that portion of the show was made forgettable by Byrd, the Kennedys, Hightower, and later, the Jacksons. Little doubt, Coelho was right, it was a good night to be a Democrat; yes, a fine evening for Democrats, but unfortunately for the Atlanta convention, the finest show occurred *that* night.

Nomination Night: The Choral Number—Atlanta Style

By its very nature, if a party has more than one name placed in nomination, this part of the four-night production is the most disjointed. Sign choreography (when to raise red "Jesse" signs and lower blue "Dukakis" posters, etc.) and demonstration-time inequities make for a naturally uneven show. In 1988, a show that was supposed to serve as a transition from a Jackson-based convention to a Dukakis-controlled assembly instead brought closure to the Jackson campaign and left everyone wondering what Bill Clinton thought he was doing. Perhaps Tom Shales (1988e) put it best when he lamented: "Watching the third night of the Democratic convention on television, one couldn't help but get nostalgic. For the second night of the Democratic convention. As Jesse Jackson had electrified the hall on Tuesday, Gov. Bill Clinton of Arkansas calcified it Wednesday night" (p. 21).

Wednesday's session traditionally features the huge choral number that is the roll call of the states. This act contained three parts in 1988 that began with nomination speeches and their corresponding demonstrations, moved to the roll call, and closed with a "nomination by acclamation" resolution. Prior to this choral performance, the DNC recitative featured congressional candidates, Democrat governors, tributes, and a segment on women, farming, and education. In essence, the party recitative paid homage to its past, showcased partisan hopefuls, and dabbled in statements of policy. Early in the Wednesday session the DNC turned to a faceless announcer as its "master of ceremonies" who introduced speaker after speaker for addresses on a variety of topics. Of course, they all shared a common villain; still, "them" aside, these speakers said more about "me" and much less about "us." Senate candidates Richard Licht (RI), Leo McCarthy (CA), Frank Lautenberg (NJ), Howard Metzenbaum (OH), Joseph Lieberman (CN), and Jeff Bingaman (NM) appeared before the invocation. Senators Patrick Leahy (VT) and Kent Conrad (ND) were joined by congressman Claude Pepper for a brief series of speeches after Ben Hooks' invocation (that appeared virtually unannounced) suddenly ended. A film on American workers (with no introduction) provided no link to what it followed, or what followed it.

With a musical interlude paving the way, Colorado governor Roy Romer initiated a segment on Democratic governors. It was at this point that disjointed aspects of the show's schedule became distracting. Following the governors, the convention offered a tribute to Arizona's Mo Udall; featured three speeches that seemed to be on the drug problem; cut to a second tribute for, and speech by, Coretta Scott King; cut to yet a third tribute for former House Speaker Carl Albert; and concluded with a return to the governors (this time as they appeared together on stage, announced one by one). If delegates paid any attention to the potpourri at all, they had to puzzle at the uneven pacing as they awaited the hoopla over the Big Scene, the nomination.

By this evening of the four-day show, impresarios either settle into production routines or deal with the ever-present and unpredictable damage control. An example of the latter was Arleigh Greenblat's public battle with convention venders (those who sell sweatshirts, convention memorabilia, and other items) over their assigned locations to peddle their wares.

The venders publicly aired their complaints that the party had provided "out of the way" locations and that their business suffered as a result. Eventually, Greenblat negotiated a settlement. Such are the backstage squabbles that require arbitration during the week-long production lest they, not the convention, become the story. By Wednesday the flap that had occupied impresario attention the previous evening had abated a bit. The Tuesday convention hall lockout, now the street talk of media village, put everyone on notice. News organizations and delegations made sure their crucial personnel were safely inside the Omni by eight o'clock lest they, too, join the growing number of external conventioneers gathered in the GWCC for the closed-circut, Smith-Hemion feed, or in the many hospitality rooms sponsored by a variety of private and public entities.

Inside the now-locked Omni, a segment featuring Martha Lane Collins, Lindy Boggs, Chris Dodd, Bob Matsui, Bill Richardson, and John Kerry was drawing to a close. The show finally turned to the nomination speeches and their demonstrations. The Jackson speeches by William Winpisinger, Olga Mendez, and Maxine Waters followed tradition: they praised their candidate's virtues and basked in the glory of the historic moment. The Dukakis strategy emphasized one speaker, Arkansas governor Bill Clinton, hoping to use the opportunity to introduce "Duke the Man" to the American people. That was the plan, but what happened was a nightmare, for Clinton took on the hated features of the Phantom of the Opera.

The orchestra foreshadowed the Clinton performance when it played the theme for *Chariots of Fire* as he appeared on stage. Little did they know that, indeed, a marathon would follow. Clinton's speech dragged on so long that most networks cut away in midstream, the delegates' inattentiveness grew, crowd noise became a crescendo, and Dwight Hemion wrote messages on the teleprompter urging Clinton to *Please* stop (as a red time light flashed on the podium). Eventually, he did, but the damage was irretrievable: the transition from Jackson to Dukakis had been mishandled.

After a demonstration that celebrated both Dukakis's nomination and Clinton's absence, convention secretary Dorothy Bush appeared on stage and initiated the roll call of the states. Though just as scripted as any other part of the show, this choral number suggests that the "ghost of conventions past" is still among us. Some 1988 roll call verses included: "Arizona, home of the Grand Canyon"; "Historic Delaware, the state that started our nation"; Idaho, "the home of scenic beauty and, of course, the great potato"; Louisiana, "home of the Superdome and the next Democratic National Convention"; Michigan, "home of the Detroit Tigers"; Texas, "the crown jewel of Super Tuesday ... the home of 16 million hard-working Texans and one tourist from Kennebunkport, Maine"; and Washington, "whose union labor built the planes that flew you to Atlanta." In a strategic move, selected states passed on the roll call to allow California to put

Dukakis "over the top." Afterward, the obligatory demonstration of celebration ensued. Following the demonstration, the roll call resumed to its foreordained conclusion.

Once all states had cast their votes, California's Willie Brown appeared and, upon Jesse Jackson's request, made a motion that the convention suspend the rules and nominate Dukakis by acclamation. The motion passed. Jim Wright followed convention tradition and appointed the useless "committee to inform" the nominee. The session closed with Dionne Warwick's singing, with conventioneers holding hands and swaying to her music.

For many in Atlanta, the 1988 Democratic National Convention ended that night. After three days of celebration, the Jackson forces would now have to endure a final night dedicated to someone they seemed to dislike. Though the tide should have turned toward Dukakis with Clinton's speech, it did not and the burden now fell squarely on Dukakis's shoulders to make this fortieth gathering of the Democratic party his entrance into the fall campaign.

Lead Singer's Night: The Ellis Island Story

"The fall campaign begins tonight" is a rallying cry often intoned for Thursday night's role in the convention process. After three days of orchestration, cordial concurrence is at hand. At least that is how the drama is supposed to play. Though the Ellis Island fantasy was the motif of the previous three shows, it reached its crescendo on Thursday evening. This three-act evening featured an opening segment that praised the city of Atlanta (the convention passed a series of resolutions honoring the host city) and, once more, paraded party congressional candidates before the convention. A second act routinized the vice-presidential nomination (party rules allowed the convention to skip a roll call on Bentsen's nomination), featured the ritual demonstration, and culminated in Senator Lloyd Bentsen's acceptance speech. And the show's final act showcased the presidential nominee's acceptance aria, the show's largest demonstration, and a Grand Finale of considerable proportions.

This closing production traditionally features less emphasis on the recitative than do the previous evenings' shows. Conventions typically emphasize the two acceptance arias and, as a result, move away from the steady stream of speeches that constitute the recitative. So, once the evening's first act interlude of congressional hopefuls (and their wives) came to a conclusion before a very inattentive audience, convention chair Jim Wright expressed his pride in his team and the show temporarily recessed. Following the recess, Wright returned to lead a strange departure from the scheduled order of business: a geographically based pep rally ("Are we gonna carry the South?"). If nothing else, Wright seemed to enjoy himself. In any case perhaps everyone was by now accustomed to the uneven qualities of the Democrats' scheduling, for when the party returned from recess with "opening ceremonies," paused for Wright's cheerleading, moved to Bill Bradley's speech on the presidency, nominated and seconded Bentsen, and *then* offered the invocation, well, no one seemed to care. After all, this was their style—it all seemed normal.

As the convention reaches its closing session most impresarios are ready to get out of town. Arleigh Greenblat planned on Thursday morning to go on vacation and *never* return to Atlanta (he assured us it was nothing against the city). The gallery superintendents were packing to head back to Washington (and quietly looking forward to New Orleans). The pool producers, party officials, and network producers were anticipating the show's end so as to ready themselves for the RNC. And, the Atlanta '88 crew prepared for its huge postconvention party in the GWCC. Sundown was about to fall on Dodge City, and quite a few people anxiously awaited the nightfall well before the Democratic presidential nominee had even made what would be his only appearance before the convention.

Back in the locked Omni, the assembled Democrats witnessed one of the week's more smoothly orchestrated segments. The Dan Rostenkowski, Tom Dachle, Barbara Jordan, and John Glenn performances that nominated, seconded, and later introduced the party's vice-presidential nominee left the few delegates paying attention with something to cheer about. Chicago's Dan Rostenkowski pleaded with Reagan Democrats to "come home to the party of your parents" and Barbara Jordan offered a "reasoned" review of how the country was turning away from "hurray for Hollywood" and back toward the logic-based task of managing the people's affairs. Jordan's remarks joined Robert Byrd's to constitute the two rare convention performances dedicated to expositions of party philosophy. Ohio's John Glenn introduced Bentsen with a rousing tune of anti-GOPisms ("we cannot talk like Rambo and act like Bambi in foreign affairs") and expressed sincere confidence in his fellow senator.

Once on stage, Bentsen sang a song of contrasts: he identified his party as a "mirror of America," contrasting Democrats with those who "march lockstep behind some narrow, rigid ideology of indifference." In a telling metaphor, Bentsen declared "we are not gray grains of oatmeal in a bland porridge of privilege." Bentsen concentrated his early remarks on the enemy. He argued how "America has just passed through the ultimate epoch of illusion: an eight-year coma in which slogans were confused with solutions and rhetoric passed for reality." The Texas senator told his "fellow Democrats" that it "is easy to create the illusion of prosperity" since "all you have to do is write hot checks for two hundred billion dollars a year." With the enemy established, Bentsen turned to Ellis Island and the American Dream. The nominee described his father "as a symbol of what people of courage and vision and daring can achieve in America." He had "lived the American Dream." The Texan told of his family's voyage to

America and of a "homestead in South Dakota back when the government would bet 160 acres that you couldn't make it through the winter." The Ellis Island tale ended with Bentsen urging that "like your ancestors, they made it through the storm." Now the party must rally behind Michael Dukakis to preserve the "American Dream we have nourished and protected for more than two centuries."

Bentsen's demonstration and exit paved the way for another verse of the Ellis Island story. The "immigrants' song" did not cease in Texas, for the entire Dukakis family would sing that tune. With the "Fanfare for Michael Dukakis" composition by John Williams—conducted by his father-in-law, Harry Ellis Dickson—the DNC offered one of the smoother segues of their 1988 show. An off-stage announcer introduced Olympia Dukakis (the nominee's Academy Award–winning cousin), who introduced a film on Dukakis (which also starred Olympia Dukakis). She took her audience through "Michael's" childhood neighborhood, and his high school, and wheeled out his ancient snow-blower (as evidence of his "frugality"). This intimate glimpse at her cousin's life previewed what would be a very personal acceptance aria.

Michael Dukakis entered the Omni from a side door and made his way through the crowd to the tune of Neil Diamond's "Coming to America" (played at a volume loud enough to be heard even by those locked outside). Once upon the stage, the nominee stood and accepted his supporters' adulation. Some observers thought Dukakis was tearful in his appreciation of the crowd's response. Actually he was not. According to drama critic Robert Brustein (1988), Dukakis is simply "the only actor since Ben Gazzara who seems to be crying when he smiles" (p. 25). The governor opened and closed his remarks with references to marathons, employing the metaphor to express his feelings about both the presidential contest and his Greek heritage. Very quickly, however, he turned to the American Dream: "We're going to win [this race] because we are the party that believes in the American Dream"; moreover, "I know because, my friends, I'm a product of that dream and I'm proud of it." As evidence he reviewed his father's trip to America ("with only $25 in his pocket") and compared that experience with others in the Democratic party. With Ellis Island in the background, Dukakis defined what the 1988 election "is all about." He said, "this election is not about ideology. It's about competence." With references to the evil the Republicans have wrought and, in virtually every case, contrasting examples of "old-fashioned" American values, he went on to establish his notion of "community" and how "by working together to create opportunity and a good life for all—all of us are enriched—not just in economic terms, but as citizens and human beings." To underscore the point Dukakis recited a litany of individual Americans who have climbed the ladder of economic success and, in so doing, "enriched and ennobled" everyone.

Here is a marked departure from traditional Democratic philosophy (after all, he told us this contest was *not* about ideology) and toward the notion of an "opportunity society" made fashionable in the 1980s by, of all people, Ronald Reagan. Nowhere did Dukakis support Robert Byrd's view of government's role, but instead he talked of people helping people and government–private sector cooperation. Though he made several references to American "character" and the value of "what we believe," the nominee probably said more about what *he* believed, not his audience's world view. It was as if the Democrats' show, as traditional Democrats, had ended Tuesday.

After negative appraisals of the Reagan years, Dukakis praised, in turn, his vice-presidential nominee Lloyd Bentsen, keynoter Ann Richards, and, most of all, Jesse Jackson—singling out his daughter Jacqueline for a curtain call stand-up. Dukakis closed with a pledge uttered after important Greek ceremonies: "This is my pledge to you, my fellow Democrats." With that, the convention erupted into the traditional postacceptance demonstration—the Grand Finale, if you will—in which Dukakis's family, the Bentsen family, the Jackson family, and virtually any Democrat of any significance appeared on stage with singer Jennifer Holiday for a rousing version of the "Battle Hymn of the Republic." As each Democrat appeared on stage, Jim Wright introduced the notable to the audience. After the benediction, the convention joined in singing "America" and, with a motion to adjourn approved, Wright told his audience to "go in peace and enjoy. Thrive and spread the word."

We offer concluding observations about the Atlanta convention after our review of the New Orleans show. Nevertheless, two points stand out here. First, the up and down sides of the Democrats' facility. Although the Omni looked commodious on television, the locked doors, crowded floors, and noise were serious distractions. Second, the Atlanta assembly's rejection of the party's philosophy in preference to a promotion of the politics of personality invited Republicans to stress philosophy and attack their opponents for interpreting the world through purely Democratic personal experiences. Locked doors and an ideological void set the scene for the ideologically oriented, open-door policy paraded before those who entered the Superdome a month later.

THE NEW ORLEANS REPUBLICANS

Driving into New Orleans one could easily locate the site of the 1988 Republican National Convention. A huge red, white, and blue elephant balloon tied atop the Hyatt Regency New Orleans and a stream of "New Orleans—Host to the Future" banners indicated the way to the Superdome and the GOP production. Inside the cavernous convention hall, with its extraordinary dark blue, 90-foot-high curtain dividing the stadium, one was immediately moved by the contrast with the Omni. With a long press stand stretching from each side of the rostrum, spacious delegate and alternate sections on the convention floor, large skyboxes dispersed around the dome's rim (but above the lighting grid), and thousands of seats available to party faithful, donors, and guests, there would certainly be ample seating for the expected "thousands" to be "included" in the week's festivities.

Contrasting set designs are reminders of how staging impacts a show. For purposes of comparison, consider the differences between two recent productions of Richard Wagner's four-part series *Der Ring des Nibelungen*. One, performed at the Bayreuth Festival by the Bayreuth choir and orchestra (staged by Patrice Chereau, conducted by Pierre Boulez), used Wagner's famous opera house to stage a contemporary version of the *Ring*. Singers wore unimaginative costumes and set design was sparse with minimal props. The Bayreuth show emphasized music far more than other production concerns. The other version, aired by Public Broadcasting stations in the summer of 1990, took place in New York's Metropolitan Opera House (produced by Otto Schenk, set design by Gunther Schneider-Siemssen, conducted by James Levine) and featured elaborate made-for-television sets and costumes. Whereas characters in Bayreuth wore work clothes or business suits, those in New York appeared in lavish outfits, against a background of striking sets suitable for viewing with an electronic eye. This extravagant, telegenic version of the *Ring* cycle spared little expense. The stories were the same and the talent exemplary in both productions. Yet the shift in staging created markedly contrasting spectacles. The 1988 party conventions displayed a similiar contrast. The Met-Omni vs. Bayreuth-Superdome comparison is a direct one. The Omni showcased telegenic stage preparations and visual casting; the dome stressed the continuity of the music.

The *Atlanta Journal and Constitution*'s theater critic, Dan Hulbert (1988a), described how "in the real-life theater of a political convention, as on Broadway, the set sells the show" (p. 7C). Hulbert noted that convention sets of an earlier era "used to be simply platforms plopped into arenas." Atlanta designer Rene Lagler's stage was a serious departure from that tradition. According to Hulbert, Lagler created a "hermetically sealed world-unto-itself" or "one vast television studio." Hulbert labeled Lagler's creation an "environmental set" that related how "the action on the floor was as integral (and more colorful than) what was happening at the microphone." Pool producer Charles Frey's observations about set lighting and the Democrats' propensity to dim the lights suggest the opposite. The Republicans lit the hall and created an environmental set; the Democrats lit the podium and, subsequently, killed the stage-floor interaction and the environmental qualities of the show.

With regard to casting, the CNN–*Los Angeles Times* poll indicates the

GOP enlisted a more experienced, convention-wise troupe than did Democrats in Atlanta. To be sure it was the first convention for 47 percent of the delegates. But it was the second assembly for 25 percent and the third for 14 percent. There were more males than females (67 percent to 33 percent) and *far* more whites than minorities (91 percent white, 4 percent black, 4 percent Latino, 1 percent other). Thirty-four percent of the Republicans' families earned over $100,000 (22 percent $50,000–75,000; 17 percent $75,000–100,000; 11 percent $40,000–50,000) and 71 percent of the delegates were Protestant (22 percent Catholic, 3 percent Jewish, 4 percent other). Fewer Republicans had graduate degrees (35 percent) than Democratic delegates in Atlanta and more of them worked in business—31 percent (20 percent in government; 14 percent law; 13 percent other professional—8 percent of the delegates claimed to be housewives). Finally, 54 percent considered themselves to be "somewhat conservative"; 22 percent described their politics as "very conservative," 21 percent "middle-of-the-road," and 3 percent "somewhat liberal"—nobody was "very liberal." And 87 percent said they had no connection to unions or teacher organizations. Thus the chorus was slightly more experienced than Atlanta delegates and far more homogeneous in race, gender, and earnings. Although few in number, the GOP minorities paraded in prominence on stage, even more so than the Democrats' minorities in the Omni.

The GOP program, as it must, opened with official business on Monday morning, but the afternoon and evening schedule was dedicated to Ronald Reagan. Hence, the official keynote occurred on Tuesday and the party's presidential nominee did not arrive in town until late Tuesday morning. In fact, there was an "official changing of the guard" scene on Tuesday, as Reagan and Bush met at the airport—one arriving as the other departed. Reagan would have his night and gracefully leave town to allow Bush to assume the limelight. Monday evening's production was virtually a convention unto itself as it emphasized the Reagan years and, true to convention melodrama, attacked the Carter-Dukakis Democrats. We begin our account of staging with Monday morning and the GOP's first session.

Opening Day, A.M. and P.M.: Welcome to the Politics of Inclusion

At ten o'clock Monday morning, national committee chair Frank Fahrenkopf called the 34th GOP convention to order. A ten-second video (that Mark Goode also used in 1984 in Dallas) signaled the beginning of the RNC Network telecasts; Fahrenkopf's declaration "we are here at the appointed place, at the appointed time" initiated the stage show. With that pronouncement, the delegates rose for the presentation of the colors and comic Yakov Smirnoff led the Pledge of Allegiance. The national anthem, invocation, and removal of the colors followed in short order. Here was the first contrast with Atlanta's production: the opening ceremonies occurred in a single segment and foreshadowed an orderly program to follow.

The morning session's five acts consisted of official business and local greetings (Act 1); two speeches by presidential primary season losers Pierre DuPont and Alexander Haig (Act 2); the recitative's introduction via a series of speakers whose mere presence suggested the "inclusion" plot (Act 3); an official business segment (Act 4); and a concluding Campaign '88 routine in which GOP candidates addressed a near-empty Superdome, the RNCN, and C-SPAN cameras (Act 5).

Unlike the DNC, the Republicans passed resolutions to thank the city of New Orleans as a first item of business. After speeches by local personalities and party business (e.g., the acceptance of the 1984 rules as the 1988 convention's temporary rules), Act 1 closed. DuPont's Act 2 aria was a "letter to Jesse" Jackson inviting the Democrats' runner-up to join the "party of Lincoln, Reagan, and Bush." Although DuPont expressed his admiration for Jackson's work in "the projects" and his rise to national stature from a "broken home," he reminded Jackson that the Democrat was also "from America." He urged Jackson to adopt a patriotic stance and join America's party. DuPont's tactics initiated the RNC's inclusion strategy as a patriotic leitmotif, underscored by a portrayal of Dukakis as not representative of mainstream Democrats. Following DuPont, Alexander Haig opened with praise for Reagan and Bush, then assured delegates that Dukakis would "trash" everything the Reagan administration had achieved. Dukakis, said Haig, endorsed the "sterile policies of George McGovern." Haig cast the Democratic ticket as "an off-broadway revival of *The Odd Couple*, starring the diminutive clerk from Massachusetts and the tall stranger from Texas." Singing a parody of Jackson's "it takes two wings to fly" verse, Haig compared the Democratic ticket to a bat "flying erratically for brief periods at low levels and hanging upside down for extended periods in dark, damp caves up to its navel in guano." This was the GOP strategy: cast the DNC's ticket in dark tones and invite the rest of the Democrats to join the Republican chorus.

Act 3 introduced another twist to the politics-of-inclusion recitative. It featured a Hispanic teenager (Johnny Martinez), a blind athlete (Craig MacFarlane), two women (Judy Hughes and Anna Chennault), and Jewish leader Max Fisher. The theatrical tactic is an old one—display social diversity and tolerance through casting. Urged by the U.S. government, for example, Hollywood in World War II made films illustrating that people of all races, religions, and creeds made up American fighting forces. The "platoon" films cast as members of a fighting unit a Protestant, Jew, and Catholic; Polish, Italian, and Irish Americans; and so on. After the fourth act's business assignments (which would be completed Tuesday morning), Republican House and Senate candidates addressed the rapidly emptying hall. Eight speeches constituted this segment in which candidates spoke directly to their constituents and attacked their opponents with minimal references to the national campaign. With this routine's completion, business assignments made, and the inclusion recitative established, the party recessed until evening.

As the opening day of the GOP assembly continued, various impresarios adjusted to the production phase. For example, the press galleries—in particular, the print galleries—were busy capping off credentials dissemination. A problem arose concerning a limited number of floor passes available in the cavernous dome. The Atlanta convention—with its crowded floor—actually provided more floor passes than the RNC (225 to 160). Retired superintendent Don Womack's observation that floor passes are "the lifeblood of a reporter" suggests the significance of those credentials and, in turn, provokes curiosity as to why the huge dome could not handle more reporters on the floor. In the give-and-take of convention orchestration, was this a calculated GOP tactic?

The Republicans' stage production had its first prime-time airing Monday night: a three-act performance entitled "The President and his Lady." It opened with a segment on House candidates (featuring Michigan Congressman Guy Vander Jagt and Helen Barnhill—a black congressional representative from Wisconsin), a bel canto number by Reverend E. V. Hill (a GOP version of Jesse Jackson), and a closing selection by Minnesota's Rudy Boschwitz on U.S. Senate candidates. The second act involved a detailed tribute to Barry Goldwater, in which William Armstrong introduced both a video on Goldwater and the former GOP presidential nominee to the audience.

Act 3 was an extended celebration and adulation of the First Family. Although Arizona senator John McCain's video and speech (on "Duty. Honor. Country.") had little to do with the president, each speaker who followed celebrated the Reagan presidency—Senator Alan Simpson; "First Friend" Paul Laxalt (who introduced the Reagans as they entered the dome by saying, "Ladies and Gentlemen, the President and his Lady"); temporary chair Elizabeth Dole; and Congressman Jack Kemp. Kemp, in fact, repeatedly turned to Ronald Reagan and created an impression he was talking with the president.

Nancy Reagan performed briefly on center stage after her introduction by actor Tom Selleck. Elizabeth Dole then introduced a film, about the "Reagan Years," that was a segue to President Reagan's appearance. Reagan's aria was a collection of "golden oldies"—lines, references, and anecdotes he had employed in timeless fashion for eight years. For example: "I can still remember my first Republican convention. Abraham Lincoln giving a speech that sent tingles down my spine," or Reagan's "shining city on a hill" metaphor. He repeated his verse that he didn't leave the Democrat party, "they left me," and his lyrics on party philosophy: "We have a healthy skepticism of government—checking its excesses at the same time we are willing to harness its energy when it helps improve the lives of our citizens." Reagan's aria may have been a collage of previous campaign speeches, clichés, and acceptance speeches, but it was also a ringing endorsement of party principle and a clear response to the Democrats' "Where was George?" attack.

When Reagan finished, the convention erupted into one of its three major demonstrations of the week. With balloons floating and confetti flying, Nancy joined her husband on stage (protected by GOP impresario Mike Miller fighting off network podium correspondents) for Lee Greenwood's closing rendition of "God Bless the USA." Following Greenwood's performance and Billy Graham's benediction, the session ended. With close to 60,000 people in the dome and an emotional Lee Greenwood–led closing act, the GOP thus raised the curtain on its 1988 stage production in a dramatic fashion.

On the Second Day: Party Business and the Fab Four

The two three-hour morning sessions—complete with their routines, uneventful business affairs, and addresses by party candidates for various offices—separated mundane nontelegenic activities from the prime-time show. In that vein, Tuesday morning's production was in an orderly three acts. Act 1 staged opening ceremonies, speeches by GOP co-chair Maureen Reagan, Van Hipp, Newt Gingrich, Art Fletcher, George Voinovich, and Helen Delich Bentley. Act 2 dealt with the committees on credentials, rules, permanent organization, and resolutions reports. Most of that segment involved a Kay Orr–led review of the party platform. The final act featured a closing round of candidate speeches in an empty Superdome.

In party business, Iowa's John McDonald summarized "contests" on credentials, all eventually resolved. Following Dick Cheney's report on rules and Herbert Eddington's presentation of the permanent organization report (during which Robert Michel was voted the convention's permanent chair), the party turned to its platform. Seven speakers summarized seven sections of the GOP document—a voluminous response to the "Democrat happy talk" (in Ralph Knoble's words) contained in the seven-page Atlanta platform.

The GOP platform is so long (104 pages) it includes a table of contents, preamble, and subject headings for organizational purposes. Entitled "An American Vision: For Our Children and Our Future," the platform stresses the "blessings of liberty." The GOP portrays optimistic belief in the "American miracle," a party that values freedom, opportunity, prosperity, and—perhaps most importantly—continuity. The "party of Lincoln" that believes in "free enterprise, free markets, and limited government" is in conflict with the villainous forces of "liberalism" personified by Michael

Dukakis. Unlike Democrats in their brief, centerfold document, the New Orleans GOP devoted ample space to party history and philosophy. For instance, the party identified itself as "the party Abraham Lincoln helped to establish—the party of Teddy Roosevelt, Dwight Eisenhower, Ronald Reagan, and George Bush." Moreover, the inclusion theme was paramount in the party's claim to be "the natural champion of blacks, minorities, women, and ethnic Americans," and in its self-description as "the party of real social progress," a party that "since its inception has stood for the worth of every person." Thus, the platform rhetoric reinforced the "inclusion" recitative just as the Atlanta platform did the "competence and compassion" tale. However, unlike the DNC platform, the RNC platform did not reflect party compromises over personal themes, but transcended individual orientations by way of philosophy. The GOP was inclusive not merely because of its personnel but because of its ideology.

The morning session closed with another "platoon" segment—nine speeches featuring a Jewish, Hispanic, black, female (in that order), and five white male candidates. Of the lot, Virginia's Maurice Dawkins (a black minister and U. S. Senate candidate) was, by far, the most entertaining. The few delegates still in the hall heard Dawkins speak at length, honored his request that everyone "stand up against drugs" (the Virginia delegation dutifully rose), and joined him in song ("God Bless America"). This morning session, in short, was the GOP's not-for-prime-time production of the week.

As convention orchestrators looked toward Tuesday evening's session, they grappled with a technical problem that had plagued the previous night's production. During President Reagan's speech, for example, those seated on the press stand and delegates and spectators on the floor and in the balconies could barely make sense of the president's remarks. The party-installed sound system required constant adjustment. A *Wall Street Journal* article captured the dynamics of the audio snafu. Langley and Davidson (1988) wrote of an incident involving CBS's Leslie Stahl. Stahl reported "on the CBS Evening News that a 'miscalculation' had been made with the Superdome and *its* sound system." A local TV reporter asked to interview Stahl. The reporter noted "the sound system was the Republican's—not the Superdome's" (p. 10). Asked if she "stood by her story, Ms. Stahl threw up her hands and walked off—all dutifully shown on the local news show." Apparently the occasional on-camera stonewall is a response to inquiring reporters not confined to politicians but practiced by TV journalists themselves in a pinch.

As the Big Easy buzzed with news of the announcement that Dan Quayle was to be the GOP vice-presidential nominee, Republicans convened their second prime-time show. The "Politics of Inclusion Goes Prime-Time: The Fab Four" was a five-act production: Act 1, opening ceremonies and Robert Michel's speech; Act 2, a segment on GOP governors;

Act 3, Kay Orr on the platform; Act 4, a Recitative Revisited; and Act 5, the Fab Four (Jeane Kirkpatrick, Tom Kean, "Pat" Robertson, and Gerald Ford). Each act had its own identity and internal continuity. Overall, the show represented a steady progression through a variety of topics.

Michel's Act 1 plea to "send us more Republicans" to the House of Representatives combined with gubernatorial appearances in Act 2 to complete the GOP's nonpresidential electoral promotions. For two days, the party faithful heard from the House, Senate, and gubernatorial hopefuls who received podium time to perform and tape fall campaign video. But, unlike the DNC, these tryouts ended on Tuesday evening; the Democrats featured congressional candidates as late as Thursday. Following Kay Orr's presentation of the party platform, Carroll Campbell, Bob Kasten, George Deukmejian, and John Sununu made up a jam session of speaker-soloists. Sununu, in particular, criticized Michael Dukakis in relentless fashion, first introducing a negative point about the Democrat's record, then adding an "and it's worse than that" refrain. Sununu declared "what you see is more than what you get" and described Dukakis's administration not as the vaunted Massachusetts miracle but as the "Massachusetts mirage."

The overall continuity in GOP messages, recitatives, and leitmotif was spotlighted in the four arias that made up the show's final act, the Fab Four. Jeane Kirkpatrick's "lecture" on foreign affairs, Tom Kean's "official keynote" speech, Pat Robertson's review of party values, and Gerald Ford's forceful endorsement of George Bush all took on the "evil liberals" and smoothed a steady segue from Reagan to Bush. All four focused on what Reagan and Bush shared: party ideology. For example, Kirkpatrick reminded delegates that "we ... cherish our freedom and our self-government," then attacked Democrats on foreign policy. Kean quoted Abraham Lincoln, declared "his creed is our creed," and described how all Americans believe in the American Dream, however "the answer to those dreams will not come through bigger government in Washington." Robertson proclaimed: "We are Republicans and we believe in government that is our servant, not our master. We believe that the wisdom of the millions who make up the marketplace is greater than the wisdom of the few who serve in government. ... We are conservatives and we are proud of it!" Lastly, former President Ford told the nation "we stand for individual freedom, for equal justice and opportunity, and for safety at home and peace in the world. ... We believe that a government big enough to give you everything you want is a government big enough to take from you everything you have."

A convention's melodramatic imperative contrasts the party's hero (in this case party philosophy as personified in Reagan-Bush) with the evil enemy. Virtually all of Kirkpatrick's speech pursued that objective as she consistently attacked the Democrats for foreign policy inexperience, especially the Carter administration. Kean used humor to attack Dukakis for the DNC's "pastel patriotism." Kean complemented Kirkpatrick's "George Bush knows better" line with: "All I can add is one warning. The Dukakis Democrats will try to talk tough. But don't be fooled. They may try to talk like Dirty Harry. But they will still act like Pee Wee Herman." Robertson described the "liberal" Democrats as "one . . . big . . . family" featuring: "Jim Wright as the Daddy, Barbara Milkulski as the Momma. And Teddy Kennedy as Big Brother. I can't speak for you, but I believe I would rather pick my own relatives." In the evening's final aria, Ford referred to the "Democratic ticket" as "a tax increase on its way to happen." Ford begged Lloyd Bentsen to "speak up now" and correct his party's failings. The strength of Ford's remarks was in his review of Bush's record and his intense conclusion: "I'll be *damned* if I will stand and let anyone with a smirk and a sneer discredit the honor, service, accountability and competence of George Bush." Thus ended the final performance by a revered member of the GOP production company on Tuesday.

Nomination Night: The Choral Number: N'awlins Style

New Orleans may have been buzzing with word of Bush's vice-presidential choice on Tuesday, but Wednesday saw the city vibrate with journalistic inquiry. During a morning Bush-Quayle press conference a question emerged about Quayle's military background. Quayle, who served six years in the Indiana National Guard, denied he had joined the Guard to avoid Vietnam and, from there, the story exploded (see Chapter 6). Wednesday night, as the fourth session convened, Quayle would face the nation in what the *Washington Post*'s Tom Shales (1988h) described in this fashion: "Dan Quayle ran the triathlon Wednesday: ABC, CBS, and NBC. And CNN, for good measure. He submitted to ordeal by anchor. He underwent trial by booth. . . . Quayle did prove his boothability, however, and at this convention, perhaps at all conventions now, it's the booth that counts. The anchor booth is second only to the voting booth. It's all a matter of boothmanship" (p. C2). Boothmanship or not, the show on the podium stage must go on and it did. The Choral Number: N'awlins Style show was a three-act production that featured opening ceremonies and a "Why I'm a Republican" recitative (Act 1); a Robert Dole aria (Act 2); and the final act, the choral performance.

Actor Charlton Heston led the hall in the Pledge and ten-year-old Heather Ostrom sang the national anthem before co-chair Olympia Snowe introduced the evening's "Why I'm a Republican" recitative. The second of the GOP's black U.S. Senate candidates, Maryland's Allan Keys, opened with a ringing "party of Lincoln" solo lauding party values and attacking the Democrats for "pitting" minority groups against one another to gain votes. Bill Bennett, Donna Owens, Dan Vasquez, Manuel Lujan,

Pete Wilson, Jim McClure, and Pete Domenici all sang songs of Republican philosophy during this initial act. Vasquez's Spanish version of "Why I'm a Republican" included the claim that Dukakis may "speak Spanish, but he doesn't speak our language."

At this point the convention abruptly paused for the "offical photograph." Then came a glitch. After Mitch McConnell and Ann McLaughlin spoke, Nancy Kassebaum tried to introduce Robert Dole. But a drummer in the orchestra refused to stop his solo. Apparently, convention producers had instructed the orchestra leader, Manny Harmon, to continue the solo (without advising the podium, one presumes) while the show awaited Dan Quayle's post-triathlon appearance in the dome. Once Quayle was safely seated, Kassebaum presented Dole to the RNC.

In his unique style, Dole described the election as "a crossroads" in which the "alternatives have never been more obvious, the consequences more important." Using this melodramatic opening, Dole declared Dukakis to be "undoubtedly a fine man" but he is "one of those liberals who does not know where to draw the line; and this puts America at risk." Dole attacked Dukakis by calling him "one of those liberals with strange ideas—Dukak-eyed ideas" and claimed "liberals define arms control this way: the Soviets arm, while we control." From these attacks, Dole praised the qualifications of the Bush-Quayle ticket and, in his closing, recalled a trip to Moscow's Red Square and his feelings that his country needed a president who knows where to "draw the line" with the "hard-as-nails communists."

The stage spectacle moved into its final segment, the long-awaited nomination ritual, with Michel's review of the voting rules. NFL Hall of Fame quarterback Roger Staubach introduced Texas senator Phil Gramm to sing the praises of the GOP nominee. Gramm reviewed the Bush record and portrayed him as a family man (yet another leitmotif to ring across the show's final scenes and the next four months), public servant, and brave soldier. Gramm attacked Dukakis's "tax and spend policies" and described the Democratic nominee's home as "Taxachusetts," where the governor "taxed the poor, taxed the rich, taxed the young, taxed the old, and taxed the middle class." Then, when Dukakis "got a second chance as governor in 1983 . . . he proved he could spend as well as tax." With the Democratic dragon slain, Gramm turned to the "George Bush Story" and contrasted the Bush record with his melodramatic portrayal of Dukakis. In closing Gramm reiterated the recitative established throughout the week: "America is not a great nation because brilliant and talented people came to live here. America is a great nation because our system offers incentives and opportunities for greatness. . . . The genius of America's success lies not in the brilliance of a few but in the spirit of enterprise, work, and family of all of us who call ourselves Americans." With those remarks, Gramm both placed Bush's name in nomination and reinforced the party's ideological stance.

After an 18-minute demonstration the GOP turned to its seconding speeches by Helen Hayes, Penn State football coach Joe Paterno, Elaine Chao, Ninfa Laurenzo, Joane Collins, Robert Dornan, and Columba Bush (along with her husband, Jeb). All but Hayes spoke from the convention floor. The mix of five women (of various ethnic groups) and two men restated the party's casting commitment to the inclusion theme.

The roll call of the states, led by party secretaries Pat Saiki and Lynn Gunderson Martin, appeared to observers (see Chapter 6) to take more time than the choral number in Atlanta. In fact, it did not. As states announced their vote they played jokes, offered long digressions before passing to assure Texas would put Bush "over the top," and, in five cases, allowed Bush children to cast delegation votes to spotlight the family-man leitmotif. Memorable lyrics included Kentucky's claim to be the "state of beautiful women and fast horses"; Missouri's comical effort to cast one vote for "The Shadow" and its subsequent correction; and Oklahoma "where we don't pass, we run the ball." In another comic moment, the Michigan chair announced "as I approached the mike this evening, I have compiled a list of all those things people wanted me to mention in my report to you. In the interest of time, however, I'll only mention those things for which I've been paid." Such were the *opera bouffe* qualities of the New Orleans choral number.

After yet another demonstration once Bush was over the top, convention orchestrators bowed to huckersterism over efficient procedure. All delegations were allowed to vote, even after the magic number was attained. The Virgin Islands took its vote as an opportunity to give a long speech and introduce the entire delegation.

The session ended with the traditional (and totally useless) announcement of the "committee to inform the nominee," the benediction, and adjournment. On the stage of the dome, the 1988 RNC performed the joy and celebration that is nomination night. Inside TV anchor booths, however, the party endured the scrutiny of Dan Quayle. For the party, their ideologically based show continued; for the 15,000 journalists in town, as we see in Chapters 6 and 7, that message was beside the point: Dan Quayle was the real story.

Lead Singer's Night: The Magical Mission

The New Orleans convention's final segment borrowed a page from the DNC's program as the show opened with entertainment and vice-presidential business, then presented its opening ceremonies, and followed with the Quayle and Bush arias, respectively (a three-act show). Thursday night was "personality night" as the party acknowledged Barbara Bush, Dan Quayle, and its standard-bearer, George Herbert Walker Bush. Offstage the relentless pursuit for information on Quayle's background continued. While most impresarios were preparing to leave town, the news media were still tracing leads on Quayle's National Guard duty.

By Wednesday's session, the audio problem had been corrected and everyone had grown used to the facilities. There were, of course, complaints. Pool producer John Reade expressed reservations about the presence of RNC Network videographers on the floor (they seemed to know what was about to happen before anyone else—and they probably did). Print journalists continued to complain about the limited number of floor passes available. Yet the show had either settled into its own groove or people were so preoccupied with the Quayle story they no longer cared about hotel problems or floor credentials. After all, the convention floor yielded few leads about the Quayle story.

The Thursday program opened with the Oak Ridge Boys. Afterward, the hall made the acquaintance of Barbara Bush via Louis Sullivan and a video. The Barbara Bush segment was relatively brief (the Atlanta convention never presented Kitty Dukakis to the delegates, through either video or speech), and echoed the George Bush, Family Man leitmotif throughout.

The vice-presidential nomination process featured an all-star cast starring Robert Dole (he nominated Quayle) and seconding numbers by Richard Lugar, Nancy Kassebaum, Alan Simpson, and Jack Kemp. Dole continued his attack on Dukakis, Lugar described Quayle as an "undefeated" candidate, Kassebaum expressed her appreciation for Quayle's values, and Simpson discussed "Dan the senator, Dan the leader, and Dan the man." (Simpson truly seemed to enjoy himself.) The Quayle nomination was by acclamation and touched off a programmed seven-minute demonstration. The opening ceremonies followed with the Oak Ridge Boys, Robert Scheuler's invocation, and a Marine playing taps in honor of all those who died for their country. (This was the only time the RNC dimmed the lights as a single spotlight focused on the Marine.) The stage was now set for the two closing arias and the Grand Finale that would end the show.

Lynn Martin introduced Quayle with the understatement of the week: "You are about to meet the best surprise of the 1988 convention." She then contrasted him with Lloyd Bentsen ("he doesn't have breakfast with $10,000 lobbyists, he has breakfast with Marilyn and the kids") and yielded the stage to the nominee. Quayle began by announcing that in "82 days" the GOP ticket would win one for the party, "America's future," and "the Gipper." After thanking Bush for his selection, Quayle reviewed his background as a senator, as a member of the House, and "as a young man, I served six years in the National Guard" (a solid applause line). Quayle told of his Hoosier background and that "our small town" believed in "hard work, in getting an education, and in offering opportunity to our families." The thrust of Quayle's opening remarks was to create a humble Hoosier persona. In classic convention melodramatic style, the vice-presidential nominee said George Bush stood for "freedom, family, [and the] future." To preserve these values, Quayle argued, the GOP must defeat the party of "George McGovern, Jimmy Carter, Walter Mondale, Ted Kennedy, and, now his buddy Michael Dukakis." Quayle's closing left the "us vs. them" motif; he thanked Bush's generation for an "era of peace and freedom and opportunity" and announced his generation's challenge to repay that debt in kind.

After Quayle's demonstration, James Thompson introduced the film that provided the segue to Bush's acceptance aria. This film, much shorter than the Reagan version from 1984 (a mere seven minutes), applied the family man leitmotif with scenes of Bush and his grandchildren along with World War II footage, comments by President Reagan, and other heroic scenes. The convention erupted on cue when Bush walked out to the podium for the production's capstone aria. Bush expressed his thanks for the many "who have honored me with their support" and announced his intentions to "run hard, to fight hard, and to stand on the issues" and "win." After applauding Quayle and Ronald Reagan, Bush declared: "And so tonight is for big things. But I'll try to be fair to the other side. I'll try to hold my charisma in check. I reject the temptation to engage in personal references. My approach this evening is, as Sergeant Joe Friday used to say, 'Just the facts, ma'am.' " In other words, Bush would follow the strategy of the previous three evenings. By rejecting "the temptation" to project the politics of personality and preferring instead the politics of ideology, Bush achieved two things: first, he related his "mission" involved the completion of the Reagan agenda (the ideological continuity theme) and second, he portrayed Dukakis as ideological-less, self-indulgent, technocratic.

Bush argued for the Reagan record and for his party's philosophy. Bush sang: "Some say this isn't about ideology, that it's an election about competence. Well, it's nice of them to want to play on our field. But this election isn't only about competence, for competence is a narrow ideal. Competence makes the trains run on time but doesn't know where they're going. Competence is the creed of a technocrat who makes sure the gears mesh but doesn't for a second understand the magic of the machine."

With those verses, Bush issued the capstone appeal required by his acceptance aria's institutional role. For three days, the Republicans had described the "magic" that is their ideology. As Gramm had stated the previous evening, America was a product of "magic," not personalities. Bush merged those thoughts, as well as other statements of philosophy, to wrap himself in his party's values and launch an attack not on Democrats but on liberalism and Dukakis. Moreover, Bush's "thousand points of light" metaphor, his "missions" declaration, and his Pledge of Allegiance closing established the fall campaign's themes. For George Bush and the GOP, the campaign *did* start that night.

As with virtually all conventions, the four-day production closed with a Grand Finale that included balloon drops (the largest in history), a popular artist singing (Shirley Jones), a long benediction, and a closing final number ("God Bless America"). The party had completed its business and its spectacle. The house lights dimmed and the show was over.

THE ORCHESTRATION OF CORDIAL CONCURRENCE: 1988 REVISITED

After Jesse Jackson's stirring performance in Atlanta, columnist George Will (1988) offered the following assessment that, in some ways, captures not only Jackson's aria but the entire Democratic convention: "Most political disputes concern programs and policies, and seasoned politicians can split their differences. But Jackson practices politics as autobiography. His aspirations are intensely personal: status, acceptance, respect. He has teetered on the edge of turning megalomania into a political philosophy" (p. A15). Perhaps Will's conclusion is overstated, but he does identify the DNC's "politics of personality" that we have contrasted with the RNC's "politics of philosophy." The Atlanta program stressed characters while the New Orleans show focused on plot.

Consider the two shows' highlights for purposes of comparison. Recall Ann Richards's and Tom Kean's keynotes in which both attacked the other side; Richards focused more on Bush the person while Kean directly contrasted the two ideologies. On Tuesday Democrats witnessed two all-star families who told of their personal sacrifices and aspirations, whereas Republicans heard the Fab Four speak about party values and philosophy. Wednesday saw Bill Clinton attempt to introduce "Dukakis the Man," while Gramm attacked liberal policies as a setup for his articulation of America's "brilliance"—a brilliance based not on people but ideology (although Gramm did sing a "Bush the Man" stanza). Finally, Thursday's voyage past Ellis Island was predicated on personal experience, Bentsen and Dukakis personified the DNC's American Dream tale. In New Orleans, though Quayle spoke of his Hoosier values, Bush resisted the "temptation" to indulge in "personal references" as he directly followed through on the "magic of the machine" plot. Both presidential candidates relied on "pledges" to end their arias. It was telling that Dukakis invoked a Greek pledge offered before important Greek events (yet another personal reference); Bush recited the Pledge of Allegiance.

In conclusion, return to the convention's institutional function in our electoral system, the orchestration of cordial concurrence. Did the two 1988 assemblies stage a transition from the primary season to the fall campaign? Did they transform the individual campaigns of the spring into the party contests of the fall? The answer is no and yes. No, the Atlanta Democrats did not produce an effective transition to the general election. While they received the traditional "convention bounce" in the polls, they effectively closed their primary season with their convention. In this sense, the DNC was more Jackson's than Dukakis's. As DNC impresario Mike Mc-Curry told us some time later, the party did not initiate the fall campaign in any meaningful way. The yes goes to the Republicans for their choreographing of ideology to transcend primary differences and incorporate Reagan's persona in the plot. Law and order, the Pledge of Allegiance, a thousand points of light, George Bush—family man, and ideological continuity ("mission") themes informed the GOP fall campaign.

Two 1988 shows, each orchestrating cordial concurrence. In Georgia, the party agreed to end the primaries; in Louisiana, the party revisited their "party of Lincoln" ideology and agreed to "stay the course." Both productions featured state-of-the-art orchestration tactics: satellite networks, spin operations, party lines, and hymnals. The stages differed but both the Omni TV studio and the Superdome open-air theater provided a setting conducive to the orchestration of cordial concurrence. The principal difference between the two 1988 conventions came not to the stage but to the staging. Ideology provided the recitative device to transfer loyalty from Reagan to Bush, tie performances together, isolate the opposition, and move into the fall campaign. Ideology created harmony among RNC singers and their individual songs. Reviews of personal histories—especially stories based on Ellis Island—are touching melodies, but they display little harmony when those personal histories differ. Democrats overlooked Robert Byrd's call to party principle. The show looked good on TV, but it featured personal melodies at the sacrifice of the party's institutional character.

Chapter Five

Melodies and Discords:
TV Coverage of the Democratic
Convention in Atlanta

It is July 18, 1988, the opening-night session of the Democratic National Convention in the Omni in Atlanta. Well before Paul Kirk, the party chairman, gavels the convention to order journalists from wire services, newspapers, and newsmagazines wander in to occupy assigned seats in tiered rows along each side of the speaker's podium. A reporter from a major news service sets up shop a few rows back and slightly to the right of the podium, a prized position affording a sweeping view of the floor, delegates, TV and radio anchor booths, and skyboxes housing local TV outlets. The reporter checks the telephone at her desk. Satisfied, she seeks aid from a co-author of this study to plug in her portable personal computer. Satisfied that it too works she plugs in a small portable TV set and tunes it to the feed of CNN, the Cable News Network. As final preparation she lays out before her advance copies of principal speeches to be delivered so close to her press position that the speaker's TV makeup is clearly visible. Each copy has been worked through with a highlighter pen. Everything in order, she undertakes her first-hand coverage of the 1988 Democratic National Convention. For the next four days her accounts appear in newspapers across the nation, and readers assume that they are witnessing unfolding events through the reporter's eyes. Readers of H. L. Mencken's columns on party conventions published in the *Baltimore Sun* in the 1920s, 1930s, and 1940s assumed as much. Had anything changed?

Paul Kirk calls the convention to order. Since it is still late afternoon, the opening ceremonies are less glitzy, less star-studded than the made-for-television formalities that will mark a second opening—that is, when prime-time coverage begins with the sign-on of the three over-the-air TV networks. For now only viewers of C-SPAN and CNN have any inkling of the convention witnessed by those gathered in the Omni. During these and ensuing proceedings the news service reporter works away on her PC, writing and filing copy via telephone modem. Rarely do her eyes scan the growing numbers of delegates in the hall, the milling and conversing on the floor, delegates' attention or inattention, or the parade of party officials and speakers to the podium. Instead, she divides her attention between the advance texts of speeches before her and the CNN broadcast on the TV monitor. From time to time as CNN's anchors, Bernard Shaw or Mary Alice Williams, comment, or as a CNN floor correspondent conducts an interview, the reporter turns up the sound on the TV set, takes a few notes, lowers the sound, and returns to pecking away at the PC. Throughout the four evening sessions the reporter continues her vigil and her reporting, filing copy, not of her first-hand observations of what is happening in the convention hall, but her impressions gleaned from advanced texts and CNN coverage. Instead of providing readers with what "it is like" to be "live in convention hall," she will hum themes orchestrated for her by speechwriters and TV broadcasters.

And she was not alone. One month later, August 18, 1988, the front page of the *Washington Post* carried a story by a staff writer headlined "Quayle's Service in Guard Stirs Favoritism Question" and "Senator Strives to Explain Vietnam-Era Record." The story dealt with the crescendo of controversy surrounding the vice-presidential nominee's entry into the Indiana National Guard and whether, as the story asked, "he used favoritism" to "avoid military service in the Vietnam War." The front-page substance of the story was based on two interviews with Quayle the preceding evening, one in the CBS convention anchor booth with Dan Rather, the other in the NBC booth with Tom Brokaw. The *Post* writer was but practicing what this study found repeatedly to be a theme in interviews conducted with journalists at both party's conventions—namely, TV coverage not only is key in its own right but also drives convention proceedings and, frequently, the way newspapers, newsmagazines, and radio cover the convention. Here are sample responses: "That's the whole thing. You've got 15,000 journalists here . . . and we in a sense have created the story. I mean they put on all of this particularly for the TV cameras" (David Treadwell, *Los Angeles Times*); "The conventions are now designed for TV. It's like covering a play, or a movie. It's a TV process and the role for the print journalist is to, sort of, describe that; they [sic] can't change it, so they sort of have to describe the process of the convention as a TV show" (Christopher Madison, *National Journal*); "We always have it [the TV] on. When we're not watching the RNC feed, we're monitoring CNN, or something like that. There's always a consciousness, not just here but in all matters of what we do, of what was on the morning shows and what's going to be on the night shows. Oh, Dan Rather had him, or Brinkley had him, or we missed this guy" (Neva Grant, National Public Radio); "Television is there to bring out whatever story comes with the convention. But the convention *itself* is a show" (Ken Bastida, KCBS, San Francisco).

Granted, not all convention coverage in newspapers, newsmagazines, or on radio is TV-driven. Many journalists insist upon an axiom—namely, "render unto print what is print's, render unto TV what is TV's." For example, Frederick Allen, political analyist for CNN, told our interviewers:

A plane crash is a TV story. A convention is a TV story. Other things are newspaper stories. The five-chapter version of Dan Quayle's military record will ultimately be written in a newspaper. We'll report the highlights on television. They're different mediums [*sic*], and it's just like weather. The weather page in the newspaper isn't very big, but it's quite a colorful little TV story.

Yet the weather pages in newspapers grow larger and more colorful, looking much like what is on the TV screen. And so, too, in 1988 did print coverage of the two-party conventions grow larger and more colorful and also—as our news service and *Washington Post* examples illustrate—report events *after* they had been mediated via the TV screen. With that in mind this chapter examines what television coverage of the Democratic National Convention was like in 1988. We focus upon what viewers saw on five networks: C-SPAN, CNN, ABC, CBS, and NBC. We are interested in the similarities and differences in themes, motifs, and pictures across the networks during each convention session.

THE DEMOCRATIC ORCHESTRATION:
THE FUTURE IS NOW

In a variety of public statements prior to the opening of the Democratic National Convention, the convention's chief executive officer, Don Fowler, stated what the Democrats sought to accomplish with their four-night mini-series. He insisted, according to news accounts, that there would be "No glitz. Glitz is out." There would be a message to the convention: "Capable, forceful, future, future, future . . . the Democratic Party is a unified, strong, committed party that can handle the future" (O'Brian, 1988, p. A-19). In an interview conducted for this study Fowler later spelled out in detail what Democrats tried to do and assessed how well they had done it. "Our message was that the Democratic party is a political organization capable of solving the real problems of the average American in the 1990s. That was the message." That "prospective message" had "a lot of implications to it." It implied a de-emphasis of traditional Democratic legends— that is, "not to talk as much about Harry Truman, Jack Kennedy, Franklin Roosevelt, as we had in previous conventions." (Although, Fowler said, "we talked more about that than I frankly wanted to.") The message "dictated in part the color scheme." It "dictated in large part the selection of speakers," featuring those "younger, less well known, and less encumbered with the perceived difficulties of the Democratic party." For, said Fowler, "frequently in the media age the messenger is more important than the message."

Fowler judged that "on the whole I thought we were pretty successful," perhaps, he estimated, "we were 75 percent successful" in doing the things "that would both in substance and in some respects, *more importantly*, symbolically," tell the American people "what our message was." Mike McCurry, director of communications and press secretary for the Democrats, when interviewed for this study, also judged that "the whole production worked well from the point of view of television." Telecasters got "a good picture . . . to put on the air." That was an achievement for, as McCurry had told *USA Today*'s Gregory Katz (1988a, p. 8E), "We don't have a lot of time available so we have to make every microsecond count. We're trying to recognize that the music and the nonverbal aspects contribute to the message we're sending." Yet McCurry was not as positive as Fowler that the intended message had been achieved, simply because there was some muddling of intent:

I remember calling . . . Dukakis's press secretary; it was like the Saturday before the convention. And I said, "Give it to me—what is this show going to be about? What's the theme that's going to drive what we're going to do everyday here?" And he had like six things. And I just knew then that we were going to have a long road ahead because it was not clear how they were going to put all these things together.

ONE CONVENTION OR FIVE? NETWORK ORCHESTRATIONS

Whether the orchestrated motifs were limited to future and unity, or perhaps included others, what message emerged from TV coverage? Did party melodies play outside the Omni? Or were there discords? To answer that question let us examine what each network did for each evening's session.

Keynote Night in the Omni: One Convention, Five Renditions

Once the three major commercial networks had signed on for prime-time coverage of the opening night of the DNC, party organizers repeated the evening's opening ceremonies. This time Garrison Keillor, an entertainer celebrated for his radio series "Lake Wobegon Days," joined a group of children in leading delegates in the Pledge of Allegiance. In the CBS anchor booth Dan Rather and Walter Cronkite stood with hands over hearts repeating the pledge. Across the Omni, seated—indeed, slouching—in the NBC anchor booth were Tom Brokaw (who had introduced Keillor as an "American folk hero") and John Chancellor. Chancellor glanced over at the CBS booth, punched Brokaw, pointed, and both NBC broadcasters jumped to their feet, each with hand over heart. If cameras caught CBS saying the pledge, so too would they picture NBC. No act is too trivial in the contest for viewer ratings! (In the ABC booth, located at the side of the CBS booth where Peter Jennings and David Brinkley were obscured from the scenes of anchor pledging, neither responded.) So began prime-time coverage of keynote night in the Omni.

C-SPAN: Motifs of Future, Unity, Compassion, and a Little Stargazing. "America's Network," as promoters like to bill C-SPAN, has a simple formula for convention coverage. As Brian Lamb of the network told a taskforce hearing on the future of party conventions, "we . . . carry those conventions from gavel to gavel . . . everything" (Commission on National Political Conventions [CNPC], 1989, pp. 27–28). Since "everything" includes all speeches from the podium, the network faithfully records the message orchestrated by party leaders. Said Lamb, "We really don't care if we are used by politicians. That is why we exist" (p. 28).

Not limited to prime-time hours, C-SPAN signed on for the *de facto* opening of keynote night and viewers had an early taste of the party message. Chair Paul Kirk, introducing convention CEO Don Fowler, proclaimed him a man taking the party "miles into the future." Fowler's remarks sang the futurist theme as did that of subsequent speakers: the party enters a "new Democratic era," said one; Kirk introduced the "state-of-the-art election process" for tabulating delegate votes; Tom Foley, U.S. House of Representatives majority leader, explained the computerized process, as C-SPAN showed viewers close-up shots of floor computers; and the chair of the credentials committee, K. Leroy Irvis of Pennsylvania, proclaimed it time to "enter the 21st century" and "*march* into the 21st century."

Irvis previewed a second theme scripted for the opening session, one sung by a series of soloist speakers featured before the C-SPAN audience of political junkies not only in the United States but in 13 million households in 22 European countries. Irvis reported that all 24 of the disagreements brought to the convention had been resolved before the committee had even met. This was then a *unified futurist party.* Following Irvis to the podium, Representative Pat Schroeder of Colorado, co-chair of the credentials committee, spoke of a "unifed" party with "unanimous appeal"; turning to women's issues, she linked them to the future of America's children, then stressed "we're showin' the world we can run this convention, we're showin' the world we can run this country." Paul Kirk closed credentials business by declaring the committee's report accepted "without a single challenge . . . the first sign of unanimity in this party, and we're on the move!"

Kathleen Vick, chair of the party's rules committee, gave voice to the third motif featured in C-SPAN's coverage. Her introduction of Marion Barry, mayor of the District of Columbia, spoke of the Democrats as a party of "compassion" as well as of unity. The lyrics of Barry's remarks restated the compassion theme: Jesse Jackson's supporters "represent the guilt of America"; the convention must turn from guilt to fairness "*now*"; and, he stressed, fairness would also mean statehood for the District of Columbia. Senator John Breaux (LA), speaking on the report of the rules committee, combined fairness, compassion, and unity in one metaphor: the committee, he said, had moved "down the road of cooperation." The convention accepted the report with "not one dissenting vote," sang Kathy Vick, and with "no opposition," harmonized Paul Kirk: "Don't tell me the Democratic party doesn't know how to do its business."

Convention lyricists echoed the refrains of future, unity, and compassion in scenes leading up to the keynote address later in the evening. Here are samples from C-SPAN's coverage: "Unified and unanimous again" (Paul Kirk after Representative Jim Wright's selection as permanent chair of the convention); the party will make a "difference into the 21st century. . . . Let us resolve . . . [to show a] picture of a party that has its act together and is ready to govern . . . united, hand in hand" (Jim Wright); "Aren't *we* beautiful. Why? Because we don't look alike" (Democratic National Committee vice-chair Polly Boca); a party of "a new American energy" (DNC vice-chair Sharon Pratt Dixon); a party of "basic concerns" that will "drive" and "move" and "push *forward*" (Washington governor Booth Gardner); and Democrats stand for "fair treatment" of every constituency (Atlanta mayor Andy Young). Leading into the keynote address by Ann Richards, Texas state treasurer, were two remarks that foreshadowed the more colorful gloss on the unity and compassion motifs to come in Jesse Jackson's address the following evening: Jim Wright yelled "We have togetherness" out of a "rich fabric"; Congressman Mike Espy (MS) recalled a black, female delegate had been locked out of the 1968 Democratic convention (Fanny Lou Hamer), but he, also black, reflects the "patchwork quilt that is the Democratic party." Finally, when former president Jimmy Carter called for party "unity," repeated, "Unity—one more time so you will not forget—UNITY," C-SPAN captured Carter's plea with a close-up.

The coverage by "America's network," however, was not confined to podium soloists. C-SPAN cameras sought out political celebrities and media stars, offering shots of their comings and goings as podium speeches sang out. Thus, viewers watched noted politicians including Congressman Richard Gephardt (MO) shaking hands, repeated shots of Senator Bill Bradley (NJ) on the floor, Georgia's senator Sam Nunn, Senator Al Gore (TN) shaking hands, Senator Fritz Hollings in the South Carolina delegation, and arrivals and departures from the various VIP boxes— Geraldine Ferraro, the Dukakis family, and so on. Celebrity delegates came into focus, most notably TV actor Mike Farrell of "M*A*S*H." And C-SPAN, which conducts no floor or booth interviews, featured shots of TV networks that do. Viewers saw, but could not hear, network interviews with Jim Wright, Walter Mondale, and Jesse Jackson (in the CNN booth, then in the CBS booth). They also saw Diane Sawyer and Leslie Stahl (CBS), and Lynn Sherr (ABC) tracking down celebrities and preparing for interviews. C-SPAN captured NBC's Tom Brokaw peering at the convention through binoculars from time to time. And at the prime-time opening, C-SPAN pictured Dan Rather and Walter Cronkite in the CBS booth, standing with hands over heart, during the Pledge of Allegiance; and Tom Brokaw and John Chancellor in the NBC booth, standing but no longer hands over heart. In sum, a national party convention is a congregation of party and media prima donnas. C-SPAN showed performances of both.

CNN: The Unity Note, Real or Deal? CNN, like C-SPAN, offers gavel-to-gavel coverage, even prides itself on being the "network of record." Gavel-to-gavel, however, to CNN simply reflects points in time, not the podium where the gavel resides. As a network that has made a reputation for its coverage of breaking stories, CNN does not, as does C-SPAN, cover everything the political party does. It searches instead everywhere for a breaking story about what the party is *not* doing, or *not doing as it appears.* Employing numerous snippets and visual or sound bites (ranging from ten seconds to a few minutes each), co-conductors Bernard Shaw and Mary Alice Williams, a chorus of floor reporters, a program of duet correspondent interviews (featured solo performances by Linda Ellerbee, Frederick Allen, Larry King, Mark Green, Pat Buchanan, Rowland Evans, Robert Novak), and cameo appearances by celebrity delegates (Margot Kidder, Casey Kasem, Morgan Fairchild), and a comic, Al Franken, CNN's coverage alternates between thematic unity and a fragmentation of contradictions.

For CNN, party motifs—future, unity, compassion—served merely as opening lyrics for probing the Big Story, an imperative that drives the CNN production and justifies the network's large cast and production crew. Thus CNN opened with a series of quick booth-to-floor-to-booth-to-floor cuts typical of the network's coverage. The theme was that the party, Michael Dukakis, and Jesse Jackson *seemed* to be operating in a spirit of harmony and unity. The "key word all day has been *unity, unity, unity,"* reported floor correspondent Charles Bierbauer. But wait a minute. Are there discordant notes? CNN thought it possible. An interviewed delegate said Jackson supporters had not been included in making the vice-presidential selection; another wanted Jackson as the vice-presidential nominee and was *not* satisfied; another reported that not everything was resolved between Dukakis and Jackson forces, not all questions answered; and, reported CNN anchors, negotiations over the party platform were "going down to the wire."

With large blocks of gavel-to-gavel airtime to fill, and reluctant to focus network cameras on the podium except for major speeches, CNN throughout the evening pursued the question, "Is the unity for real?" Sometimes the answer was yes, at others no. Whether yes or no, the time either judgment remained current was fleeting—just long enough for CNN to switch from one anchor, correspondent, interview, or analyst to another. No sooner had a Georgia delegate acclaimed the "spirit of unity" pulled together by Jesse Jackson than a delegate interviewed from Indiana proclaimed that changes in party rules were "a step backward from a unified party." CNN correspondents sang contradictory responses as well: one was skeptical and called the convention a "unity show"; another believed and reported the "theme of the evening has been unity"; a third hedged, "unity *seems* to be the theme of the day."

Twice CNN's co-anchors solemnly judged the big story of the day to have been a unity conference between Dukakis and Jackson. Shortly, however, anchor Bernard Shaw reported himself "mystified" by the meeting. In the anchor booth Shaw, Williams, and "political analyst" Frederick Allen devoted seven minutes to debating whether there was unity or a deal: Shaw now thought there to be no deal, but Williams and Allen were not so sure. Sure or not sure, it was a motif of CNN coverage that Shaw would not give up, raising it again in an interview with former President Jimmy Carter. Finally, CNN's duets of political commentary provided discordant responses to "unity or deal?" An exchange between Pat Buchanan and Mark Green concluded that the party was united, with Dukakis "the quarterback." Rowland Evans and Bob Novak sang "deal"; Jackson had "yielded."

A muted theme of CNN coverage, one that struck yet another discordant note to the party theme of harmony, was a focus on Congressman Jim Wright. Correspondent Frank Sesno interviewed Wright about the "ethics" problem—that is, charges of unethical conduct brought against Wright as Speaker of the House. Wright denied the problem. But in the anchor booth Bernard Shaw reported "the fact is that the ethics issue is serious." Later in the evening CNN devoted eight minutes to a videotaped feature on Wright's ethics controversy, concluding that Wright's problems "undercut the sleaze issue" Democrats hoped to use against the Republicans.

CNN concluded its opening coverage by showing in its entirety musician Phil Driscoll's trumpet solo from the podium, followed by swaying delegates singing "God Bless America." Remarked Bernard Shaw, the Omni had been "orchestrated to make it look like a big TV studio." With its plurality of reports, judgments, and performances CNN used the studio to orchestrate an opera with a cast of thousands.

ABC: An Evening of Rap. Although Bernard Shaw and Mary Alice Williams sat at the same anchor desk in the CNN booth, they operated more as two single anchors than as co-anchors. They looked at one another only occasionally, seldom interacted, and rarely talked about the same subject. That was not the case with ABC's Peter Jennings and David Brinkley. The interaction was so continuous and so dominant that homey co-anchor chats, not convention proceedings, became the leading motif of ABC coverage on opening night.

As party convention orchestrators were presenting their second, prime-time round of opening ceremonies on the podium, Jennings signed on ABC's coverage by quoting a DNC official that this convention was "organized, orderly, and short, just like our candidate." Jennings and Brinkley conducted a joint interview with Michael Dukakis speaking from his hotel room. Using many of the phrases that would later appear in his acceptance speech, Dukakis assured ABC that Jesse Jackson "will campaign shoulder-to-shoulder with us." The six-minute interview concluded (an interview conducted as CBS and NBC anchors were on their feet for the Pledge of Allegiance), ABC cut to the podium for the close of the national anthem. Without pause, the anchors moved to a six-minute interview with Jesse Jackson seated in the ABC booth. "Are you happy?" they asked. Yes, said Jackson *but*, there is a "challenge to define our relationships." People should stop asking, said Jackson, "What does Jesse Jackson want?" and ask instead "What has Jesse Jackson built?" The interview, as with Dukakis, was informal, chatty, conversational; the anchors lyricized questions, Dukakis and Jackson sang rehearsed responses.

This opening segment set the tone of ABC's brief evening coverage. Although ABC covered two podium speeches, the keynote, and that by Jimmy Carter, no substantive theme emerged in the telecast. For ABC the medium was the message and the medium was chit-chat. Correspondent Sam Donaldson opined that Dukakis was "pleased" with the "unified party" without giving Jackson anything, Charles Murphy profiled Ann Richards as keynote speaker, Lynn Sherr interviewed Walter Mondale, followed by three more floor interviews and reports. Little dealt with the future, unity, or compassion themes. Interviews frequently had a chatty tone as Jennings interrupted to ask questions or make observations (in one instance clearly to Sam Donaldson's irritation). Moreover, the network's political analysts, Hodding Carter and George Will, did not confront one another as antagonists (CNN's faceoff coverage); nor did they simply offer solo renditions of thoughts (the CBS-NBC motif). They engaged instead in discussions with Peter Jennings or David Brinkley.

Thus, aside from podium speeches, the bulk of ABC's evening turned on what Jennings and Brinkley had to say: about Ann Richards (while C-SPAN viewers and delegates were watching a Democratic video on Richards); her address—namely, a "highly successful keynote," "not orating, but talking," and "eloquent"; why Democrats lose (with correspondent Jeff Greenfield); the nation's problems (with New York governor Mario

Cuomo); memories (with former Speaker of the House Tip O'Neill); the Dukakis-Jackson "arrangement" (with Lynn Sherr interviewing Walter Mondale); and the "good day" for the Democrats (with Will and Carter). CNN orchestrated a cast of thousands, ABC a cast of two.

CBS: Twin Peaks, Competing Podiums. In Richard Wagner's four-part opera, *The Ring of the Nibelung,* the leading character is Wotan, a god of the sky come to earth to try to understand and conduct human affairs in accordance with that understanding. CBS coverage features its own Wotan, anchor Dan Rather. No single podium speaker, no single correspondent, no anchor from a competing network commands as much airtime as Rather. Prominently pictured seated behind a plate-glass window overlooking the convention hall, Rather presides, comments, interviews, discusses, explains, and moves the orchestrated CBS telecast through its prime-time hours. Whereas other networks capture the convention primarily by featuring shots over the heads of anchors gazing into the camera, CBS frequently shoots up at Rather gazing down on the floor, or places the camera close to Rather as he surveys the scene below. Rather, too, is a god come to earth to understand and preside over convention coverage in accordance with his understanding. The anchor booth is his domain, a podium where he conducts in competition with the party podium and its shouting chairs, speakers, and other lesser mortals.

Party motifs largely ignored, CBS's Rather opened the telecast on keynote night with a judgment that conventions "once every four years showcase . . . the democratic process." The CBS charge is to show "behind the scenes," to sort out "substance" from "hype, hoopla." Moving quickly to a three-minute interview with Michael Dukakis he alluded to "three people running for two offices"—Dukakis, Jackson, and Lloyd Bentsen for president and vice-president. Dukakis retreats to motifs of unity and team effort. Then it's to Diane Sawyer, who gets 24 seconds to comment on Kitty Dukakis. Rather announces a commercial break, informing viewers that this is the first Democratic convention held in the South since 1860 (overlooking the Democratic meeting in Houston in 1928). Returning to the air, Rather engages his predecessor as CBS's Wotan, Walter Cronkite, in remembrances that the Dukakis-Jackson unity conference was nothing new: Dwight Eisenhower and Robert Taft did the same in 1952, Richard Nixon and Nelson Rockefeller in 1960. As the national anthem sounds a CBS camera shoots from below into the anchor booth. Rather, not Garrison Keillor at the speaker's podium, seems to be conducting the opening ceremonies.

"And," to borrow CNN commentator Linda Ellerbee's signature line, "so it goes." Or so it went with CBS coverage. Twirling in his chair between the floor below, the camera facing him, and an occasional "guest" (Jesse Jackson, Walter Cronkite, Eric Severeid, or Bruce Morton) in the booth, Rather dominated CBS coverage. Here are sampled Rather refrains:

Dukakis moved in his "usual careful, cautious way"; there would be a controversial vote on the party platform Tuesday evening (repeated three times during the telecast; no such vote took place); Congressman Mike Espy, who would introduce the keynoter, hailed from Yazoo City; a sweeping history, for 14 seconds, of the origins of the ritual of the convention keynote address; that Richards delivered a "scalpel-style attack" on George Bush; that correspondent Leslie Stahl might, as she did in an interview with Congressman Charles Rangel, see problems in the Dukakis accord, but Rangel, although not totally satisfied, was comfortable with the ticket; and Jimmy Carter was the "Pride of Plains"; and the "big story of the day—the show of unity!" Hovering on the periphery, if not on center stage, of CBS coverage, Rather inserted himself into Diane Sawyer's post-keynote interview with Ann Richards. Richards fretted over her "loss of eye contact" with the audience. Always the chief conductor, Rather implored Sawyer to assure Richards not to "worry about eye contact," all was fine. Moving below the throne room that served as Rather's podium, CBS correspondents did manage to conduct a rare interview without the anchor's comments. Diane Sawyer spoke with Kitty Dukakis twice; Bob Schieffer with Ann Richards before her keynote, with Texas party leader Bob Slagle, and, stressing that "we've talked to a lot of celebrities tonight," with a "regular delegate." Yet of eight interviews, Rather conducted two, as well as leading discussions with Cronkite, Severeid, Morton, and Ed Bradley (featuring Rather looking down from his podium to Bradley looking up from the floor, a visual exchange that became the logo of CBS convention coverage).

NBC: Issue Refrains Sung Upstairs and Downstairs, All 'Round the Hall. In interviews conducted for this study Joe Angotti and Lloyd Siegel, producers involved in NBC's convention coverage, described the network's preconvention plans. Said Siegel,

We all came to the conclusion early on that we wanted to do something different, given the fact that we knew that one, and probably two, of the conventions were going to have foregone conclusions. We had to do something to *justify all this effort and all this time* [emphasis added] on the air. We thought there was an agenda of issues that was important.

This emphasis resulted in two issue motifs in NBC's opening night coverage. One directed floor correspondents to seek out "issue interviews," and they did—on platform items, taxes, unions, drugs, and the like. The other involved convention-without-walls segments, wherein man-in-the-street interviews away from the convention were conducted in conjunction with discussions with delegates in the hall about those issues. In all, a dozen correspondent and/or anchor reports or interviews were issue-oriented in content.

Also during portions of the evening's coverage anchor Tom Brokaw and analyst John Chancellor were placed in separate booths on different levels. One booth had an open window to catch crowd noise from the convention. Said Angotti,

The idea was that for years and years John Chancellor has always said that he wanted to be out in the convention hall. He didn't like the idea of being in an air-conditioned isolated booth where you couldn't really hear the crowds, smell them, feel them, touch them. This was an idea I had based on Chancellor's feeling to touch and feel the crowd and what was going on—to have the lower booth with windows that slid back that would actually allow him to sit there and really feel the emotion of the crowd and what was going on.

The "upstairs-downstairs" exchanges between Brokaw and Chancellor, although a featured motif of NBC's opening evening coverage, did not work. Said Angotti, "It was an experiment, it kind of worked and they loved it, but it didn't allow the kind of control that we have over other things like sound and picture and things like that as when they are up and inside the booth." Moreover, "we [also] discovered . . . that Chancellor and Brokaw are always better when they are together." For, "they play off each other better, they are more inclined to get into discussions with one another, amplify and explain, than when they are separated." So, "it was best to have John next to Tom."

A third motif of NBC coverage consisted of "segment" reports. Unlike CNN, ABC, or CBS that moved in a booth-to-floor-to-booth-to-floor sequence, NBC anchor Tom Brokaw introduced a floor correspondent who, having completed an interview or report, simply introduced another correspondent who would then pass airtime to a third, and so on. Composing a melody from this "round the hall" coverage were instructions for each broadcast segment to cover a specified topic. Here are Angotti's reasons: "We had in mind specific things that we wanted to address . . . so I would tell them [the correspondents] between 9:30 and 10:00 sometime, let's talk about religion and politics. Go out and find people who can address that. Let me know who you have in mind to talk to." Of course, "sometimes they would have in mind the same person and I would have to negotiate." Or "sometimes we would have to throw those things entirely out. . . . We just never could get to them." Anyway, "it gives the impression of being an impromptu kind of whip round, but it really isn't. *It is planned out well in advance.*"

Issue segments and musical-chair anchor booths reduced Tom Brokaw's role in NBC's first-night coverage. Left to provide the interpretive opera glasses for viewing the performance, he lip-synched selected themes: the "big issue—who will raise taxes?"; the keynote was "like lighting the fire"—folksy, humorous, tough and showing George Bush's vulnerability;

but signing off, "the most important symbolic image to come out of Atlanta this far" happened not in the Omni but was the joint Dukakis-Jackson press conference before the session even started.

One Keynoter, Five Keynotes. This summary of coverage suggests differences in themes and tone across the five networks. Network contrasts are particularly pronounced when all five cover a single convention event such as a major address. The words of the address, of course, do not change from network to network, but the visual presentations do. We recorded, tabulated, and categorized several types of visual camera shots for selected major addresses—Ann Richards's keynote, Jesse Jackson's speech, and Michael Dukakis's acceptance for Democrats; Ronald Reagan's address, Tom Kean's keynote, and George Bush's acceptance for Republicans. Here we collapse those categories into four. They are, regardless of camera angle, (1) close-up and/or tight shots on the speaker showing no more than his or her head, shoulders, and chest; (2) distant shots of the speaker, podium, and audience members; (3) tight shots on individual delegate's head, shoulders, or entire body; (4) distant shots showing delegates in group clusters.

Consider Ann Richards's keynote address. During the address C-SPAN used 105 separate camera shots, two-thirds being of the speaker, with above-the-waist shots featured over distant shots by a 3-to-2 ratio. The average time of a shot was 19 seconds. By contrast CNN carried 171 shots during the speech, 53 percent being of delegates and primarily delegates in groups. Average shot time was 12 seconds. CBS moved the TV picture frequently with 248 shots averaging 8 seconds each; 56 percent were delegate shots almost evenly distributed between individuals and groups. ABC provided 179 shots averaging 11 seconds in duration; two-thirds were on the speaker and two-thirds of those were distant shots. Finally, NBC provided viewers 171 shots averaging 12 seconds, distributed roughly evenly between speaker and delegates but emphasing distant shots of Richards, tighter reaction shots of individual delegates.[1]

These raw data provide interesting contrasts. C-SPAN's tendencies to use fewer shots, lingering over longer duration and emphasizing the keynoter, suggest a slow-paced portrayal of the classic speech situation—namely, a speaker talking from a distance to clusters of audience members. The visual depiction is speaker-driven. So also is ABC's depiction, but by using a preponderance of speaker shots of Richards on the podium with large numbers of delegates also in view, the keynoter appears to be speaking to a crowd, not to clusters of delegates; with considerably more shots of shorter duration, however, ABC's coverage is faster paced. CNN and CBS offer delegate-versions of the same speech; reactions to Richards's remarks, not the remarks themselves, constitute the story. The delegates are viewed not as individuals but as congregated in groups. Where CNN and CBS differ is that CNN, in using shots of the speaker, employs tight shots while CBS emphasizes Richards against a background of crowds of delegates; moreover, CBS's use of many more shots averaging a shorter duration than is the case with CNN makes for a fast-paced presentation. Finally, the NBC focus is as fast paced as CNN's (the same number and duration of shots), but there is a balancing of the numbers of shots between speaker and delegates, seemingly giving equal weight to each as part of the keynote act. As we shall see (in this book's Finale), combined with findings from analyses of visual presentations of the remaining five major addresses, data reveal a pattern of single speakers performing in five musical dramas that differ depending on the network of coverage.

Planks, Patches, and Pouts: The Night They Closed the Concert Hall

In selecting Atlanta's Omni and fabricating it into a TV studio to showcase their nightly DNC sessions, convention orchestrators knew they were running a risk. Installation of a massive podium ("It looks like someone had backed a battleship into a movie theater," said a former DNC press secretary) and of TV equipment and booths reduced the arena's seating capacity from 16,000 to 11,000. Crowding in more than 5,000 delegates and alternates, a few thousand working journalists at any given time, party officials, pampered party financial contributors, entourages of party notables, countless celebrities, and members of the general public produced a "shoebox convention." As prime time approached for Tuesday evening's second session, fire marshals, fearing overcrowding, closed the hall. Delegates, journalists, and notables not inside at the time were denied entry. The son of Martin Luther King, Jr., credentials in hand, argued with security guards, but to no avail. The previous evening's keynoter, Ann Richards, was left waiting at the gate. Many journalists, unable to get to their assigned seats in the hall's press gallery, complained, pouted, and sulked. It seemed "the party of inclusion," as some Democratic speakers called it, was excluding Democrats from their own convention.

Even network TV celebrities were shut out. CNN's Linda Ellerbee related her experience during one evening's lockout. Ellerbee had been in the hall all day working on her commentaries to be presented during the network's telecast. She decided to leave the hall for a "breath of air." When she tried to return she was refused entry by convention security guards. She explained that she had to return to deliver her TV commentary. An Atlanta policeman recognized her. He whispered to her, "Get in an argument with me." She did. The policeman then "took her into custody" and marched off into the hall, and by the convention security guards, where the Atlanta police had an office. Once inside Ellerbee was released with "Have a good evening, courtesy of the Atlanta Police Department!"

C-SPAN's Party Refrains, Attentive and Inattentive Listeners. Although newspapers (as well as the Republicans a month later) publicized the Democratic lockout, it received scant attention as a TV network story. C-SPAN, covering the convention essentially as party leaders orchestrated it, presented the evening's musical in three acts. The first two, a 90-minute and an 80-minute act set apart by a suspension of the rules, were devoted to debates over planks of the Democratic platform. Both preceded the prime-time signing on of ABC, CBS, and NBC. C-SPAN viewers were actually treated to parallel proceedings during these acts. First, in each act a succession of speakers came on stage to present and to support or oppose aspects of the platform. C-SPAN viewers witnessed an orderly, smoothly presented series of soloists. There was but one glitch: the highly sophisticated electronic device for voting on planks proved slow and cumbersome. Chair Jim Wright repeatedly called for delegations to enter votes electronically, urging that it was impossible to vote on one plank until voting had been completed on the preceding plank. In the end, electronic tabulations on the platform planks were not completed until well after consideration of the platform had ceased being a key scene in the evening's drama.

Second, while continuing to carry the sound of each speaker's words during the platform debates, C-SPAN cameras frequently moved about the hall in search of another story—namely, who was in the hall and what were they doing? Viewers witnessed delegates conversing, reading newspapers, waving Dukakis and Jackson banners, milling about, or holding up signs to capture the cameras' attention—"ERA Yes," "Gender Gap," "NO MX," "No First Use," "Pro-Choice," "Palestine Statehood Now," "Middle East Peace," and "What's More Important Than Investing in Our Kids?" Sometimes the signs related to the platform plank under debate, sometimes not. In either event the "lobby by banner" coverage amplified single-issue, special-interest demands that belied the unity and futurist themes crafted for the convention. Moreover, C-SPAN cameras continued to stargaze. As on the previous evening there were shots of Margot Kidder (Lois Lane of *Superman*) and "M*A*S*H" 's BJ (Mike Farrell). C-SPAN cameras kept viewers up to date with what was going on in network anchor booths as well, picturing Dan Rather (the camera shot upward into the CBS booth), Peter Jennings (head on in ABC's booth), Bernard Shaw at CNN, and Tom Brokaw and John Chancellor both upstairs and downstairs, with and without binoculars, at NBC.

The third act in C-SPAN's coverage was prime time. The unity theme sounded but was muted by the string of soloists featured by convention orchestrators: California congressman Tony Coehlo (introduced as a "rising young star of the Democratic party") introduced a "Where was George Bush?" refrain, but without audience response; former House Speaker Tip O'Neill was a reminder of the past, not future; John F. Kennedy, Jr., received a wild, cheering, waving, standing ovation as he introduced Sena-

tor Ted Kennedy; Kennedy's "Where was George?" chant was more successful than Coehlo's and drew such a delegate response that he lost control of it; and, Texas agriculture commissioner Jim Hightower attacked
George Bush as a "toothache of a man."

It was now time for the lead baritone of the evening, Jesse Jackson. First
came introductory remarks by Jackson's five children, then a DNC film on
Jackson. C-SPAN's visual coverage of Jackson's address paralleled its coverage of the keynote of Ann Richards. With only 153 individual camera
shots (averaging 19 seconds in duration), C-SPAN cameras devoted one-
third to bust shots of Jackson. Although shots of delegates outnumbered
those of Jackson 75 to 65 (there were also 14 shots of VIPs in reserved
boxes and network anchor booths), by holding the camera on Jackson longer than on individual or clustered delegates C-SPAN produced a speaker-
driven address. That was not the case with CNN.

CNN Sings "No Blood on the Floor." CNN's gavel-to-gavel coverage
missed the opening of the second session—indeed, CNN came on the air
after the debate on the taxation plank in the platform had closed, just prior
to C-SPAN's second 80-minute act. Anchor Bernard Shaw found "no
smoking gun in this platform," correspondent Charles Bierbauer noted the
"last minute of suspense out of this convention" would be the vote on the
plank calling for no first use of nuclear weapons by the United States, and
Linda Ellerbee expressed disappointment at the absence of "chaos" at a
Democratic gathering (CNN's co-anchors said they would "try to find
some" for her). Finally, anchor Mary Alice Williams summed it all up: "No
blood on the floor" this evening.

CNN, however, sought to spill some. Frederick Allen, reporting on the
results of a CNN–*Los Angeles Times* "focus group," found disagreement
among delegates; they were divided along candidate lines! CNN's Tom
Braeden and Pat Buchanan staged a series of *"Crossfire"* segments endeavoring to work up conflict over platform issues. Analysts Mark Green and
Pat Buchanan faced off on the platform plank on taxes; later Rowland
Evans and Robert Novak debated the "milk toast" platform. And, away
from studio booths CNN correspondents roved the floor probing for discontent. Correspondents queried delegates about a rumor that Jackson
supporters would seek to replace Lloyd Bentsen on the ticket with their
man; the rumor died. They repeatedly asked other delegates about dissatisfaction with the platform. This finally prompted Ron Brown, Jesse Jackson's campaign manager, to exclaim "we won" on the platform, "What
do you mean contention? We won . . . the media are looking for a story!"

With, as co-anchors Shaw and Williams agreed, matters of the party
rules and platform "out of the way," CNN ceased searching for chaos and
blood and looked to the lighter side. Larry King conducted celebrity interviews with actress Morgan Fairchild and the once but not future Gary
Hart. Comedian Al Franken did a routine on the *L* (liberal) word, "ru-

mors," then read a *TV Guide* description of a "Matlock" episode, a repeat, that NBC was airing at the very moment CNN carried live convention coverage. Threatening to read it again, he provoked Mary Alice Williams to say "please don't repeat." Only eight minutes later Frederick Allen *repeated* the same 3¼-minute "focus group" segment he had lip-synched 10 minutes into the beginning of CNN's evening coverage. This repeat was apparently more justified than NBC's "Matlock" repeat.

The remainder of CNN's evening focused on two families: first, the Kennedys and Ted Kennedy's address, then the Jackson children's introduction of their father and his address. The emphasis, however, was on Jackson. It is "the Reverend Jackson's moment" said the anchors; "this is his night," said Frederick Allen. CNN's visual coverage of Jackson's address emphasized that it was not only Jackson's "moment," there were also moments for each of his supporters. During his speech CNN gave viewers 271 separate camera shots averaging 12 seconds in duration. Of those, 110 were of Jackson, evenly divided between tight close-ups or shots showing him against a background of cheering delegates. Matching the focus on Jackson were 111 tight reaction shots of individual delegates. As Jackson likened the Democratic party to a quilt made of patches, CNN focused on delegates appropriate for each patch—women, blacks, the young, the elderly, the farmers, the teachers. When he repeated the refrain "I understand," the camera cut quickly to tight close-ups of tearful delegates nodding with approval. "His night" was their night.

ABC's "It's Jesse Jackson's Night." ABC's second-session coverage was brief and in two acts. Act 1, the shorter, was The Beloved Kennedys. Both floor correspondents and anchors dwelled on the Kennedy legend. "Will John F. Kennedy, Jr., run for something?" they asked. Sam Donaldson spoke of the rebirth of the 1960 Massachusetts-Texas "axis" of John Kennedy and Lyndon Johnson in the pairing of Michael Dukakis and Lloyd Bentsen. Dukakis's gestures are "Kennedy gestures." ABC covered in full the speeches by both John F. Kennedy, Jr., and Ted Kennedy. The latter, said Peter Jennings, was a "speech that stirred people more than any other" here in this convention. "These delegates love Ted Kennedy," said Sam Donaldson.

Act 2, Here's Jesse, was ABC's featured coverage. That eclipsed almost any talk of the party platform adopted earlier in the evening; Jennings simply gave a brief summary. It also overshadowed any efforts to find controversy. When ABC asked Atlanta mayor Andrew Young if Jackson had been left off the ticket because he was black, Young replied no, that it was "not blackness" but inexperience in office that kept Jackson from being vice-presidential nominee. The only disagreement ABC finally found with that opinion was expressed by Republican Lee Atwater, George Bush's campaign manager. He said Jackson had not been left off the ticket; it was, he said, an "extended ticket—three persons on the ticket."

The Jackson focus remained through ABC's camera coverage of his address. Over one-half of ABC's 190 camera shots were on the speaker and closely divided between bust shots or against a delegate backdrop. Each shot averaged 15 seconds but ABC's penchant for lingering for long periods on the talking-head shots, and only momentarily on shots of delegates, resulted in a Jackson story not a reaction story. So also did ABC's summing up: "a tour de force," said David Brinkley; a "rapt" audience, said Jim Wooten; "he is their Ronald Reagan who transcends politics," said Jeff Greenfield. If the Democrats indeed had a unity theme, for ABC it had a loud and lingering Jackson note to it.

CBS: "Get Grandmother from the Other Room." "It's Jesse Jackson's night to shine," said Dan Rather as CBS signed on for prime time. Perhaps. But since Rather from his anchor podium conducted 56 minutes of airtime on the network that evening and Jackson only 48 from the speaker's podium, one wonders. After dismissing all platform proceedings—they "took place before television cameras came on" (that is, before CBS came on)—Rather and his correspondents and analysts devoted the first portion of their telecast to nostalgia about the Kennedys—John F.; John F., Jr.; and Ted. He's "not out of the running ever," Walter Cronkite said of Teddy. Following Senator Kennedy's speech, Rather and Cronkite discussed the party platform. Cronkite concluded that platforms "may be meaningless," but the "permission" and "tolerance" for groups to be heard helps achieve consensus—that is, cordial concurrence. Rather, then correspondent Bill Plante, briefly concluded CBS coverage of the orchestrated unity over the platform with a report on the tax plank.

Rather presided over the "main moment of the evening" that would be coming up, the Jackson address, "so get grandmother from the other room." If "grandmother" came in, she found out from Diane Sawyer that convention orchestrators would allow Jackson to "go on as long as he wants"; and that this, said Rather, meant "chaotic (Did CNN's Linda Ellerbee take note?) rearranging of the schedule of the convention" in the "hall the podium ate" during this "shoebox convention." Watching CBS's visual coverage, grandmother would have seen 258 separate camera shots during Jackson's address of an average 11 seconds in duration. Of those, 55 percent were not of Jackson, but of delegates. Moreover, of delegate shots, over 70 percent were tight shots of individual delegates. "Jesse's night" was for CBS reactions to Jesse—by Rather, by correspondents, and by delegates. Jackson "had the audience," concluded Rather, "he connected."

NBC's Elegy for Liberal Issues and Icons. NBC anchor Tom Brokaw dubbed Teddy Kennedy and Jesse Jackson the Democrats' "two most liberal icons." Even the "Dukakis people" are calling it "liberal night." *Liberal,* however, for NBC meant more than Kennedy and Jackson as icons; the network also treated as icons the issues arising out of passage of the

Democratic platform. No sooner had Brokaw completed his lead-in than NBC correspondents conducted their first wrap-around of the evening—Ken Bode on taxes; Chris Wallace on "guns, butter, and national security," and Lisa Myers on the platform. Brokaw and John Chancellor completed the segment with a discussion of liberals. Later in the evening NBC devoted a convention-without-walls segment to a discussion of taxes.

Although NBC carried the remarks of John F. Kennedy, Jr., and the address of his uncle, the other focus of NBC's coverage was Jesse Jackson. Two wrap-around correspondent interview segments before his speech discussed Jackson; a wrap-around segment of stand-up reports evaluated the speech afterwards. Brokaw and Chancellor moved to the open-air booth and used hand-held microphones to catch the crowd response. For NBC the Jackson speech was a response-reaction story, not a speaker story. During the address NBC used 326 camera shots, 226 quick cuts from 69 tight shots on Jackson's face to close-up shots of individual delegates. The plethora of quick cuts and brief duration of the average shot (9 seconds) provided a rapidly paced viewing experience. The effect was intentional. NBC's director of cameras, George Paul, deliberately sought quick flips from Jackson to crying delegates, yawning reporters, and preening celebrities. "What counts isn't what we're seeing inside the hall; what counts is what they are seeing out there on television" (Diamond, 1988c, p. 16). "The pictures," said Paul, "are judgment calls. You have to get it the first time—there are no Take Twos." For Paul and NBC the effects of Jackson's remarks, not the remarks themselves, were the theme song of the evening.

Transition Night in Atlanta

The pace and tenor of TV coverage from all five networks shifted considerably Wednesday evening. C-SPAN viewers watched a line of six Democratic candidates for the U.S. Senate march to the podium to speak of the importance of family, fairness, and the future to American lives (and, more important, to build a stock of video coverage that could later be discreetly edited for use in their campaigns' TV commercials). There followed another parade, this time of Democratic governors and gubernatorial candidates stressing compassion and also making videotapes. Once the "congress and governors" scene had ended, C-SPAN followed with the nominating speeches (the only network to carry Arkansas Governor Bill Clinton's lengthy nomination of Michael Dukakis in its entirety and without comment) and the ritual of the roll-call vote. Stargazing remained in vogue as C-SPAN cameras peeped at Tom Brokaw and John Chancellor at NBC, Bernard Shaw (with binoculars) and Mary Alice Williams at CNN, Peter Jennings and David Brinkley at ABC, and Dan Rather in his glass-encased roost high above the convention floor.

CNN finally sounded the unity theme loud and clear Wednesday eve-

ning. Not, however, without a struggle. Interviews by network correspondents failed to generate any evidence that Jesse Jackson's name would be
placed in nomination for vice-president. Frank Sesno reported "trouble in
the ranks" of Jackson delegates and a potential "walkout" by Michigan
delegates as an "expression of displeasure." Tom Mintier reported negotiations within the Michigan delegation to avoid the walkout; later he interviewed Detroit mayor Coleman Young, who assured Mintier there would
be "no walkout." CNN retuned from discordant notes to reporting that the
"convention from here on belongs to Dukakis." This was on the same evening that Linda Ellerbee's commentary concerned too many efforts at the
convention by journalists to "drum up mini-crises" and to "write an entire
column about having nothing to write a column about." As if to under-
score how hard it was to drum something up in a "convention without cri-
ses," Charles Bierbauer filed a report that not everything was well orchestrated: the evening before Jim Wright had been forced to "wing it" in a
speech about congress because Senator Robert Byrd's speech, not
Wright's, was running on the teleprompter. Sesno took one final crack at
controversy and reported that delegates were yelling "shut up," "can it,"
"sit down," and "boo" during Bill Clinton's address.

CNN's correspondents reluctantly departed "drumming something
up"; ABC's scarcely tried. Indeed, anchors and correspondents alike "sang
a song of no news, pocketful of talk." Sam Donaldson reported that only
four Michigan delegates shared the view that Dukakis had stabbed them
"in the back" and, thereby, downplayed any walkout threat. Jim Wooten
explained delegates' discontent at Bill Clinton's speech by saying merely,
"They want to get to the Duke's coronation." Jeff Greenfield was even
more charitable, saying that Clinton was talking "to the count.y" not to
the delegates, "a chat" with the video audience. "Chat" was most certainly the accurate description of the thrust of ABC's night. Viewers
learned from such chatter that the convention "seems to be as well organized" as Democrats can get, which is "not saying too much" (Brinkley);
there is a "transition from Jesse Jackson's to Michael Dukakis's convention" (Jennings); "we don't really have demonstrations anymore" (Brinkley); and between George Will and Hodding Carter, the discovery of "the
fickle beast—television."

At CBS there was also chatter but it was one-sided and focused on the
harmonic trio of Dukakis, Bentsen and Jackson. Dan Rather opened and
closed the telecast hyping the unity theme among the three. He later
judged that Dukakis has "orchestrated this very well," now "can he take
that orchestration and use it with . . . harmony?" Walter Cronkite summed
things up by saying it's the "most unconventional Democratic convention
in recent history" with "scarcely any contention." At a subsequent point
in the telecast Rather defended conventions as "part of the dance of democracy" that are not "crazy" for "that's the way *we* do things." Eric

Severeid observed there is "obviously going to be a troika" of Dukakis, Bentsen, and Jackson. Will such troika harmony continue? Rather seemed to think it would because of Jackson's "classy performance; he's helped to turn the spotlight on Michael Dukakis." With unity triumphant in the CBS throne room floor correspondents below were left to hum such tunes as those of the future (Leslie Stahl on Bill Clinton as a "new face" and a "break with the past"), the present "two-front war" (Bob Schieffer on how Bentsen on the ticket would make Texas a battleground and reduce the time George Bush could woo California), and the past (Bill Plante on what Martin Luther King would think).

NBC's coverage of nomination night remained true to the network's formula. Tom Brokaw and John Chancellor opened in the upstairs anchor booth; a correspondent wrap-around discussed the schedule, William Winpisinger's nomination of Jackson, the "brush fire" in the Michigan delegation, and, again, the schedule. After Winpisinger's speech another wrap-around assessed Dukakis's chances in New Jersey, the South, and mid-America. This ended with a brief lecture by John Chancellor on how Michael Dukakis would present himself in the fall campaign: "People want a manager," he said, not another era of Ronald Reagan's charisma. With Bill Clinton's speech Brokaw and Chancellor had something else to evaluate ("timing is very important" opined Brokaw) and floor correspondents had something else to (w)rap about ("bad for TV" was the consensus). With the roll call upcoming Brokaw and Chancellor moved downstairs to their open-air "sportscaster" booth, as Brokaw called it. Chancellor, hand cupped over his ear, complained it was "so hard to hear so close to the action." Hear or not, Brokaw managed to comment throughout the roll call—the only anchor, including Rather, to do so. Brokaw concluded the evening's session by observing there was "no suspense" and "this was organized for television." But, said Chancellor, Dukakis and Jackson did *"terribly* well."

Singing We're "Coming to America": Acceptance Night at the Omni

Convention orchestration called for a televised celebration from the Omni acceptance night and the TV networks covered it in different ways.

C-SPAN and Songs of Celebration. C-SPAN highlighted the celebration itself. The network covered the podium's soloists, building to the climactic virtuoso performance by the party nominee. First came a series of candidates campaigning for election and reelection to the U.S. House of Representatives, each enjoying a few seconds on center stage that would reappear in video commercials in the fall campaign. Then came the festive nomination and acceptance of Lloyd Bentsen for vice-president. Finally there was the colorful, visually impressive entry of Michael Dukakis into the Omni along a runway at the bottom of the battleship podium, a runway conceived and constructed just moments before the opening session. With Neil Diamond's "Coming to America" throbbing over the sound system, and the close quarters through which Dukakis appeared to walk surrounded by admiring supporters, the eight-minute demonstration was reminiscent of scenes from Leni Reifenstahl's *Triumph of the Will*. Only the loudness of Diamond's rendition detracted from the scene: on C-SPAN it drowned out the chorus of cheers for Dukakis.

As in the case of the keynote address and the Jackson speech, C-SPAN economized on the number of camera shots during Dukakis's performance. There were only 128, less than half of any other network, and each shot averaged over 21 seconds in duration—an eternity on TV. Again C-SPAN portrayed a speaker's speech: shots of Dukakis outnumbered those of delegates 77 to 37. Of those Dukakis shots 48 were of him alone without any delegates in the picture. Delegate shots were evenly divided between individuals and clusters, but none were close-ups yielding intimate reactions to Dukakis. For C-SPAN viewers Dukakis was left primarily to celebrate himself with a cheering chorus provided audibly but rarely visually.

CNN: The Speech as Aria. CNN's Mary Alice Williams, alone in the anchor booth, opened the network's coverage of the final session of the DNC noting that most Americans "do not know" Michael Dukakis. Floor correspondent Charles Bierbauer followed with an opinion that the Democrats had a "four-day window of opportunity" to make Dukakis known, but had "squandered three-fourths of their opportunity" and now the window had "narrowed to just one day, one shot." Co-anchor Bernard Shaw shortly materialized with a stand-up report from the floor describing the "made for TV convention," scripted so that there was, once again, no blood on the floor. Williams, Bierbauer, and Shaw foreshadowed CNN's own script for the evening, one which Frederick Allen neatly summarized: Thus far Dukakis had made but a "cameo appearance" in prime time, as he watched roll-call returns seated in his hotel room wearing running shoes "without socks." Said Allen, "If there is a TV show, then the message delivered to the people at home," differs from the message to delegates. To that end, Dukakis's acceptance speech would be a "personal conversation" inside a hall of limited space, obeying a strictly timed schedule, accompanied by an orchestra, with a musical overture composed in Dukakis's honor, and Dukakis would make a "grand entrance." In short, TV viewers would see a soloist attempting a virtuoso performance in his maiden, prime-time, made-for-television aria.

CNN's emphasis did not shift throughout the proceedings placing in nomination and seconding Senator Lloyd Bentsen's selection as Dukakis's running mate. Rising and falling during these proceedings was a muted theme—namely, alleged "unhappiness" among supporters of Jesse Jackson with the choice of Bentsen. But by the time Bentsen spoke to accept the nomination that theme had faded. Even Jackson's arrival in the hall was but a muted motif. As the moment for the convention's finale approached CNN journalists used floor reports and interviews to prompt discordant notes with the convention's overall unity theme, observing at one point that "Bush bashing" may have been the keynote of the Democratic gathering and may have gone "too far"—so far that it might come back to haunt the party. CNN carried actress Olympia Dukakis's introduction of her cousin and the network showed the brief film that accompanied her remarks. Shaw and Williams described Dukakis's grand entrance in detail, "well rehearsed," then settled back to listen to the speech that would help Americans "find out who he [Dukakis] is."

CNN devoted a considerable portion of its buildup to Dukakis's address to predicting a personal and conversational tone, a "getting to know you" approach; the network's actual coverage turned out to be something else. The CNN visual version of the aria left the impression that the speech played better in the hall than at home on TV. As with coverage of other speeches CNN did employ a large number of camera shots (299) of brief average duration (slightly over nine seconds). Whereas CNN had covered Jesse Jackson's speech as a delegate-driven spectacle that featured a preponderance of camera reaction shots of individual delegates and a majority of shots of Jackson that were close-ups, with Dukakis's address CNN reverted to a visual style more akin to that in covering the Ann Richards keynote—delegate-driven, but delegates reacting in clusters and groups (54 percent of shots of delegates were of clusters). Moreover, of 123 shots of Dukakis, 57 percent featured him against a backdrop of delegates. Instead of a candidate conversing intimately with each delegate, CNN depicted a standard stump speech of an orator to cheering throngs.

Be that as it may, political analyst Frederick Allen judged "he has brought it off very well" in *this* studio. Co-anchors Shaw and Williams also thought Dukakis had "pulled it off," and concluded that the Democrats had indeed put on the unity show they wanted in what, said Shaw, was the "largest TV studio I've seen."

ABC: The Speech of His Life (or Else). If party orchestrators hoped that all TV networks would feature Michael Dukakis's acceptance speech as the finale of their convention, it was a wish only partly fulfilled by ABC. The network hyped the forthcoming address as floor proceedings were occupied with nominating the vice-presidential candidate: Peter Jennings said it would be "the most important speech" of Dukakis's life; Jeff Greenfield predicted it would stress competence, efficiency, and integrity; Peter Jennings responded that party leaders were playing the "politics of diminished expectations," minimizing the speech's importance just in case it did not play well. Before airing Senator Lloyd Bentsen's acceptance speech the verdict was in: Dukakis had to do well in the "speech of his life" or suffer serious setbacks to his image.

Hyping the speech as a grand finale, however, did not lead ABC to permit the drama surrounding the address to unfold precisely as party orchestrators would have wished. ABC showed Olympia Dukakis's introduction and the videotape that went with it. But as Michael Dukakis made his carefully scripted entrance, ABC resumed its patented formula for convention coverage—chit-chat. As Dukakis moved along the runway below the podium to the beat of Neil Diamond's "Coming to America," ABC correspondents provided voice-over running commentaries: Sam Donaldson on what Dukakis must do, Bret Hume interviewed an old friend of Dukakis, Peter Jennings and David Brinkley chatted about Dukakis, Jeff Greenfield commented on Dukakis. Suddenly, ABC broke for advertising, then resumed chit-chat between Jennings and Brinkley until Dukakis began to speak. Not only did ABC step on Dukakis's entry, but the chatter about "silver half-moons and stars" (reminding viewers of Olympia Dukakis's role in the film *Moonstruck*) and Brinkley's appreciative view, "That was *excellent!*" for Olympia Dukakis's introduction, made the "speech of his life" fade by comparison.

ABC's visual coverage of the speech paralleled its style in covering other addresses. The network favored camera shots of the speaker over delegate shots 55 to 45, evenly distributing close-up and backdrop shots of the speaker along with individual and cluster shots of delegates. Visual cuts between shots were fewer (260) than with any network other than C-SPAN and each shot averaged 11 seconds. ABC used more fades and zooms than other networks, leaving an occasional sense that Dukakis was melting into his audience. Sam Donaldson gave the only extended evaluation (68 seconds) of the speech—namely, it was a "well-delivered speech," that was "unspecific," but "for now, Michael Dukakis has risen to the occasion" and "has done better than . . . expected." Jeff Greenfield gave Dukakis higher marks, insisting that George Bush had probably sent out for Maalox because of the speech. The closing 20 minutes of ABC's coverage were largely put aside as correspondents and anchors chatted about balloons, Dukakis's mother, Walter Mondale, flags, the upcoming campaign, and assorted happenings.

Who's Night to Shine on CBS? Presiding from the CBS podium anchor Dan Rather proclaimed the closing convention session to be "a night to shine" for Dukakis to "fill in the blanks." As the national anthem began, CBS cameras first pictured Rather singing in the booth, then went to actress Linda Carter's rendition at the speaker's podium. The anthem completed, Rather spoke briefly of the Democrats having "orchestrated harmony the Republicans are famous for." The remainder of the evening, including the period of floor proceedings involving the vice-presidential nomination, centered in CBS's coverage of the task assigned by Rather—that is, to "define Mike Dukakis." Here are samples of what viewers learned: Dukakis had "vetoed" all, or about all, of the entertainment, star, and Hollywood aspects of the convention (Bill Plante); he was the "son of immigrant parents" and an "unemotional man" (Walter Cronkite); his "most important base is Greek-Americans" (Charles Kuralt); and the "party wants a better sense" of him because in elections the "party counts for 10 percent, program 40 percent, and personality 60 percent" (Eric Severeid).

In the effort to define Dukakis CBS did not show the videotape prepared by the DNC and aired in the Omni following Olympia Dukakis's remarks. Olympia Dukakis may have introduced her cousin from the speaker's podium, but it was Dan Rather who introduced the candidate to CBS viewers. Rather talked over the sound of Diamond's "Coming to America" during Dukakis's entrance, thus detracting from the spectacle. Dukakis is, said Rather, "as his dad puts it, a product of the American Dream." Quoting author Louis L'Amour, Rather observed "Victory is not won in miles, but inches." Looking at a close-up of Dukakis, Rather said that in "this one" (the camera picture) there were "tears in his eyes: nobody I know has ever seen a picture of Michael Dukakis with tears in his eyes, not until this one." (In fact, there were no tears in his eyes.) Also in an effort to define Dukakis, Rather described the candidate's wardrobe. Finally, noting that American politics "is theater," and that delegates were chanting "we want Mike," Rather turned the podium over to Dukakis.

CBS's visual coverage of the address combined close-ups of Dukakis (60 percent of all shots of the speaker) and of delegates (57 percent of all shots of delegates were of individuals); using 303 shots averaging 9 seconds in duration CBS thus provided a defining picture that captured Cronkite's judgment of the "importance of the speech just as much in this hall" as with the national audience. Although it was a visual definition more closely delineated on CBS than on C-SPAN, CNN, or ABC, CBS's camera portrayal fell far short of the intimacy depicted at its rival NBC.

At NBC It's Meet Mike AND Lloyd Night. Until Senator Lloyd Bentsen had completed his acceptance of the vice-presidential nomination NBC's coverage made few allusions to the upcoming acceptance speech of Michael Dukakis. Tom Brokaw opened the evening's telecast observing that this would be the night to meet Dukakis and that Dukakis would "make the most important speech of his political career." Brokaw's discussions with John Chancellor, however, dwelt on Bentsen. NBC carried a portion of Barbara Jordan's seconding speech for Bentsen, covered the vote by acclamation that nominated Bentsen, and carried Senator John Glenn's remarks introducing Bentsen. Moreover, one correspondent wrap-around dealt solely with the topic of Bentsen's nomination. A second wrap-around covered the question of "what might have been," consisting of separate interviews with Richard Gephardt, Bruce Babbitt, and Paul Simon who had each fought Dukakis for the nomination.

Once the convention's attention was turned solely to Dukakis, however,

NBC underscored it for network viewers. NBC carried Olympia Dukakis's remarks, the DNC video, and the grand entrance. Brokaw spoke of the "unusual entrance"—from the floor rather than the podium—then devoted six minutes of the ensuing demonstration to introducing viewers to Dukakis with voice-over remarks. With the Dukakis address underway NBC provided 323 separate shots averaging 8.5 seconds duration. As with coverage of Jesse Jackson's speech, NBC employed quick cuts from close-ups of the speaker (96 of 125 shots of Dukakis were close-ups) to close-ups of individual delegates (144 of 170 delegate shots). The effect was of a one-to-one, head-to-head relationship between speaker and listener—in effect, the conversational style that CNN correspondents spoke of but CNN cameras did not depict. Moreover, the incorporation of more fades than other networks added to the sense that speaker and listener were consubstantial and "in the same boat together." Finally, NBC's placement of microphones in the hall added a dimension of intimacy not captured by the other networks, as the words of chants could clearly be distinguished in response to Dukakis's remarks: "Duke," "We want Mike," "We're all right," "Where was George?" and "Let's go, Mike." John Chancellor's final judgment on the convention—namely, "the unity is genuine"—was problematic, but as presented in the relationship of speaker and delegates during the Jackson and Dukakis addresses, there was certainly a visual unity placed before NBC viewers.

A PARTY CONVENES, NETWORKS BROADCAST

Democrats convened in Atlanta to concur cordially in the nomination of Michael Dukakis for the presidency of the United States. An orchestrated theme of unity sang the cordiality of the gathering, refrains of future and of compassion were to see the party through the election. Aside from a little stargazing, C-SPAN's cameras and microphones reported the four-night mini-series the Democrats staged. It was for C-SPAN a podium convention; what was seen and heard from the speaker's podium was the story. For the commercial networks the story was elsewhere, the songs were not party songs. Of course, the very fact of being commercial networks accounts partly for orchestral differences. From 14 to 16 percent, depending on the network, of total airtime devoted to coverage of the DNC by the commercial networks consisted of advertising breaks (as much as one-fifth for ABC during the opening session).[2] There were other orchestral variations as well.

CNN, the "network of record," devoted less than one-third of its airtime to what transpired on the speaker's podium—least by far of the four commercial networks. For CNN the DNC was a floor correspondent's convention. Endeavoring to uncover breaking stories, CNN gave floor correspondents one-fifth of the total airtime—more than twice that afforded by

ABC, CBS, or NBC to its correspondents. In orchestrating a floor correspondent's convention CNN reduced the role of its anchors, giving 17 percent of airtime to its co-anchors (who rarely interacted with one another), less than any of its rival networks. Finally, CNN's coverage of the DNC involved peripheral commentary (15 percent of airtime)—interviews by Larry King, "Crossfire" segments, segments of political analysis, even comedy routines. Add to these considerations CNN's coverage of major speeches—with an emphasis on speaking to clusters of delegates—and CNN emerged as a network of many voices singing many tunes.

ABC divided its coverage of the DNC among the podium (49 percent of airtime), the anchor booth (24 percent), and floor correspondents (11 percent). The podium, however, was less the center of attention for ABC than a reference point. Around it anchors Peter Jennings and David Brinkley organized their anchor chit-chat; in anticipation of what would happen on the podium Jennings directed his chats with floor correspondents. Coverage of major podium addresses for ABC was speaker-driven, featuring the remarks of the speaker and not the reactions of the audience. If the adage "politics is talk" is accurate—namely, talk among politicians—then ABC coverage offers another adage: "news is talk," the chatter of anchors and correspondents.

In CBS's convention coverage the party's podium was rivaled by Dan Rather's. Of CBS's coverage 47 percent was of events from the speaker's podium and involved the principal addresses; 27 percent was from the CBS anchor booth. With sole possession of the anchor booth (aside from "guests") Rather's share of network airtime was largely his and his alone. If C-SPAN reported a party podium convention, CNN a correspondents' convention, ABC a chattering convention, CBS reported a spectacle orchestrated through Rather's eyes from his lofty perch above the convention hall. Add CBS's tendency during visual coverage of major addresses frequently to picture a speaker far above the audience below. For CBS it seems politics is predominantly communication from elites to masses.

Finally, NBC gave more time (53 percent of airtime) to covering podium events than did the other commercial networks. A plethora of correspondent wrap-arounds minimized shifts from floor to anchor booth after every report, and thereby reduced anchor time at NBC to one-fifth of total coverage. Correspondents' alloted portion of airtime (10 percent), however, did not differ appreciably from the 11 percent at either ABC or CBS. Yet the fact that wrap-arounds were topically and/or issue oriented lent a harmony to NBC coverage missing from CNN's discordant efforts to discover breaking stories, a sense of plural voices singing in unison not characteristic of ABC's chit-chat, or of Dan Rather's solo renditions at CBS. These aspects combined with the orchestrated efforts of NBC camera directors to focus on reactions of individual delegates to specific appeals made by major speakers. NBC's coverage was set apart from other networks as a coherent whole: a podium convention, correspondents' convention, convention of talk, and anchor's convention, yes, but overall a convention in its own right neither taking precedence over, nor overwhelmed by, TV's presence.

NOTES

1. In subsequent discussions of visual treatments of major addresses by the five networks we shall minimize the presentations of numbers. In the interests of space, tabular presentations of the results of the coding scheme employed are not included in this volume.

2. Tabular distributions of the percentages of total airtime devoted to podium events, anchor booths, floor correspondents, other events, and advertising for each network are available from the authors.

Chapter Six

Grand Old Party or Ruptured Harmony?: TV Coverage of the Republicans in New Orleans

On a warm, clear, blustery Thursday afternoon, October 22, 1987, more than 400 reporters, editors, and technicians from the nation's major news outlets; officials of the U.S. House and Senate press, periodical, photographers,' and radio/TV galleries; members and staff of the Committee on Arrangements of the Republican National Committee; and assorted bystanders (including the authors) traipsed off the floor and up a ramp, went outside, circled around, and re-entered the Superdome in New Orleans, Louisiana. Eavesdropping on conversations revealed the provocative topics to be how much money the journalists had lost in the Black Monday crash of the stock market three days earlier (a lot), and the prospects for the Minnesota Twins to bounce back and win the World Series against the St. Louis Cardinals (they did).

The occasion for this assembly was the Republican walk-through for its 1988 presidential nominating convention, a guided tour for the news media of the Superdome and Hyatt Regency Hotel. The tour would afford journalists the opportunity to examine work space, calculate if sky-boxes were plentiful and big enough to serve their needs, and determine if parking areas around the dome could handle scores of KU-Band trucks beaming satellite coverage of the convention. The tour completed, the gathering marched back up the street to the Hyatt, led by a Dixieland jazz band playing "Way Down Yonder in New Orleans" and "When the Saints Go Marchin' In." It was not the first, would not be the last, but to date was the most lavish of efforts kicking off the GOP's orchestration of the convention that would offer the rhapsodious melody of "the politics of inclusion."

THE GOP LOOKS TO THE BIG EASY: THE POLITICS OF INCLUSION

Interviewed six months after the RNC, convention manager Bill Phillips spoke of GOP intentions:

I like to say it was a convention of inclusion instead of exclusion. It was inclusion in several ways. It was inclusion in the program in that we had 150 to 170 people actually involved [as speakers]. It was inclusion in that we had an arena that, for the first time, not only could we get all of our delegates and their guests in, but people in local areas got in. . . . Probably it emerged when we found and looked at the Superdome. . . . We had looked at Atlanta, we knew the restrictions of the facility, and when the Democrats said they were going to that facility, I saw an opportunity to play up our inclusion while the Democrats were excluding people.

Phillips concluded, "And as it turned out, the fire marshal closed the doors on them and left delegates standing outside; we had nobody standing outside knocking on the door. Anybody who had the credentials could get in. [It was] *a little bit of political opportunity as well as physical* [emphasis added]."

Little in the orchestration of the four-night musical drama, "Politics of Inclusion" was left to chance. It was detailed down to any subthemes or topics:

If we wanted to emphasize foreign affairs . . . during the night, talking points would be printed up the next day and slipped under the door of delegates' hotel rooms so that they know on, say Tuesday, it's foreign affairs and here are some things you might want to say. People are going to say what they're going to say, but you could plant the seed of thinking. So *you get a common humbug going*, everybody's got to *sing from the same page of the hymnal* [emphasis added].

EXITS, ENTRANCES, AND UPSTAGINGS: NIGHTS AT THE OPERA

Inclusion, then, would match the Democratic orchestrators' stated intended themes of "future, unity, and compassion." How did inclusion play in the five networks' teleconventions? Unlike the Democrats, the Republicans at recent conventions have continued an older tradition of holding daytime sessions as well as prime-time stagings. They did so on the first and second day of the RNC in New Orleans, convening for morning sessions on each. C-SPAN, CNN, and the RNC Network carried sessions from gavel to gavel. For C-SPAN and the RNC Network, the televised message was the orchestrated message. Monday morning's session showcased 15 congressional candidates, GOP national chair Frank Fahrenkopf, and other officers of the convention. The Tuesday morning session presented cameos by 16 congressmen or congressional candidates (suitable for use in TV campaign commercials), and 9 women and 8 men in supporting roles during proceedings dealing with credentials, rules, platform, and so on. The speakers' list for the second session was drawn to highlight inclusion as well: 12 featured women speakers, 3 blacks, 1 black woman, 1 Hispanic, 2 Asian-Americans, and 1 Greek.

Very little of what C-SPAN covered from the podium in the two morning sessions appeared on CNN. Instead, CNN composed the following themes: (1) rumors of dissatisfaction that included unhappiness with Pierre DuPont among George Bush staff members for DuPont's "Letter to Jesse" speech during Monday's morning address that publicized Jackson, not Bush; (2) rumors of dissension among supporters of Pat Robertson, who had contended with Bush for the nomination; (3) rumors regarding whom Bush would name as a vice-presidential nominee, when, and what party factions would be unhappy with particular possibilities; (4) rumors of a floor fight over Bush supporters' efforts to conduct voting on the vice-presidential nominee by acclamation rather than by roll call; (5) an absence of delegates at the morning sessions, usually attributed to "partying on Bourbon Street last night;" (6) a showcasing of what CNN anchors called the network's "four on the floor"—that is, CNN's four floor correspondents conducting interviews and doing stand-up reports; and (7) exchanges between columnists Rowland Evans and Robert Novak speculating on who would be the vice-presidential nominee and why. In sum, lacking a breaking story, CNN sought to compose one. The results, as at the DNC in Atlanta, hinted at a drama with a "cast of thousands."

Ronnie and Nancy Cross the Rainbow Bridge: Opening in Prime Time

The closing scene of *Das Rheingold*, the first opera of Richard Wagner's four-part cycle (a mini-series by today's standards), *Der Ring des Nibelungen*, is striking. The venerable god Wotan and his wife, Fricka (he the one-eyed guardian of treaties, she the guardian of morality) cross a rainbow bridge to their fortress home of Valhalla. Their peaceful departure scarcely portends the havoc yet to come in the three remaining operas. They would never again control events on earth. The opening session of the RNC closed on such a note. President Ronald Reagan addressed the delegates. When his speech ended Nancy joined him on the podium. Cheers roared, balloons fell, Lee Greenwood sang "God Bless the USA," and the GOP's guardians of treaties and morals exited stage right for their ranch in California, never again to command the Grand Old Party. Would the heir to the party, George Bush, be as Wotan's son Siegmund and triumphantly yank the golden sword of victory from the campaign? Bush in his acceptance did. Bush's words, "I am that man!" sounded like Siegmund's,

"Siegmund be ich" ("Siegmund am I"). Would Bush's heir-apparent, Dan Quayle, be the next generation's heroic Siegfried? We await the verdict on that.

C-SPAN: Singing the Praises on a Night of Tribute. Throughout, C-SPAN cameras depicted a spacious podium area, uncrowded and orderly—a marked contrast to the smaller podium at the Omni, where friends and relatives of prominent speakers congregated. The GOP's podium themes sounded on C-SPAN in three keys. The first showcased Republican candidates for the U.S. House and Senate and worked in the refrain of the politics of inclusion. Congressman Guy Vander Jagt introduced a group of GOP challengers for House seats; Senator Rudi Boschwitz, emphasizing his migration to the United States from Nazi Germany as a counterpoint to the Democrats' "Coming to America" theme, spoke on GOP Senate candidates. Sandwiched between Vander Jagt and Boschwitz was a ten-minute fire-and-brimstone address by Pastor Edward Hill, the GOP answer to Jesse Jackson, castigating Democrats for unfulfilled promises to ethnic minorities.

The second GOP–C-SPAN theme consisted of nostalgia for fading stars, a welcome to rising stars. The nostalgia was for Senator Barry Goldwater, the party's 1964 standard-bearer. Two sets of remarks by U.S. Senator William Armstrong and a film constituted a tribute to Goldwater of approximately a quarter of an hour. After brief remarks by Senator Alan Simpson (WY), looking and sounding like Jimmy Stewart in *Mr. Smith Goes to Washington*, former senator Paul Laxalt foreshadowed the tribute to nostalgia yet to come as he spoke of his "best friend," Ronald Reagan. It took C-SPAN's cameras a long time to find the Reagans entering the hall during these proceedings. Their arrival, timed so they would sit in a VIP box listening to speeches by such "rising stars" as Elizabeth Dole, Congressman Jack Kemp, and Senator John McCain, had another purpose. It enticed the commercial networks to sign on in prime time and catch the entry.

The final C-SPAN key was the GOP's tribute to the Reagans. Actor Tom Selleck introduced Nancy Reagan; her remarks were brief. An 18-minute film (an updated version of the 18-minute film shown at the 1984 GOP convention that sparked a debate regarding TV network coverage) introduced the president. C-SPAN's visual coverage of Reagan's address emphasized a podium speech, a talking head appearing in a cavernous hall. Of 120 camera shots, 45 were close-ups of Reagan and the camera dwelled at length on the speaker; of shots of delegates, those of clusters outnumbered those of individual delegates by a 2-to-1 margin. With each camera shot enduring for an average of 21-plus seconds, coverage was slow paced. Although news stories on the commercial networks and in newspapers would hype the Superdome's faulty sound system that made it difficult for delegates to hear, there were no problems with the TV sound.

Indeed, when a pop gun went off and Reagan quickly retorted "Missed Me!" both the pop and Reagan were clearly audible. Finally, C-SPAN's penchant for stargazing so evident in Atlanta was virtually absent in New Orleans—one shot of CBS's Dan Rather and Bruce Morton in the network's anchor booth-podium.

CNN and Reagan's Farewell. The "network of record's" co-anchor, Mary Alice Williams, signed on coverage with a preview of coming attractions for the convention:

The Republicans are going to give as good as they got from the Democrats in Atlanta and they're going to do it as a play in three acts with a surprise ending. The first act: tonight when the convention gives a nostalgic tribute to Ronald Reagan and his revolution, capped by a valedictory from the president. The second act: the difficult transition from the party of Reagan to the party of George Bush. And the final curtain comes down after Bush reveals his running mate, and *that's* the best kept secret in town.

Briefly into the evening's coverage Williams noted offhand that there would be no roll-call vote for the vice-presidential nomination—a bland dismissal of what the network had covered as a "major" controversy during the morning's session. Aside from noted orchestra leader Lionel Hampton's Pledge of Allegiance as part of the opening ceremonies, CNN covered nothing from the podium until the tribute to Barry Goldwater well into the telecast. Co-anchor Bernard Shaw mentioned GOP convention director "Mark Goode's hands-on, behind-the-scenes" efforts to make sure certain proceedings ran smoothly, yet CNN ignored the proceedings themselves.

Prior to the Reagan tribute CNN coverage consisted of three refrains. The first was "analysis." Thus Frederick Allen assured viewers that Reagan's address would follow a "three-movement orchestration" similar to Jesse Jackson's—an endorsement of the party's presidential candidate, a review of accomplishments, and a personal-nostalgic close (2 minutes). Tom Mintier previewed the fall debates between the presidential candidates (6 minutes). Larry King's guest provided impersonations of noted political figures (4 minutes). And, Linda Ellerbee reported on a survey she had conducted of what CNN "stars" would miss about Ronald Reagan (2:30 minutes). The second buildup refrain for CNN was "Who will it be?" (vice-presidential nominee). Floor correspondents asked the governor of South Carolina (Carroll Campbell) what kind of candidate the South wanted; learned from Bush adviser Stu Spencer that the selection process was "no charade;" and discovered that a circular was making the rounds in support of Jack Kemp. Finally, CNN covered the Goldwater tribute: Shaw and Williams recalling the 1964 campaign, Bill Armstrong's remarks, a video tribute, and Mary Alice Williams in a 6:30-minute filmed interview with Goldwater finding that the former senator thought "LBJ had a thicker hide than Dukakis, but was not as bad!"

Preliminaries almost, but not quite, completed CNN moved closer to the "nostalgic tribute" to the Reagans. CNN cameras caught the Reagans' entry into and walk through the hall. Charles Bierbauer meandered through a videotaped interview with Nancy Reagan. Mary Alice Williams reported how the president had "surprised" the First Lady by appearing at a luncheon in her honor. These hymns, however, were still hummed against a backdrop of interviews by floor correspondents that revealed Senator Pete Domenici smokes, but is trying to give it up (to be a vice-presidential contender?); Reverend Jerry Falwell believed the "religious right" would be happy with Bush's VP selection; an interviewed delegate wanted Jack Kemp; George Bush, Jr., knew not his father's will; and Bush's campaign manager, Lee Atwater, was "waiting on a call" from the presidential candidate. The call came with Atwater in the Texas delegation, but CNN's Gene Randall found Atwater's comments on the call unenlightening and yielded his airtime to the anchor booth just as he was being muscled out of the way by ABC's Sam Donaldson.

For the high note of the evening CNN covered the remarks of Tom Selleck, Nancy Reagan's thank-you, the 18-minute video introducing the president, Reagan's remarks, and an 8-minute filmed report by Frank Sesno, "The Reagan Years." In covering Reagan's address CNN used more camera shots than any of the other networks (266 averaging 10 seconds in duration). Shots of delegates outnumbered those of Reagan 56 to 44 percent. With shots of Reagan being predominantly bust shots and of delegates being on individuals, there was a *mano y mano* quality—person to person but without intimacy. As with C-SPAN's coverage viewers had no problems hearing the address, nonetheless at its conclusion Mary Alice Williams called attention to the Superdome's "sound."

ABC's Rap Music on Changing of the Guard. "Anyone who says this is all cut and dried is too much of a cynic," said ABC's Peter Jennings as he opened a telecast of proceedings for "Reagan's valedictory." Without further ado ABC anchors and floor correspondents chatted about the "changing of the guard from Ronald Reagan to George Bush." Sam Donaldson stressed the transition theme in an interview with Texas senator Phil Gramm; Lynn Sherr spoke of Bush's "take over" from Reagan; and Bret Hume asked "Can George Bush step out of Reagan's shadow?" As ABC cameras caught the Reagans entering the hall Jeff Greenfield mused it would be an "unusual kind of autumn to see how Bush and Reagan work together," Jennings judged Reagan's popularity to rest on being "not a politician," and David Brinkley said he's "simply a nice man."

ABC paid lip service to the Goldwater tribute, but not by covering podium events. Instead, Sam Donaldson interviewed Goldwater and found that the 1964 TV speech by Ronald Reagan in support of Goldwater (a legendary performance) had originally been written for Goldwater, but the candidate said "give it to Reagan." ABC also entered the "Who will it be?" sweepstakes on the VP nominee by interviewing Senators Alan Simpson (not interested, "I am a legislator'), Peter Domenici (he was interested), and Robert Dole (still interested but knows nothing). The most shrill vocalizations of the VP theme came when George Bush allegedly phoned Lee Atwater in the Texas delegation. Not to be scooped, Sam Donaldson pushed aside other network correspondents and tried to overhear the conversation on the made-for-television phone call.

Throughout ABC's coverage Jennings and Brinkley conversed in the anchor booth, sometimes about the convention ("organized to the nth degree," said Jennings) but frequently about matters having no bearing on the gathering. Finally, the time came for the Reagan tribute. Jennings and Brinkley again agreed the president was not "a politician." Instead of showing the 18-minute film introducing Reagan, Jeff Greenfield exercised his network's journalistic independence with a 5-minute taped report comparing the 1984 and 1988 films; then Sam Donaldson offered an 8-minute taped report assessing "The Reagan Years." ABC's coverage of Reagan's address was speaker-oriented: the plurality of shots (39 percent) were bust shots of Reagan; a minority of shots were of delegates, 55 percent of those were clusters of delegates; and the coverage was the slowest paced of the commercial neworks (shots averaging 13 seconds each). As the postspeech demonstration unfolded on the floor, George Will, Jennings, Brinkley, Hume, Jim Wooten, Sherr, Greenfield, and Donaldson exchanged evaluations. Consensus: good, but not Reagan's best effort.

CBS: "Ronald Reagan's Night" from Rather's Roost. Aside from podium coverage of Ronald Reagan's address, the bulk of CBS's opening-night coverage of the RNC centered in the anchor booth, the CBS podium using 30 percent of airtime compared to 42 percent for the GOP's podium. From his perch Dan Rather declared it would be "Ronald Reagan's Night," informed viewers that the decision to name the VP nominee had been moved "up" to Wednesday night, and noted that Reagan's "win one for the Gipper" line that would appear in his speech had been suggested by Nancy. Also from the CBS booth-podium Rather interviewed Nancy Reagan in a pretaped interview that ran during the Reagans' arrival in the dome; portions of the tape served as voice-over for pictures of the entry. Hence, a *taped* segment described a *live* event. And CBS ran taped coverage of the Goldwater tribute *after* it was over on the floor.

Executives at other networks took note of CBS's taped orchestrations and commented critically. Said one in an interview for this study:

The thing that strikes me and disturbs me and was done a lot in 1988 was the pretaped interview (that was only very lightly glossed over as being pretaped) and made to look live. So [for instance] pretape something with the governor at 7:26. Fine. Somewhere in there you find a way to word it so you can say, "Well, we said that this interview was recorded earlier." But if everything you did on that box made it look like it was happening right there and then, even right down to the end of it, say, you cut back to Dan Rather or Tom Brokaw and he says, "Thank you, Governor," and turns . . . Well, is it a nice TV technique or have you just gone a bit over the line and misled your audience? I feel it is misleading the audience. That is cheating.

From the Rather Roost came interviews with Robert Dole (on the vice-presidency); conversations with Walter Cronkite (saying Reagan was the "most successful" Republican president since Lincoln), Eric Severeid ("one of three truly popular presidents of this century—FDR, Ike, and Ronald Reagan"), and Bruce Morton (speculating on the vice-presidency). When checking in with floor correspondents, Rather talked more to the correspondents than the correspondents did with those they interviewed. Leslie Stahl pursued the VP story with Senator Pete Domenici only to be corrected by Domenici that he was of Italian descent, not Greek as was Michael Dukakis; hence, there would not be a Greek-American on each party's ballot if Domenici were Bush's pick. Bob Schieffer pursued the Bush telephone call to Lee Atwater in the Texas delegation. When Schieffer was shoved aside by ABC's Sam Donaldson, Rather concluded the whole incident was "chicken feeding for reporters." Returning again to the vice-presidental sweepstakes, Rather followed an interview by Leslie Stahl with Dan Quayle with the judgment that "pros believe" the nomination is "Bob Dole's to lose."

Preliminary to Ronald Reagan's address CBS covered portions of speeches by Elizabeth Dole, Jack Kemp, Senator John McCain, and the remarks by Tom Selleck and Nancy Reagan. Like ABC the network asserted its editorial judgment, not showing the 18-minute Reagan film but instead a 6-minute taped report by Bill Plante *on* the Reagan film. CBS's coverage of Reagan's address opening the "four-night celebration" (Rather) paralleled CNN's. Of 242 shots (11 seconds average duration), delegate shots outnumbered those of the speaker. Shots were Reagan bust shots rather than against a backdrop of delegates (70 to 30 percent) and individual delegates rather than delegate groups by the same 70 to 30 percent ratio. As with CNN, the visual was of a person-to-person speech lacking intimacy. Bob Schieffer reported the address hard to hear in the hall. Afterwards Rather and Cronkite concurred it had been a "very successful first evening." Thursday night would be "very important," for Bush would then have an opportunity to deal with his "purely . . . public speaking problem." Viewers should stay tuned.

Oh, He's "A Grand Old Man" on NBC. Likening the evening as the political equivalent of the Yankee Stadium farewells of Babe Ruth and Lou Gehrig, Tom Brokaw signed on NBC's prime-time coverage speaking of Ronald Reagan as the "Grand Old Man of the Grand Old Party." There followed a correspondent wrap-around on the possible vice-presidential nominee. Saying "I looked it up in the history books," John Chancellor judged that delaying the announcement of the vice-presidential selection was not hype, just the normal process. In quick succession, interspersed with ads, came another segment on the VP possibilities, a wrap-around on the GOP platform, a portion of Jack Kemp's address, a convention-without-walls segment—also on the platform—and a portion of Senator John McCain's speech.

Thus did NBC's coverage build toward the "Grand Old Man." Along the way NBC cameras missed the arrival of the Reagans in the hall (ads were running at the time) but caught up with them in the VIP box. Brokaw dubbed Reagan "an absolute thoroughbred when it comes to being a political warhorse." Owing to its convention-without-walls segment, and unlike the other networks, NBC did not get caught up in the shoving match accompanying the alledged phone call by George Bush to the Texas delegation: "a well-orchestrated phone call" was Brokaw's judgment. Following remarks by Tom Selleck and Nancy Reagan, NBC opted to have Brokaw discuss the 18-minute filmed introduction of the president, then showed the last 6 minutes. Visual coverage of Reagan's address was distinct from that provided by other networks. Of 90 shots of Reagan, 81 were close-ups; of 134 of delegates, 116 were of individuals, often shots tight enough to picture tearful eyes and a rich diversity of faces. Here was indeed a "convention of inclusion." In addition to delegate shots NBC had a dozen views of Nancy Reagan in the VIP box. These shots were planned well in advance; said camera director George Paul, "She has a great face for the camera to look at . . . and her eyes, they were looking out with all the emotion she has for her husband" (Diamond, 1988c, p. 16). Combined with pictures of Reagan so tight his face filled the screen and tight close-ups of delegates, the result reduced the cavernous Superdome to intimate interpersonal space between Reagan and his admirers. GOP orchestrators could have asked for no more.

Scarcely mentioning sound problems in the dome, Brokaw regarded it a "tough hall in which to give a speech because it is so ominous." Correspondent Lisa Myers spoke of "delegates in tears." Finally, before crossing the Rainbow Bridge the president wandered to the back of the podium and was besieged by reporters. But, as Brokaw noted, he was "rescued by Mrs. Reagan." Perhaps, as Reagan said in his speech his "twilight" would be but a "new beginning, a new day" after all.

The Night the Keynote was Not the Key Note at the Superdome

Convention orchestrators planned a night singing the praises of George Bush for the second prime-time session. Jeane J. Kirkpatrick would sing that Bush was strong on defense; keynoter Tom Kean, governor of New Jersey, would extol the GOP and Bush record; Pat Robertson would sing of unity; and Gerald Ford would sing that he was "mad as hell" about attacks on Bush (he turned out to be mad as well at not getting on the air until after prime time). But, except with C-SPAN, the drama turned elsewhere.

C-SPAN Speaks the Speech "Trippingly on the Tongue." Viewing C-SPAN's coverage, and thereby witnessing what the GOP wanted viewers to see, one sees little of the "future" motif so prominent in the Omni in Atlanta. The whole of the second session of the RNC showcased two sets of party notables: Republican governors who might or might not have a future in higher office and Republican holdovers from earlier times. For the "governors' night" portion of coverage, convention orchestrators paraded out for walk-on performances all the incumbent Republican governors. Governor Michael Castle (DE) introduced and rhapsodized of the accomplishments of each. Moreover Governors Orr (NE), Campbell (SC), Deukmejian (CA), Sununu (NH), Martinez (FL), and Kean (NJ)—as keynoter—spoke during the evening. Following the segment on the governors, C-SPAN's podium coverage carried the speech by Kirkpatrick, then the keynote and speeches by Robertson and Ford. Introducing Robertson was political consultant Clifford White, architect of Goldwater's 1964 campaign. C-SPAN's cameras panned to two female delegates as White came to the podium: "Who's he?" one could read the lips of one asking the other.

As the keynote began C-SPAN ran a crawler on the screen informing viewers that 31.5 million Europeans in 20 countries could receive the network's coverage. What did they see? They witnessed a talking bust (35 of 44 shots of Kean) speaking to groups of delegates (30 of 32 shots being on clusters). They witnessed a slow-paced performance with each shot averaging almost a half-minute duration. They did *not* see a pro-life, anti-Kean demonstration (with "Kean Kills Babies" banners) in one tier of visitors' seats in the Superdome. Party orchestrators moved quickly to turn off the lights in that section of seats, too quickly for C-SPAN cameras to picture the protest. The convention of inclusion did not include unorchestrated demonstrations.

CNN: A Quayle and a Quartet. Podium speeches were not the thrust of the coverage of the commercial TV networks. Prior to going to the podium to cover a portion of the remarks of New Hampshire's Governor Sununu, a speech by Congressman Henry Hyde (IL), and the address by former U.N. Ambassador Jeane Kirkpatrick, CNN devoted all of its airtime to repeating the question, "Why Quayle?" As GOP governors spoke from the podium, Mary Alice Williams merely reported that the convention was "hearing from various politicians on the party platform" (in fact, this was *not* the gist of the gubernatorial remarks). Moving from anchor booth to floor, floor to booth, booth to floor, CNN featured its "four on the floor" team of correspondents in a series of repeated quartets—asking in interviews and answering in stand-ups the identity of George Bush's running mate and why he had been selected. Although CNN would find the Quayle theme loudly discordant for the RNC during the Wednesday and Thursday evening sessions, the quartet of correspondents on Tuesday managed to find a tentative, later discarded, harmonic consensus prior to the keynote address. Quayle had been chosen for several reasons— namely, he was "a pretty face"; he would help with the "gender gap"; he was from a new generation; he was a Midwesterner; he had a record as a "proven vote getter"; he reflected Bush's effort to "reach across generational lines"; and he reinforced the GOP emphasis on "family."

In constructing this consensus CNN reported various sidebars. One continued to dwell on the previous evening's phone call by George Bush to the Texas delegation. Bernard Shaw asked James Baker, recently named Bush's manager for the general election campaign, if there was "trouble" in the Texas delegation because of the way outgoing campaign manager Lee Atwater had handled the matter. Baker, a Texan, said he had heard nothing about the phone call. Later, Gene Randall asked Atwater to comment on the phone call: were there "repercussions" he asked? "Not at all," said Atwater. Other sidebars were the staples of CNN's gavel-to-gavel coverage: Frederick Allen analyzed Quayle; Linda Ellerbee analyzed Quayle; Rowland Evans and Robert Novak revealed the "inside story" on the timing of the Quayle announcement; and Mark Green analyzed Quayle. Mary Tillotson tried to work a video report on the evangelical right into the Quayle quartet, but it was lost in the chorus from the floor.

With little to add on the Quayle story, CNN rediscovered the speaker's podium. The network carried the addresses of Kirkpatrick, Robertson, Kean, and Ford. CNN identified Kean's authorship of a book, *The Politics of Inclusion*, then settled back for the keynote. The visual coverage was speaker centered. Of 164 camera shots (not counting 15 of VIPs) 35 percent were bust shots of Kean, 19 percent of Kean against a backdrop of delegates; 25 percent of individual delegates; and 21 percent of clustered delegates. With each shot lasting an average of 12 seconds the pacing was quicker than for other networks, but few shots of Kean or of delegates were facial shots. The result was again a person-to-person, person-to-crowd motif without intimacy. As the pro-life demonstration unfolded in the visitors' gallery, CNN managed, by using its own cameras with lights attached, to picture the "Governor Kean Is a Baby Killer" protest. Overall, however, speculation not speeches constituted the key note of CNN's second-night coverage.

ABC: Quayle Talk. Speeches also were not uppermost in ABC's coverage that evening. The network carried only a small portion of Jeane Kirkpatrick's address, joined even the keynote in progress, but carried addresses by Pat Robertson and by Gerald Ford. As with CNN, ABC's coverage centered on Dan Quayle in efforts to answer three questions posed by Peter Jennings: How well is Bush doing on the floor with Quayle? Why Quayle? What is unique about Quayle? In interviews, but mostly with stand-up opinions and/or anchor-booth chatter and analysis, ABC constructed its picture of Dan Quayle's selection. Sam Donaldson concluded that the delegates liked Dan Quayle but didn't know much about him. Bret Hume was surprised at the choice and, he reported, so was Dan Quayle. Lynn Sherr voiced the prospect that Quayle might be "a media candidate," raising concerns of "no substance"; later, interviewing Barbara Bush, she learned that "Danny Quayle is just the *best* choice." Jim Wooten reported that the Democrats knew, and would use, the fact that Quayle voted twice against blue-collar and farm bills. Jeff Greenfield thought that the "youth of Dan Quayle elevates Bush"; and later that Quayle was "acceptable, acceptable" and "does no harm." George Will noted that the young have a "short historical memory" and "they're all pleased out on the floor." Finally, James Baker, asked by Jennings and Brinkley about Quayle, put everyone at ease (or so he thought), saying he saw "nothing that will be a problem" with Quayle.

ABC's coverage interrupted its Quayle talk for the keynote address of Tom Kean. Correspondent Jim Wooten introduced Kean with a video, noting his "lockjaw British accent." The visual coverage of the keynote was similar to CNN's, but with a higher ratio of speaker to delegate shots (63 to 37 percent); ABC's ratio of bust to backdrop shots of the speaker was identical to CNN's, and its ratio of shots of individual to clustered delegates virtually the same. A key difference, however, was that the average duration of ABC's shots was longer (15 seconds to CNN's 12), making for even more distance between Kean and his audience. ABC made no effort to cover the pro-life, anti-Kean demonstration in the visitors' gallery. The reasons can be fathomed from an interview conducted with executive producer Justin Friedland about ABC's coverage plans for both party conventions. He had informed convention orchestrators:

We are going to get angry if you take the lights down during a speech so that you can barely see the man who is speaking and you can't possibly see the people he is speaking to. That is what the speech is all about. The speech is about reaction, effect. If you can't gauge that and you can't measure it by seeing it, you've lost 50 percent of the story. If the guy is doing well we show that, if the guy is bombing we show that, too.

Jennings explained ABC's failure to catch the beginning of Kean's address by the fact that he had started ahead of schedule (at CBS Dan Rather would report that the schedule had "slipped" and the keynote was late). David Brinkley pronounced the keynote "more serious than the Democrats' keynote speech." Jeff Greenfield thought Kean's "jokes very gentle" compared to Democrat Ann Richards's more "vicious" remarks; he concluded the speech was effective on TV, not in the hall. Bret Hume, in contrast, thought the keynote "played well in the hall."

CBS: It's Quayle, But Who? Why? Why Now? So What? Peering down on his floor correspondents Dan Rather asked four Quayle questions: Who is he? Why him? Why announce the selection now? What difference will it make? Leslie Stahl responded to *why* and concluded Quayle could win votes. Diane Sawyer dealt with *who* and labeled Quayle a millionaire. Ed Bradley got *why now* and said it was the "right" night to make the announcement. Bob Schieffer tried *why now* and speculated it was to avoid the perception of "manipulation." Those responses did not end the questions. Rather discussed with CBS's Phil Jones the *who* and found that Quayle's record gave the GOP "Jack Kemp without Jack Kemp." Rather interviewed the Democratic vice-presidential nominee and found Lloyd Bentsen to be nonplussed about either Dan—Quayle or Rather. Finally, Rather found from Bush's pollster, Robert Teeter, the *why* was youth, the *why today* was that there simply was no sense in delaying once Bush had made his choice. The choice of Quayle had shifted the "story of the evening" said Rather, his questions continued to orchestrate the network's coverage as correspondents and guests in the booth sought answers.

The speaker's podium took backstage in CBS's coverage. Of Jeane Kirkpatrick's 22-minute address, CBS used 6 minutes (Rather used a minute and a half introducing her and closing the segment). Later Kirkpatrick was a guest on Rather's podium in the booth—this time for 2:30 minutes. Then, almost as if interrupting more significant booth proceedings, CBS turned to coverage of Kean's keynote address. It was for CBS a visual story evenly balanced between shots of speaker and audience. A preponderance of speaker bust shots yielded a speaker-centered production. When CBS focused on individual delegates, many were reading newspapers and books as Kean spoke. There was no coverage of the gallery demonstration protesting Kean's stand on abortion. Leslie Stahl's evaluation was not charitable. She compared Kean's keynote to Governor Bill Clinton's long, rambling speech placing Michael Dukakis's name in nomination in the Omni. The delegates, she said, paid no attention, were too tired, and the announcement of Quayle's selection had "taken the steam out of the convention." Rather chimed in that the Superdome's sound system was also at fault.

CBS covered 11 minutes of Pat Robertson's address and all of Gerald Ford's. Although Barbara Bush told Rather to quit asking "Why Dan Quayle?" and ask instead "Why not Dan Quayle?" Rather continued to focus on the whys of the Quayle nomination—the "thunderbolt that hit the Superdome." Ed Bradley interviewed Reverend Jerry Falwell who was pleased with Quayle, "a winning ticket" he said. Summing the evening

up Rather concluded "What a Night!" and noted that Falwell had endorsed Quayle in speaking to the convention. Falwell did not speak to the
convention!

NBC: The Quayle Quandry. NBC's coverage took a more light-hearted
approach to Dan Quayle's selection than did the other networks, with
Brokaw introducing it as a "gold-plated ticket." "How does it play on the
floor?" he asked. A correspondent wrap-around whistled back answers:
Chris Wallace endeavored to get a White House aide to see "problems"
but to no avail; Andrea Mitchell found that the White House chief of staff,
Ken Duberstein, thought the ticket would appeal; Ken Bode discovered
that Quayle would "help in the farm belt"; and Connie Chung learned
from California governor George Deukmejian that the governor had never
met Quayle but thought him to be "a terrific campaigner" anyway.
Brokaw and John Chancellor remained puzzled by the choice and speculated that political consultants Roger Ailes and Robert Teeter had influenced Bush's selection. Brokaw called attention to Quayle's peripheral involvement in a golfing trip with lobbyist Paula Parkinson, a "scandal" that
did not rub off on Quayle.

Until the keynote address began NBC anchors and correspondents provided viewers with nothing other than reports about Dan Quayle. Lisa
Myer tried to get Barbara Bush to admit to playing a powerful role in the
selection, but received only the response, "I guessed." Interviews with
Senator Robert Dole and Congressman Jack Kemp failed to provoke any
"disappointment" from either that he had not been selected. Correspondent John Dancy thought people would be surprised at Quayle's abilities.
After four correspondent round-robins on Quayle the words *generational,
Robert Redford look-alike, monied, conservative, handsome, baby boomer, a
gamble, inexperienced, heartbeat away,* and *spin* were finally exhausted.

Brokaw provided a one-minute introduction to the keynoter, Tom Kean,
cut to a brief correspondent stand-up on Quayle, then in 20 seconds summarized everything he had already said about Kean. NBC's coverage of
the keynote took no notice of the demonstration in the visitors' gallery.
NBC's 159 camera shots averaged 14 seconds each and consisted primarily
of cuts from close-ups of Kean (65) to close-ups of individual delegates
(57), giving viewers a picture of an intimate face-to-face relationship not
to be found on any other network. Brokaw pronounced Kean's address "a
superb job!" It was back to three more correspondent wrap-arounds dealing with Dan Quayle; interviews with James Baker and Lee Atwater, who
provided fungible answers to questions about Quayle; and a plethora of
"heartbeat away," "gamble," and "concerns" sing-along phrases. So ab-
sorbed was NBC with Quayle that the network carried only nine minutes
of Pat Robertson's address but did cover Gerald Ford's in its entirety. In
sum, there was a genuine puzzlement among NBC's broadcasters over the
selection of Dan Quayle. Viewers were left to judge how provocative that

puzzlement was, however, by Brokaw's late observation regarding Quayle's age, only "41." Said Brokaw, "Wonder what he'll do with the rest of his life?"

Strains of "Oh Danny Boy" on Nomination Night

In spite of the efforts of the networks to uncover stories that would hold viewers' interest on nomination night at the DNC in Atlanta, nothing substantial appeared. However, at the RNC the orchestrated visits of Dan Quayle to network anchor booths and the parallel endeavors of the networks' floor correspondents to pursue stories about Quayle's service in the National Guard, monied influence, and the Paula Parkinson affair resulted in a crescendo that almost drowned out the celebration songs of the evening in honor of the nomination of George Herbert Walker Bush for president.

C-SPAN carried all the podium proceedings of the evening. Those consisted principally of housekeeping chores (for example, a pause for taking the official photo of the convention); speeches by leading congressmen and senators (including Robert Dole); and cameo appearances in speaking roles by such celebrities as actor Charlton Heston (Pledge of Allegiance), former NFL quarterback Roger Staubach (who introduced Texas senator Phil Gramm to place Bush's name in nomination), actress Helen Hayes (a seconding speech), and Pennsylvania State University football coach Joe Paterno (a seconding speech from the floor saying he—like Gerald Ford—was "mad as hell" about what Democrats were saying about Bush). C-SPAN also covered the two major made-for-television demonstrations prior to the nomination—namely, the entry of Barbara Bush and Marilyn Quayle, and Dan Quayle's arrival in the VIP box. Throughout these proceedings C-SPAN's cameras kept the "convention of inclusion" theme sounding as GOP orchestrators showcased women, blacks, Hispanics, Vietnamese, and so on. This evening, however, C-SPAN's cameras, that had for the most part remained on the podium and on delegates during earlier sessions, were restless. The network also focused on TV's covering the made-for-television convention. During the speech of the party's senatorial candidate from Maryland C-SPAN found Tom Brokaw chatting with Dan Quayle in the NBC booth. During Senator Pete Wilson's (CA) address C-SPAN got a glimpse of Dan Rather interviewing Quayle at CBS. And "America's network" peeped in as the other networks' correspondents prepared for interviews—for example, CNN's Frank Sesno.

CNN's viewers tuning in to the evening's festivities in the concert hall might have thought they were caught in a time warp approximating the years when the music of Soviet composer Sergei Prokofiev (1891–1953) premiered. CNN's coverage matched what was regarded, during Prokofiev's early career, as the composer's cacophonous sounds. Anchor Mary

Alice Williams signed on informing viewers that the evening "must sell the Bush-Quayle ticket in this hall." CNN's subsequent coverage resulted in a cacophony on the Bush-Quayle sale that combined abrupt switches from anchor booth to floor to booth, 16 floor interviews, 9 stand-up reports from the floor, 7 studio commentaries or face-offs between analysts, 53 exchanges between the anchors, and 17 commercial breaks. In addition Larry King interviewed Donald Trump, although it was not clear why. Not counting the individuals casting each state's delegate votes during the lengthy roll call, there were 165 individuals appearing (the anchors and correspondents, of course, more than once) on camera in CNN's coverage. Only four were scheduled podium speakers. Whatever record the network of record recorded, it was not the GOP's.

Although CNN emphasized the Dan Quayle story prior to the roll call of the states, the presentation lacked coherence. Moreover, anchors and/or correspondents frequently filed reports that interrupted the flow of coverage. For example, King's interview of Trump was sandwiched between analyses of Quayle by Frederick Allen and Pat Buchanan ("too young, too cute, too conservative, too much a one stater," said Allen; a contrast to "Beltway Bentsen," said Buchanan) and the podium remarks of Secretary of Education William Bennett. Similarly, a taped report of almost seven minutes dealing with how George Bush had progressed in presidential primaries interrupted a series of floor reports on Dan Quayle's service in the National Guard. It was as though a Parkinson's Law was operating that noncoverage of the convention would expand to fill the time available for CNN's gavel-to-gavel presence.

Midway during the telecast Mary Alice Williams noted that the GOP had "strayed from its tightly scripted" evening. CNN's coverage of "the Quayle problem" (correspondent Tom Mintier) also strayed considerably. Floor correspondents in interviews and stand-up reports made continuous references to "problems" that had surfaced during Quayle's press conference earlier in the afternoon. Yet instead of explaining precisely what happened during the press conference, they spoke of it in the abstract, taking it for granted that viewers already knew. It was not until CNN had been on the air for more than an hour (through half a dozen commercial breaks) that correspondent Mary Tillotson summarized what had actually been said at the press conference. Only then did CNN viewers have an inkling of why the network found "problems" in Quayle having joined the National Guard to avoid the draft during the Vietnam War, possibly using "influence" to get into the Guard when openings were limited (or numerous, depending upon whom CNN interviewed), being too inexperienced to serve in the presidency if called upon, possibly culpable in the Paula Parkinson "scandal," and not being "forthright" (Tom Mintier) in responding to questions about these matters. Without Tillotson's explanation CNN viewers could only have been baffled at all the talk that Quayle might be dropped from the ticket before he was ever on it!

Several correspondents' comments caused glitches for CNN. For instance, analyst Frederick Allen assured viewers that Quayle was better at speaking extemporaneously than from a script, hence would use note cards in his acceptance speech (he used a teleprompter). Mary Alice Williams opened the 8:30-minute interview of Quayle that she conducted with co-anchor Bernard Shaw proclaiming Senator Quayle "the man of the hour, the talk of the town." When she said Quayle had "worked for the National Guard," Shaw inquired if Quayle had "ducked" combat duty, and Williams raised the Paula Parkinson question, a decided chill entered the anchor booth. Asked by Williams about his "looks" Quayle just laughed, "Ha, ha, ha" without response. Finally, co-anchors Shaw and Williams also encountered difficulties later over a non-Quayle matter. Each separately reported that Jeb Bush, George Bush's son, would make a seconding speech for his father. In fact, Jeb's wife, Columba delivered the speech and in Spanish. Neither Shaw nor Williams corrected the error; instead they dismissed the speech as an effort at "wooing Hispanics." Once the roll call of the states finally began, CNN's broadcasters fell silent. There were no comments made during the proceedings.

While CNN's interview with Quayle came well into its telecast, ABC preceded its convention coverage with a 15-minute anchor-booth interview. The interview was relaxed, chatty, and lacking much of the bite of CNN's confrontation with Quayle. David Brinkley asked where Quayle had gone to lunch. (It was at lunch that the Bush staff reached Quayle to notify him he was to contact Bush for the offer to be on the ticket.) Asked why he thought he was chosen, Quayle said it represented a "transition" to the future. Asked about the National Guard, Quayle replied it permitted him to go to law school and serve his military "commitment" at the same time. Would his campaign be "handled?" Yes, said Quayle, and that was agreeable to him. The whole interview showcased the vice-presidential nominee better than GOP orchestrators could have hoped.

Throughout, ABC's coverage of the Quayle story was largely upbeat from both floor and anchor booth. Peter Jennings found "no diminished enthusiasm among delegates" for Quayle, Brinkley said "everyone's happy," and both Jennings and Brinkley sympathized with Quayle's children who had been "pained" by the selection. ABC's floor correspondents had mixed comments: Bret Hume reported Quayle to be the "talk on the floor" as his selection had been the "Eveready Energizer" for the convention the previous evening; Lynn Sherr reported that delegates were asking "us what we're saying about him" (Quayle); Jeff Greenfield said liberal Republicans are "not making much noise" about Quayle. Later Jennings wrapped up all the chat about Quayle explaining that ABC had spent "enormous time" on Quayle and that might be a "down side" for Bush's evening; Brinkley said it was all because "he's a new face."

ABC did not dwell on the podium, covering only the remarks of Roger

Staubach, the address of Senator Phil Gramm, the seconding speech by Helen Hayes, and the roll call. Instead it filled out its coverage with over 5 minutes of reminiscing with ABC radio anchor Robert Trout about past conventions, 9 minutes of punditry with George Will and Hodding Carter, 11 minutes of reports on each of the children in the George Bush family, and talk about balloon drops, flags, and handmade signs. Jennings and Brinkley frequently spoke of the "highly scheduled, highly warranted, spontaneous" demonstrations; and the "very carefully orchestrated roll call" that Brinkley pronounced "sweet." As soon as Texas's votes put Bush over the top, ABC signed off.

CBS viewers received a different judgment about the roll call. Dan Rather lamented (perhaps to mollify CBS affiliates chafing to get their local news shows on the air) that the convention was running late, the hall had cleared out, and the "high rollers have bailed out and gone to Bourbon Street." Rather opened prime time by presiding over three solos by CBS correspondents. Viewers learned that Dan Quayle would need a "crash course on politics" (Bob Schieffer), was a "scratch golfer" (Ed Bradley), and that the GOP was "thinking visual" because George Bush and Dan Quayle "look good together." Following a commercial break Rather returned with an interview (6:30 minutes) of Dan Quayle that had been taped earlier. Rather asked the standard questions—the Guard, use of influence, Paula Parkinson—and with each explained why it was a relevant and important question. Returning to the TV screen live Rather gave his judgment: Quayle "can connect with voters." (Later he would offer his verdict that the National Guard matter was a "nonissue.")

Diane Sawyer did "Entertainment Tonight" type segments, perhaps preparing for her move to ABC to undertake "Prime Time." She interviewed Barbara Bush "as she came into the hall" (said Rather), leaving an impression that the taped interview was live; she extracted from Marilyn Quayle the judgment that her husband was "better looking than Robert Redford"; and she found Bush's aides "mystified" by his speaking style. Rather presided over correspondents' repeated reports of dissatisfaction with the hall: the "hall that ate the speeches" (Diane Sawyer); delegates "can't hear on the floor" (Rather); they can't hear high in the dome, there is no intimacy, no togetherness (Bill Plante); and one can't know what is going on (Bob Schieffer).

CBS covered two speeches from the podium (Dole and Gramm) and one seconding speech from the floor (Columba Bush). Including the time for the roll call, CBS cameras devoted 43 percent of airtime to actual convention proceedings; it devoted another 43 percent to Dan Rather (30 percent) and the floor correspondents. For CBS viewers the roll call itself was conducted not from the speaker's podium but from Rather's. He introduced each state, commented along with Bruce Morton throughout, and noted that many of the remarks introducing votes were read from "scripts" to "dig" Michael Dukakis. In fact, he concluded as CBS signed off, the "scripted statements" had produced "the longest roll call in history."

In his rounds of the anchor booths on Wednesday evening Dan Quayle began at NBC. There, Tom Brokaw taped an interview used to open the network's prime-time coverage of the RNC that evening. Brokaw thus asked first all of the questions that would be staples of interviews with other networks later—about his family values, his candidacy and the gender gap, women's issues, the National Guard, his influence getting into the Guard, Paula Parkinson, and his role in a Bush administration. So, when later Dan Rather at CBS kept pushing Quayle on the Parkinson matter and the candidate responded he had already answered that question, he had in fact done so. When during his last anchor-booth interview at CNN the Parkinson matter again came up, small wonder that it had become a red flag. Brokaw, however, did not press the Parkinson issue, but fastened on the key "problem"—namely, the use of the Quayle family's influence to enter the Guard. Brokaw was not alone. Correspondent Lisa Myers raised it with White House aide Craig Fuller; Connie Chung raised it with George Bush, Jr.; Ken Bode raised it in a delegate interview; Lisa Myers returned to it in interviews with former senator William Brock and Senator John McCain; and Brokaw returned to it repeatedly during the evening.

For NBC the Quayle story was an influence story. It was not NBC's only theme of the evening. The network also made a story out of the seconding speeches on behalf of Bush. Part of that story was the "family affair" (Connie Chung); five members of the Bush family gave seconding speeches or cast votes of delegations and NBC interviewed them *all* during the course of the evening. NBC also featured the seconding speech of Joe Paterno with tight close-ups and Brokaw's report that it was "100-yard support" for Bush. NBC also made a story out of Dan Quayle's arrival at the VIP box. Unlike other networks NBC's cameras showed Quayle's entry on the floor, followed him all the way to the box with tight close-ups, and caught the senator and his wife greeting one another with a lingering kiss on the lips. Finally, NBC exploited the roll call to showcase Brokaw's depth of knowledge of the electoral process: he reported for each state the number of its electoral votes and the historical voting record of each state, even though he found announcements of states' delegate votes a bit "windy."

Apparently CBS and NBC covered two different conventions. The convention that Dan Rather found "disorganized" and "off track," Brokaw and John Chancellor spoke of as "tightly scripted" and "innovative." Chancellor was moved to award a "medal" to the GOP for "innovations"—namely, in having seconding speeches from the floor as well as podium. And, was the conclusion, "they [the GOP] do patriotism better than anybody."

The News Is That There Is No News

From the standpoint of GOP orchestrators the closing Thursday evening session of the RNC was cut and dried. C-SPAN reported it in that fashion. This was the only evening that the Republicans waited until prime time for the formal opening of the session. Although convention chair Robert Michel had called the convention to order earlier and the Oak Ridge Boys had sung "Take Pride in America," it was not until Barbara Bush had addressed the convention, Robert Dole had placed Dan Quayle's name in nomination, Senators Richard Lugar (IN), Nancy Kassebaum (KA), Alan Simpson (WY), and Congressman Jack Kemp had made seconding speeches, and Quayle was named by acclamation that the presentation of colors, Pledge of Allegiance, national anthem, and invocation took place. Aside from picturing scheduled demonstrations, C-SPAN rapidly moved on to cover Quayle's acceptance speech, an 8:30-minute film introducing George Bush, Bush's acceptance, and the closing balloon drop, celebrity song (by Shirley Jones), benediction, and "God Bless America." Thus had C-SPAN viewers seen live, uncut, and unedited the Queen Mum (Barbara Bush), the Dauphin (Quayle), and the Royal Father (Bush) in a single evening.

There is "a pall hanging over this convention tonight" said Bernard Shaw as he opened CNN's coverage. CNN spent the evening figuratively posing the question, "Will Quayle Quack or Croak?" If he confessed on the National Guard issue that would be his quack; if he did not he might be dropped from the ticket and croak. In the end, of course, Quayle did neither, but this did not prevent CNN's cameras and microphones from passing serious, even though mixed, judgments. Here are samples: Quayle "did not answer" the nagging questions (Charles Bierbauer); Bush is "planning to keep him on the ticket" (William Schneider); the White House staff is angry with James Baker over the "Quayle fiasco" (Robert Novak); and "a lot of questions still to be answered" (Frank Sesno after Quayle's acceptance speech).

CNN's anchors, analysts, and "four on the floor" rendered all but the last of these judgments as Dole, Lugar, Kassebaum, Simpson, Kemp, and others soldiered on at the speaker's podium, largely uncovered by the "network of record." Preparatory to Quayle's acceptance speech Frederick Allen repeated his claim from the evening before that the speech "will be on cards." Bernard Shaw picked up the tune, saying Quayle was to "speak from notes." Mary Alice Williams sang to viewers that Quayle's address "isn't a tightly scripted speech, no teleprompter." The only thing left was the speech itself. "Guess What? He had a very tightly scripted speech and used the teleprompter!" reported Mary Alice Williams without so much as a raised eyebrow.

ABC treated the Quayle nomination in upbeat fashion on Wednesday evening; by Thursday, however, the beat had changed. There was "a cloud" over the night said Peter Jennings, "a nasty little surprise," said David Brinkley. Interviewing James Baker, as had CNN, they pressed him on the Quayle "damage." Baker reported that all "rumors" had been explored, "finding nothing" with regard to the "influence" issue; there was "some" political damage but nothing substantial. Jennings mused, "We all know politics is the stuff of rumor." Still, said Baker, there is no thought of dropping Quayle. By the time the interview ended the demonstration preceding Quayle's acceptance was underway on the floor. ABC's anchors and correspondents chatted away as cameras captured the celebration. The chatter was about Quayle. The overall impression left was that Quayle was proving a liability ("terrific damage" was George Will's assessment). But, then again, perhaps it only meant there were "5,000 reporters in search of a story" (Jennings).

CBS signed on for convention coverage earlier than normal to provide the "inside story" on the Quayle "privilege," according to Dan Rather. The "inside story" scarcely materialized. Instead, aside from correspondent reports and commentary from Walter Cronkite, CBS viewers received a steady series of "inside" tips and facts from Rather: Bush was a ".264 hitter"; the convention was poorly run; delegates were missing from the hall; the advance copy of George Bush's speech read "excellent," *but* "how well will he deliver?"; the failure of CBS to catch the invocation prayer was due to so many things going on; the pictures of George Bush on TV the previous evening were of him in his hotel, *not* the hall; and convention speakers and anchormen wear a regimented uniform of a dark suit and striped tie. Throughout the evening Rather referred to Quayle as "J. Danforth Quayle" and "Danforth Quayle" instead of "Dan" or "Senator," as was the practice with other anchors.

On NBC Tom Brokaw and his correspondents stuck with the influence, privilege, and character themes regarding Quayle. White House staff member Craig Fuller told Brokaw that only 85 percent of the Indiana National Guard commitment had been met when Quayle sought entry, hence "don't jump to any conclusions about Dan Quayle." North Dakota Governor Mickelson assured NBC's Ken Bode there was "no favoritism." Brokaw capped the first correspondent wrap-around by returning to the "waiting list" vs. "vacancies" question regarding the status of the Indiana National Guard in 1969. John Chancellor put it all in perspective as Quayle approached the podium, "There he is, handsome, young, and on the spot" (reminding one of Bert Parks singing "There She Is, Miss America"). In any event the GOP would "press on regardless" with Quayle on the ticket. Quayle spoke "one of the best television speeches we've heard all week," sang Brokaw, "a modern media candidate;" "the torch has passed" John Chancellor concluded solemnly.

With Quayle finally out of the way, the spotlight finally reached the

RNC's lead baritone of the week, George Bush. Once again C-SPAN's visual coverage was of a talking head speaking to a crowd of delegates; of 160 shots, lingering for an average of 18 seconds in duration, 37 percent were bust shots of Bush, 46 percent were shots of delegates in clusters. The deliberate fashion used by C-SPAN to cut from speaker to crowd resulted in depicting Bush continuously stepping on his own applause, interrupting delegates' reactions.

CNN's coverage of the Bush acceptance combined bust shots of the speaker with shots of delegates evenly distributed between individuals and clusters. Of the 266 shots (more than any other network) 52 percent were of delegates, 39 percent of Bush, and the remainder of celebrities in VIP boxes. The coverage was fast paced (11 seconds per shot) and the verdict of CNN's "four on the floor" positive: "a grand slam" (Tom Mintier); a "forceful speech" (Gene Randall); a "rapt attention of delegates" that "can't be orchestrated" (Mary Tillotson); "delegates were spellbound" (Frank Sesno); and from podium correspondent Charles Bierbauer, "delivered quite well. *Period.*"

ABC featured shots of Bush more than did the other networks; 41 percent of 226 shots alone were bust shots or close-ups and 56 percent of all shots were of Bush. The close-ups of Bush were "up close and personal" and viewers could read not only Bush's lips but his eye movements across the teleprompter. Shots of individual delegates were not as tight; of delegate shots two-thirds were of individuals, one-third of delegate clusters. ABC's microphones were well positioned to catch delegates' responses: "Well said," "Thank you, George," "Just say no" (on tax increases), and "Three Blind Mice" (Dukakis, Bentsen, and Jackson). The speech played well with all of ABC's correspondents, although Jeff Greenfield, who but a few hours earlier found no problems with the Quayle selection, likened Dan Quayle to "a shadow on his [Bush's] life."

The CBS coverage was evenly distributed between camera shots of Bush and of his audience, 51 to 49 percent. The shots of Bush were predominantly bust and close-up shots; of delegates there were only slightly more of individuals than of groups. The average duration of the 251 shots was 12 seconds, the same as ABC and but a second longer than CNN or NBC. Dan Rather started commenting on the address before Bush had finished, jumping in before Bush's Pledge of Allegiance. Rather called it a "solid speech" but asked "did it connect?" Walter Cronkite thought it did; "a good speech" that "energized" and was a "good speech for television," said Cronkite. After contemplating the 200,000 balloons rising from the floor and falling from the rafters, Rather continued his concern. How, he asked, would the ticket play with those who "carry lunch buckets to work?" And, he concluded "J. Danforth Quayle" didn't look like Robert Redford at all but like "Pat Sajac."

NBC cameras were tight, Tight, *Tight* on George Bush. Moreover, quick camera cuts from Bush to close-ups of individual delegates not only yielded a person-to-person aura but also masked Bush's tendency—no matter how the speech is written—to begin each sentence with an *And*. Of 260 shots 109 were close-ups of Bush, 103 close-ups of individual delegates. The ever-tightening shots on Bush captured facial expressions and lifts of the eyebrows more characteristic of Bob Hope or Johnny Carson than one would expect of George Herbert Walker Bush. John Chancellor delivered NBC's verdict: "a very good job at the end . . . a little off the mark" for blue-collar workers who voted for Ronald Reagan, but "a splendid job." Brokaw cut to the balloons, 200,000 of them, he said, all "hand tied."

THE SUCCESS OF GOP ORCHESTRATION: DID IT PLAY ON TV NETWORKS?

Robert Burns tells us that "The best laid schemes . . . gang aft a-gley." It can be argued that the GOP's orchestrated "convention of inclusion" proves the poet's point. Certainly the speakers who came to the podium in the Superdome presented the Republican party's leadership balanced between genders and the party's membership as composed of a rich variety of ethnic and generational backgrounds. Viewers of C-SPAN's or the RNC Network's coverage had the opportunity to grasp the message of inclusion, with respect to seeing both the diversity of speakers and the throngs of people who poured into the hall each evening. Moreover, while listening to the speakers TV viewers would have heard the "inclusion" refrain sung repeatedly. The commercial TV networks, however, ignored the podium except in the case of major addresses; NBC and ABC devoted slightly less than half their airtime to the podium, CBS about two-fifths, and CNN about one-third. Emphasized instead were other leading motifs, all bearing on the suddenly key office of the vice-presidency: On Monday, Who will it be, and when? On Tuesday, Who's he, and why now? On Wednesday, Why him with all his problems? And on Thursday, Will he remain on the ticket? Surely, then, the theme of inclusion orchestrated by convention planners took second fiddle to those sounded by the networks in response to George Bush's selection of a running mate.

And, just as certainly, the overall tone of each network's coverage, too, detracted from the GOP's orchestration. For example, the orchestrations of Republican planners and of CNN planners were not harmonious. Could a single theme of inclusion be heard in the cacophony of CNN's multitude of voices—anchors, analysts, celebrity guests, floor and podium correspondents, interviewees? What the "network of record" recorded was its own voices, not a symphony in four movements sounding from the podium. The duets performed in ABC's chit-chat coverage afforded more opportunity for GOP themes to sound above TV's mediated version. And

ABC devoted less total time to the convention, hence, by covering the major addresses covered by other networks, a greater proportion of its airtime featured podium themes, 61 percent during the closing session. Yet a good portion of that time involved the network's co-anchors in voice-over chats, frequently having nothing to do with what transpired on the podium or floor. CBS's coverage, conducted as it was by Maestro Rather from his separate podium, featured themes of his selection. They were not themes of inclusion. Aside from various renditions on Dan Quayle, Dan Rather sounded notes critical of the convention: poor sound, poor orchestration, poor scheduling, poor planning. Of all the commercial networks NBC's delicately scored coverage provided the most opportunity for viewers to hear the GOP's intended themes. The network's limited use of convention-without-walls segments at New Orleans combined with more frequent issue-focused wrap-around segments gave interviewed Republican leaders time to air their lyrics, even in the Quayle operetta, in response to the NBC quartet of correspondents on the floor. John Chancellor's didactic performances putting events into larger perspective muted Tom Brokaw's returns to the "influence" melody. And NBC's visual coverage, emphasizing close-up reaction shots to principal speakers (shots depicting a pluralist gathering), frequently trumpeted a "convention of inclusion."

It would be misleading, however, to conclude that because the "convention of inclusion" did not always rise above CNN's cacophony, ABC's duets, CBS's maestro direction, or even NBC's delicate scoring, that key themes to be exploited in the general election campaign were muted as well. For instance, ABC correspondent Sam Donaldson's interview with Barry Goldwater showcased refrains that would resound in the campaign about Michael Dukakis—pollution in Boston Harbor and the furlough issue. CNN's Mary Alice Williams's interview with Goldwater uncovered two more—low taxes and strong national defense. Keynoter Thomas Kean's address stressed another—allegiance to the flag ("not pink, azur, and eggshell" colors as in Atlanta, not "pastel patriotism"). Moreover, George Bush's "Stand By Your Man" rendition in defense of his selection of Dan Quayle sounded loud and clear. And as the Democratic party's director of communications, Mike McCurry, remarked in an interview: " 'kinder and gentler' was in Bush's convention speech, and so was furloughs, and so was Pledge of Allegiance; everything they did for the general election was in Bush's speech at the convention." He observed with regret, "They really used it to launch their campaign. Dukakis used our convention in Atlanta to conclude the primary campaign. *That was the fatal mistake I think*: we didn't begin the general election campaign in any sense at that convention."

Chapter Seven

The Number of Genuine Music Lovers Is Probably Very Low: Chanties of Criticism and Reform

On a cool, dark, and rainy seventh day of April in 1989, in a ballroom of the venerable Willard Hotel in Washington, D.C., Peter G. Kelley, chairman of the board of the Center for Democracy, called to order public hearings of the Commission on National Political Conventions. The purpose of the hearings was threefold: (1) to explore the evolving structure and organization of the national party conventions; (2) to examine the purpose of the conventions in encouraging and increasing voter interest and participation in elections; and (3) to consider the role of the conventions as the most visible means of supporting and maintaining the nation's two-party system. Invited to air their views were former and current chairs of each major political party, TV network executives, campaign managers and consultants, political journalists, political scientists, communication directors of the parties, officials of the U.S. House and Senate press galleries, and officials of previous national party conventions.

The opening speaker at the hearings was former Republican national party chair Frank Fahrenkopf. He turned directly to the point that would preoccupy the day-long hearings: "Someone used the analogy the other day of the political conventions being a lot like that ad being run by one of the light bulb companies, where a man and wife are sitting at a dinner table, and she says, 'The magic is gone; every time the lights go out, you go to sleep.' Well, they are saying that the magic may be gone because long before the lights ever come on at a convention city, everyone knows who the presidential nominee will be." The task of the Commission on National Political Conventions (CNPC), said Fahrenkopf, was to examine the political conventions and determine whether or not they are relevent in the context of contemporary American politics. They would grapple with several issues: "Should there be gavel-to-gavel coverage? What is the obligation of the media? Should they be motivated only by ratings, and how much advertising they can sell, or is there a public service obligation—assuming anyone will watch the conventions in their present form—to provide gavel-to-gavel coverage?" (CNPC, 1989, p. 1).

Fahrenkopf understood that these questions were not new. Journalists, TV executives, media critics, and politicians debated them during each party's 1988 conventions. And they surfaced four years earlier as the "dinosaur issue" during the 1984 Democratic National Convention, a conflict in news philosophies among the three major TV networks. ABC opted to show a rerun of "Hart to Hart" preceding Jesse Jackson's address. ABC vice-president David Burke defended the network: "Four years from now everyone will be doing what we did. . . ." Larry Grossman, president of NBC News referring to the Democratic proceedings said, "The whole thing could have been taped delayed." Ed Joyce (1988), president of CBS News, disagreed with Burke and Grossman: "How could anyone argue that leaving the convention for a rerun of a so-called adventure series was in the public interest?" (pp. 376–77). Moreover, eight years earlier Robert Merry (1976), correspondent for the *National Observer*, had foreshadowed the commission's concerns by expressing doubt about the "significance of conventions as major media events, not to mention major political events" (p. 4).

This chapter examines the recurring criticisms of national political conventions—first as *media* events, then as *political* events. The recurrence of the critical themes takes on the character of chanties. The chanty is a song that originated in the days of sailing ships. The orchestrated rhythm of the chanty kept sailors together as they repeated their often boring labors of hauling anchors and raising or lowering sails. The orchestration was simple: a leader set the rhythm by singing out words to be answered by another line of words repeated by the rest of the sailors in unison. Thus, "Sing me a song, oh a song of the sea" preceded the response of "Yo ho, blow the man down." Clever leaders improvised popular lyrics that passed from ship to ship. In like manner leading media and political critics improvise new complaints (or phrase old complaints in novel ways) about media coverage of conventions or the conventions themselves. The echoing chorus of responses by journalists, politicians, academics, and others help them in their boring labors of covering and convening the party conclaves. And indeed they often feel the boredom: "I am so bored with this fucking convention," said CBS executive vice president Van Gordon Sauter to Ed Joyce at the 1984 Democratic convention, "I'm on overload and it hasn't even started. I can hardly wait to get home" (Joyce, 1988, p. 373).

Critics of conventions, as both media and political events, are what Theodore Adorno, as noted in the Prelude, called *resentment listeners*. They scorn the life of conventions and find that life tedious, dull, and anachronistic. Yet much of their livelihood depends upon convention criticism; therefore, as Adorno (1976) wrote, the critic "Pays tribute to the very reification he opposes" (p. 10). Although rarely on the surface consisting of positive commentary on convention events, there is an expectation that criticism will be "constructive." As H. L. Mencken wrote, there is a "demand for 'constructive' criticism," a demand unwarranted in his view. For, said Mencken (1956), "the true aim of a critic is certainly not to make converts" (p. 436). For example, with respect to music criticism, "In the United States the number of genuine music-lovers is probably very low" (p. 549). Those not musically inclined are scarcely worth converting; music lovers make up their own minds. "Moreover," thought Mencken, "the critic must always harbor a grave doubt about most of the ideas" audiences "lap up so greedily," hence, "it must occur to him not infrequently, in the silent watches of the night, that much that he writes is sheer buncombe" (p. 436). In like manner the number of genuine lovers of politics in this nation is probably very low (if voter turnout is any indicator). Too, both the politically indifferent (those who don't care) and committed (those who are fiercely loyal) are beyond conversion. Perhaps it occurs to convention critics that their analyses are "buncombe"; however, such doubts in the "silent watches of the night" do not render them mute.

Mark Twain (1924) thought that "the trade of critic, in literature, music, and the drama, is the most degraded of all trades and that it has no real value—certainly no large value" (p. 274). One wonders how he would describe the contemporary trade of the media-political critic, the chanty leader goaded to improvise at length on conventions as media events and as political events. With respect to critics of conventions as media events we examine the commentaries in 1988 of three types: those who provide instant analysis during an individual session of the convention as a TV show; the writers of the "overnight" reviews of session proceedings as TV spectacles; and reviewers of the convention's four-nights of proceedings as a TV series. Our consideration of critics of conventions as political events focuses on those arguing for reform of the convention system.

CHANTIES OF CRITICISM: SPIN CONTROL AND POLITICAL "ANALYSIS" AT THE OMNI

Each morning at 8:30 A.M., in the downtown Atlanta Marriott Marquis Hotel during the Democratic National Convention, high-level party officials, media consultants, and pollsters met (see Chapter 3). Included were national chair Paul Kirk, convention chair Jim Wright, communications director Mike McCurry, media consultants Robert Squier and Frank Greer, and pollsters Peter Hart, Harrison Hickman, Paul Maslin, and Mark Melman. According to McCurry they gathered and said, "Look, I think things are going well, this is something we are going to try to emphasize today, we think this is how they seem to be shifting." The consultants dubbed the group the *spin patrol* (Guskind, 1988b, p. 6). At the end of the half-hour session McCurry "would go out and do a briefing for the press where we communicated that message." The target was "a small community of people who are known to the political press corps who get talked to all the time." This small set of political "analysts" and "pundits" constitute the opinion leaders who appear in TV interviews, provide sound bites for the media, and offer pithy quotations for news reporters and columnists. They, mentioned McCurry, "were all going to talk to the press," hence, "we just tried to get them all into the room with the lure of a couple of extra floor passes," said McCurry. "So they would all show up because that was their way of getting an extra credential for the day:"

And that proved to be enough of a lure that they'd all come in and listen to us about what we thought was important that day, and they all wanted to be helpful, and they all felt like they were being asked to play a role in this. . . . We figured we might as well take our shot at telling them what we're saying today, and maybe if you can work in some of this in your own analysis that would be helpful. . . . And I think it worked very, very well.

McCurry went on to say, "I think we could probably get a little more sophisticated about it next time [1992]." Why? *"It works a lot better when your're quiet about it so people don't think they're manipulated"* [emphasis added].

The spin patrol thus sought to orchestrate media interpretations of speeches, candidates, campaign strategies, and the convention itself. Since we have already seen in Chapter 5 how TV covered the speeches, candidates, and strategies involved in the Democratic convention, we will focus here on media critiques of the convention as an orchestrated media event and critiques of how the media covered that event. We begin with the instant critics—those who provide running, on-the-spot observations as each convention's session unfolds. Of the four networks only CNN and ABC dwelled at length on instant analysis of the convention as an orchestrated media event during the opening session. Bernard Shaw, as we saw in Chapter 5, made that a muted motif of his anchor role. Linda Ellerbee made it the focus of several of her special commentaries throughout the convention, beginning on the first night with the observation that, although there was much to be learned about Mike Dukakis:

The trouble is that television and politics get in the way of the learning. . . . Since the day they met television and politics have been locked in the kind of embrace that gives unsafe sex a bad name. Take conventions. Used to be conventions were political street fights. Then along came television. Politicians caught on quick, and now conventions are generally passion plays for the political party and industrial shows for television.

ABC's coverage of the opening session in the Omni was barely under-way before the network's roving critic, Jeff Greenfield, commented in ways that must have elated the party's spin patrol: "This convention . . . is about stability and order and managing comfortable, reasonable change; you can subsume every other issue into that category." ABC anchor Peter Jennings responded with a query to Greenfield concerning the convention hall: "This convention hall was picked by Paul Kirk, the chairman of the Democratic National Committee. . . . And it looks awfully *sterile* com-pared to some of the halls we've been in." Greenfield turned instant media critic and rendered a verdict not based on spin control:

Peter, this is the compromise that politics makes to show business. . . . They also decided, if you will look at the podium, that red, white, and blue was too busy, too blatant. So we're all going to stand up tomorrow and sing "Every heart beats true for the salmon, turquoise, and gray." As Jerry Ford once said in another con-text, if George M. Cohan were alive today, he'd roll over in his grave.

Co-anchor David Brinkley fed Greenfield an opportunity to continue his criticism, noting that he had yet to hear the phrase so common to past con-ventions—that is, "Please clear the aisles." Greenfield responded, "If they cleared the aisles, we'd have to leave too, and then what would they do?" Said Jennings, smiling, "We didn't set him up to do that." By evening's end, however, ABC was back in tune with party orchestration. Political commentator Hodding Carter concluded, "It's been a dream day for Dukakis; it's been a dream day for the Democrats. . . . The speeches to-night touched all the items they want to. What emerges is the idea, as Jimmy Carter said, of unity as the central theme. It's an important day; it couldn't have been any better for Dukakis and for the party." Pundit George Will agreed: "Dukakis had a very good day."

A major portion of the criticism of the national political convention as a media event derives from columns appearing in the major daily news-papers. Each newspaper has a reporter designated to prepare a column on TV. Newspapers differ in the labels used—Media Critic, TV Critic, TV Edi-tor, and so on. Not all such columnists regard themselves as critics. For example, Elizabeth Jenson, who covers TV for the *New York Daily News*, when interviewed for this study, insisted, "I'm not strictly a critic. I'm a reporter. I cover the industry. I write about it, but I don't do subjective re-porting." Whether critic or not, the responsibilities of each reporter are broader than TV's coverage of politics. Mark Lorando, of the *New Orleans Times-Picayune*, said, "I review TV's coverage of politics like everything else." Dave Berry of the *Miami Herald* claims merely to be a "humor col-umnist" who sometimes covers politics. Steve Daley of the *Chicago Tri-bune* thinks "almost every major story has a TV angle," political or not. Elizabeth Jenson put a number on it: "20 percent are political and the rest are everything else." In any event, few of the media critics interviewed for this study—as well as few of those writing columns for daily news-papers—possess any particular *political* expertise for their craft. Until as-signed to write TV columns they have been, instead, sports reporters, for-mer trade magazine journalists, and/or general assignment reporters. In sum, they critiqued the conventions not as political but as *media* events. Said Lorando: "Most TV critics have the feeling that it's dangerous to get too political in their columns. Politics is not my beat; I'm not political. I don't know much about politics."

The overnight reviews of the DNC by media critics appearing in Tue-day's newspapers presented a mixed picture. Many stressed the low audi-ence ratings of TV coverage. Ben Kubasik's (1988) article in *Newsday* was typical. Headlined "Less Of The World Is Watching," it reported that rat-ings were down from 1984. NBC had a 6.1 rating, 11 share; CBS a 5.8 rat-ing, 11 share; and ABC was third with a 5.6 rating, 10 share. In the New York City market area, according to Kubasik, a Humphrey Bogart movie, *The African Queen,* had far outdrawn any single network's coverage (7,531,000 homes). Yet considering that the WABC, WCBS, and WNBC combined coverage reached over 16 million homes (and 34 percent of TV sets), Kubasik's conclusion that "in New York, nearly all the non-convention programming on local stations outdrew any network's cover-age" (p. 5) must be questioned; that one-third of viewers watch a political event should not be dismissed lightly.

Other media critics sought to compare network coverage and ended up applauding NBC's first evening's performance. For example, the *Times-Picayune*'s Mark Lorando (1988a) described NBC's outfoxing of rival net-works by conducting the first convention interview with Mike Dukakis. Although ABC had won a coin flip to be first to interview during prime-time coverage (at 8:05 EDT), NBC signed on the air at 7:30 and inter-viewed both Dukakis and Jesse Jackson. (At the time, ABC aired the one-hour entertainment drama "MacGyver" and CBS carried "Blue Skies." NBC won the media horse race, but not without carping from competi-tors.) Lorando quoted an ABC official as calling NBC's ploy "a mindless competitive game that we won't play" (p. A9). Media critic Ed Bark of the *Dallas Morning News* improved on Lorando's version of the NBC scoop by reporting that NBC had never been a party to the coin flip for rights to Dukakis, only ABC and CBS had. NBC passed on the coin flip. In any event, asked Bark, "What can we learn from this?" The lesson, he wrote, was that "from the interviews, basically nothing. Dukakis and Jackson spewed the same unity rhetoric on all three networks . . . NBC's first-strike interviews were nothing but 'inside baseball' played to score network bragging rights. But at least NBC had the good judgment to stay away from the coin toss and make its own luck" (1988c, p. 3F). (Mixed meta-phors come easily to media critics.)

The media critic of the *Washington Post*, Tom Shales, also compared the three networks, but devoted only a passing comment to the NBC preemptive strike: "Now that the television networks have begun their convention in Atlanta, the question is whether the Democrats will get many words in edgewise. Little of what officially happened on Monday night's Democratic convention opener made it to ABC, CBS, or NBC" (1988a, p. C1). Like actor George Sanders's portrayal of the acid-tongued theater critic Addison DeWitt in the film *All About Eve*, Shales was seldom charitable to network coverage. He pointed to the "many technical snafus" of CBS; to the "handily in command . . . smart and smooth but a little stiff" Dan Rather; that neither Walter Cronkite or Eric Severeid "had anything of interest to contribute" and "those old dogs wouldn't hunt"; and that "alone in his pundit's perch [NBC's John] Chancellor brought to mind either Statler or Waldorf, the two Muppet codgers who used to sit in box seats and disparage the passing show below." Shales concluded: "With the exception of [David Brinkley] and Ann Richards, everybody was rusty Monday night, but then it has been four years since the last of these anachronistic political orgies." There seemed, he wrote, "to be too many people hanging around with not enough to do. They'll all be interviewing each other before the week is over."

The TV editor of the *Atlanta Constitution*, Michele Greppi, focused on another target, Atlanta-based CNN. The judgment was not flattering: "Although CNN touts its beyond gavel-to-gavel game plan, the network talked over some interesting early speakers, muffed lines and cues, and generally obscured the very thing it should have been able to convey better than anyone except no-comment C-SPAN" (1988a, p. 17C). However, it was the *Constitution's* theater critic, Dan Hulbert, who put the opening session into an overnight perspective that would have pleased convention CEO Don Fowler, the members of the spin patrol, the Smith-Hemion production team, and all the orchestrators. He wrote:

The evening first came to life when a multiracial group of school children, billed as the class of 2000, lined up under the sheltering arms of the tall, charmingly shambling [Garrison] Keillor. It was a living *Saturday Evening Post* cover, shamelessly calculated, and it was brilliant theater. The kids droned a shy, touchingly tuneless rendition of "The National Anthem." And as the crowd joined in for the slow, determined, almost fierce final chorus, and as the cameras panned across the cheeks beginning to glisten, that much bandied word—unity—had a fleeting reality. (1988b, p. 8C)

The network's instant critics silenced themselves during Tuesday's second session, but overnight critics did not. During his analysis of Jesse Jackson's address ABC's Bret Hume reminded viewers that one thing it had achieved as a media event was to "occupy the center stage of this conven-

tion during what would have been the 11 o'clock news for most people."
The network's Hodding Carter, however, noted that Jackson had done
something "this convention was very carefully crafted not do. This convention's going for the 51 percent of the 50 percent who are going to vote.
Jesse Jackson was talking to the *other* 50 percent, the nonvoters, the left-
outs." Jackson had sung a message not orchestrated by party planners.
NBC's John Chancellor sounded a similar discordant note about Jackson's
address: "My judgment is that it was great theater and bad politics for the
Democratic party as Dukakis would like to see it."

As might be expected the overnight newspaper reviews emphasized
Jesse Jackson's performance during the Tuesday session. Tom Shales
(1988b) deemed Jackson's address a "television triumph" that could easily
get people "swept up and swept away with the passionate musicality of
the rhetoric and the eager participation of the crowd" (p. B1). Beyond that,
however, "neither the Democrats nor the networks seemed ready for
prime time on this, the convention's second night." Shales judged TV coverage as "often clumsy and uncertain," Teddy Kennedy's address "only
a few steps short of shambles," and the convention schedule "fumbled."
He accused CBS of "erratic camera work and a very strange selection of
shots." CNN, wrote Shales, "which likes to call itself 'the network of record,' again showed that slogan to be a joke when it missed two minutes
of an appearance by John F. Kennedy, Jr." NBC's convention-without-
walls segment Shales found "dopey." Not ignoring ABC, Shales criticized
Peter Jennings who "repeatedly stepped on remarks by illustrious colleague David Brinkley, and sometimes looked irritated when Brinkley
spoke." Shales's harshest criticism was for the Democrats' failure to get
Jesse Jackson on during prime time: the political parties ought to wake up
and realize

that there is now *no purpose whatsoever to the convention except to be televised* [em-
phasis added]. If the cameras left, so would the delegates. And if you're going to
paint the hall to look good on TV, you ought to have the sense to maximize exposure of whatever big draws you have. Jesse Jackson had made himself the biggest
draw.

Media critic Bill Carter (1988a) of the *Baltimore Sun* viewed the late appearance not so much as a fumble but as a tactic that gave the networks
a story angle—namely, "great anticipation of Jackson's address" (p. C1).
Without that "this was a night of almost pulverizing boredom for all but
the most glazed-eyed political junkies." His words were less caustic but
no less pointed regarding the networks' coverage: ABC "decided it would
stick to a theme of how the fall election is going to play, rather than how
this dull convention's playing"; CNN "reported on delegate focus groups,
a cosmic exercise in boredom"; NBC brought out more just-folks for

strained counterpoint to the professional politics at hand," which "smacked of local news;" and CBS "skipped the Jackson tape that preceded his appearance after screening it in the afternoon and deciding it was a campaign film."

In contrast to Shales and Carter, Marc Gunther (1988a), TV critic of the *Detroit Free Press*, criticized the networks for what they did *not* do—namely, cover a key *political* issue. "The issue was taxes, and, when the networks did pay attention, they either trivialized or oversimplifed the story—and they let their biases show" (p. 9A). Gunther was referring to the vote on the tax plank in the party platform. Jackson supporters had proposed higher taxes on corporations and persons earning $200,000 a year or more, and a freeze on taxes for those with low and middle incomes. The proposal failed. Instead of covering the debate on the issue, each network took a different tack: NBC emphasized the party's reluctance to draft a detailed, controversial platform; CBS's Dan Rather spoke of Dukakis's "clout and the votes to get what he wanted"; ABC dismissed the tax issue as a "mock battle" over a proposal that "was defeated just as everyone knew it would be." Gunther concluded:

That's the real problem with the network analysis of the tax issue. Again and again, the reporters simply linked the Jackson tax proposal with Walter Mondale's admission that we would have to consider a tax hike in 1984. In other words, all tax increases are alike—and by implication they are bad. This is a self-fulfilling prophesy of the worst sort, since all tax increases are alike only because the networks fail to distinguish one from another.

With major party attractions Ann Richards, Jimmy Carter, Teddy Kennedy, and Jesse Jackson removed from the scene, neither instant nor overnight critics commented extensively on the convention as a media event during or after Wednesday's nominating session. ABC's George Will mentioned that "at long last" the convention focus would turn to Michael Dukakis; Hodding Carter responded that Dukakis had, in fact, always been "in charge." John Chancellor, as if to save the evening for the Democrats and for NBC, offered the view that the foregone conclusion of Dukakis's nomination had actually been "suspenseful."

Media critics such as the *Sun*'s Bill Carter and the *Post*'s Tom Shales virtually dismissed coverage of the post-Jackson nomination night. Wrote Carter (1988b), "All night long last night, the networks played the same theme: Could Michael Dukakis' nomination act follow that tough one starring Jesse Jackson the night before? The answer was a pretty emphatic no" (p. F1). Carter lambasted Governor Bill Clinton (AR) for his speech nominating Dukakis—"bad"—and the networks for starting to analyze how Clinton had lost the audience even before Clinton had finished. Carter thought even less of the roll call: "The usual endless litany of license plate mottoes, featuring an especially bumpkinized performance on national TV by the governor of the great state of Crabcakes, er, Maryland." Carter charged the networks with failing to "electrify the evening"; it was, he wrote, "scrounge night on the floor." That said, Carter critiqued each network's performance: "The biggest flop of the convention" was NBC's convention-without-walls; CBS's Diane Sawyer "needs a producer to be a real journalist; on her feet she's a lightweight"; NBC's Connie Chung was also an "overmatched podium correspondent"; ABC's Jim Wooten was a "real reporter," Jeff Greenfield "a rising star on political reporting"; and CNN "still lags badly," for "some of its floor people are truly weak."

Shales (1988d), too, criticized Clinton's nomination speech, network coverage of it, then network coverage of the whole evening. However, from Shales Diane Sawyer received high marks ("effortlessly, tends to outclass everybody in the place"); Connie Chung a B grade (for reporting that DNC chair Jim Wright implored Clinton to "shut up"); Walter Cronkite a solid physical exam ("looking encouraging robust"); Eric Severeid at death's door ("not looking robust"); and Dan Rather a concerned psychological assessment ("has not seemed as relaxed as at the 1984 convention"). Shales's highest praise for the evening's performance went to ABC's George Will for his view that the night lacked "carbonation," and to CNN's Linda Ellerbee's "there is no major story" and "the words 'trivial pursuit' do come to mind" (p. D1).

Both network instant analysts and newspaper TV critics used the closing session on Thursday evening to comment on the entire four-day series, not just the session itself. CNN's Frederick Allen was not optimistic that the media event would boost the Democrats. He said Dukakis aides "don't think it's going too well for Dukakis." He continued: "This is a TV show that's going on here this week and the man of the hour, the Democratic nominee, has had one cameo appearance so far, of two-minutes' duration last night in his hotel suite, and all anybody really talked about was the fact that he didn't have any socks on. Jesse Jackson just continued to be the show." Although, said Allen, the focus was to have shifted on Wednesday night, "that didn't exactly happen." And "if you think about it" when prime time began Wednesday night the first thing they saw "was Jesse Jackson being nominated. Then they saw a nominating speech by Bill Clinton that did not go well for Dukakis. And at the very end the whole point was to have California put Mike Dukakis over, and make a big show out on the West Coast, an important area to carry. But who was the last face? It was Willie Brown, the [California] Assembly Speaker, a Jesse Jackson man. He was the lasting impression." In short, "too much Jackson, not enough Dukakis."

Analysts at ABC largely concurred. George Will spoke of a convention of "two minds," Hodding Carter of the effort to accommodate the "past" and "looking to" the future. But NBC's Tom Brokaw concluded that it had been a "well-managed" convention that addressed the "future," and John Chancellor returned to the unity theme. Dan Rather concluded that the convention had been "tailored," reinforcing his verdict of the evening before when he concluded that Michael Dukakis had "up to now, at least, orchestrated this remarkably well." This must have come as surprising news to many of the convention planners. Communications director Mike McCurry expressed the view in an interview that such was not the case. Reflecting on what he called his "personal" and not the "party's judgment," McCurry said that "I think we had a marvelous apparatus set in Atlanta that I don't think Dukakis took particular advantage of. The reason, I think, is that he was not a message-driven candidate from the very beginning." The Dukakis entourage, he observed, "had a very curious aversion to communicating a consistent message." Dan Rather, apparently, thought otherwise.

Critics for daily newspapers divided in their assessment of TV's coverage of the Democrats in Atlanta. Monica Collins of *USA Today* called it "four nights of primetime TV extravagance, showmanship, showoffmanship, drama real and contrived, and comic relief" (1988a, p. 3D). It starred, she wrote, "an electrifying preacher, a bland governor, hyper-to-please anchor people, and a supporting cast larger than you see in a Cecil B. deMille epic." There wasn't "much news," she thought, but it was a "TV spectacle of politics" that had "flashes of brilliance, stretches of boredom, and lots of tacky excesses." With that she passed final judgment on the network performances: Best Cameo: Diane Sawyer. Best Floor Reporter: Jeff Greenfield. Anchor in Her Prime: Mary Alice Williams. Anchor in His Prime: Peter Jennings. Most Uncomfortable Anchor: Dan Rather. Most Uncomfortable Commentator: John Chancellor. Best Enterprise: NBC's sign-on with the Monday evening Dukakis interview.

Ken Tucker, TV critic of the *Philadelphia Inquirer*, was not so positive. Like Collins he found no news in the mini-series, but for different reasons. The networks' rigid packaging, he opined, had created a "bore," not a TV spectacle. In attempting to impose order on a convention that had a life and logic of its own, "television had managed to smother some good television" (1988, p. 1D). He argued, "By analyzing and catering ceaselessly, by hauling out the elder statesmen of evening news to pontificate," the networks spewed out "more verbiage per minute than your average blabbering sitcom." The worst offender, he concluded, was CBS: "Neither Rather's obsequiousness nor the pompous banalities of those he introduced was worth air time." In sum, network TV coverage was "anchorbabble."

Instant and overnight reviews of convention coverage do not end the criticism. The nation's three major newsweeklies concentrated on the four-night series as a whole. *Time*, echoing Dan Rather's questionable verdict, said "it was Dukakis who controlled the convention machinery." The result was orchestrated unity and a plus for Dukakis. Correspondent Walter Shapiro (1988) wrote a favorable review: "Successful drama demands a strong final act, an inspirational address that seemed beyond Dukakis's rhetorical range" (p. 15). Yet "in a speech that had a lilt and a majesty unlike any other he had given in his 16-month quest, Dukakis found the answer." He was a "man transformed," wrote Shapiro, "punching the air in triumph, blowing kisses to his wife: these were not the metronomic gestures of a soulless technocrat." Shapiro's colleague Jacob V. Lamar (1988) was equally positive: "As a media spectacle, the convention's only failing was so unusual for Democats that they reveled in it: the floor show was rather dull and undramatic" (p. 16). Lamar listed the spectacle's highlights: the keynote, Ted Kennedy's address, Jesse Jackson's evocation of his quest, and "with his artful orchestration of people and events, Dukakis emerged looking like . . . a strong leader." *Time*'s sidebars listed awards for the TV show: Biggest Bomb, Bill Clinton's address; Worst Theme Song, *Fanfare for Michael Dukakis*; Moment Most Like a Jerry Lewis Telethon, Garrison Keillor's "syrupy rendition" of the national anthem "complete with children, adorable on cue." *U.S. News & World Report* also lauded the surface presentation of unity of the Democrats and Dukakis's performance. The magazine's assessment was that "The Speech" (Dukakis's acceptance) was "content-free and, well, practically Republican." But "the man who had spent his entire career speaking in prose revealed an unexpected flair for poetry. . . . As a piece of choreography, too, Dukakis's performance was superb. The entrance, the music, the lighting, even the near tears . . . all lent soul to the technocrat" and, not incidentally, wrested the focus of the spectacle away from Jesse Jackson ("Charge of," 1988, pp. 12, 14).

In its August 1, 1988, wrap-up of the convention, *Newsweek* took a different critical approach by reviewing the backstage operations of the spectacle in a three-page piece. Backstage consisted of what was going on to orchestrate events from trailers under the Omni grandstand and from rooms underneath the podium. "This was to be the year the Democratic convention finally left the Era of Mencken and entered the Era of McLuhan. . . . Conventions were essentially TV shows—a 'mini-series,' as Paul Kirk, chairman of the Democratic National Committee, put it" ("Of 'Visibility,' " 1988, p. 18). *Newsweek* reviewed performances of convention workers who wore red baseball caps with the caption BITE PATROL, and who orchestrated party members' comments when interviewed on TV; "visibility whips" who promoted party spokespersons for interviews and assigned Dukakis's lobbyists to key delegations to drum up support; and the coaching and rehearsals in holding rooms before speakers went to the podium. *Newsweek*'s photos captured Jesse Jackson in his "quiet room" before he spoke; Dukakis's handlers applying his makeup; and ABC's Sam Donaldson and a producer waiting backstage to conduct an interview. The

Democratic message of unity and of a triumphant Dukakis, for *Newsweek*, was a minor achievement.

Conventions don't exist for the networks. They exist to network! The pols come to talk to the journalists; the journalists come to talk to the pols and each other. The pols-cum-lobbyists come to talk to both groups and to troll for clients among the corporate types attending this year in record numbers. (p. 19)

For *Newsweek* the play was not the thing to "catch the conscience of the king," as Shakespeare wrote, but the play's stage management. It must be noted, however, that *Newsweek*'s own conscience was staged. The magazine circulated a press release listing 19 of its own reporters and editors available "as broadcast guests" for radio and TV interviews (Weiss, 1988, p. 29). The interviews could be arranged through a spokesperson, *Newsweek*'s own "visibility whip."

Adding to the on-the-spot, overnight, and series reviews of the Democratic convention are the critiques of media-monitoring organizations. Many consider it their task to act as watchdogs over TV coverage of politics and political events. One such organization in Atlanta was FAIR (Fairness & Accuracy in Reporting), a group that lists itself as "the national media watch organization" ("Fairness &," 1988). FAIR charged that the media's use of the "pejorative" term *special interests* denigrated the "progressive" and "Jesse Jackson forces," but was never applied in news accounts to "conservative Democrats" such as Lloyd Bentsen, oil and business clients, or the Republican party. FAIR also criticized media references to Dukakis's "coddling" and "caving in" to Jackson, and media doubts that Dukakis might be "too liberal" to win.

A "conservative educational organization," the MRC, or Media Research Center (1988a), also examined media coverage, principally TV, of the Democratic gathering in Atlanta. MRC analyzed the prime-time TV coverage of ABC, CBS, CNN, and NBC, rating each network for its use of ideological labels, choice of officials to interview, questions asked of interviewees, consistency with 1984 convention coverage, coverage of controversies, criticism of Dukakis and/or the Democrats, and "the overall educational value of the broadcasts to the voter." On a 10-point scale that rates higher scores more favorable to conservatism than lower ones, NBC received a 7.3 score, CNN a 7, ABC a 5.5, and CBS a 2.5. (How MRC codes items and calculates scale scores is not clear from the press release.) MRC's critique concluded that, "thanks to the networks," the convention's efforts to "package" Dukakis as a competent manager and as a political moderate were successful. (Dukakis was characterized as liberal only 12 times in 50 hours of coverage.) Overall, according to MRC, "CNN and NBC gave viewers the greatest diversity of views without interfering with major convention events," but "CBS spent more time talking among themselves than offering viewers convention-related information."

A third media-monitoring group, the Center for Media and Public Affairs, reviewed TV with another focus. It examined prime-time coverage of ABC, CBS, and NBC (Lichter & Lichter, 1988) with respect to the number of "segments" (speeches, interviews, round-table discussions, etc.) devoted to coverage of differing topics (Dukakis, Bentsen, policy issues, campaign strategy, etc.). Network coverage devoted the plurality of segments to Jackson (98), with Dukakis ranking second (79). To no surprise, podium speakers appearing on the networks praised both Jackson and Dukakis more than they criticized either. Evaluations of Jackson and of Dukakis by the networks were also largely positive, but the center determined that "positive evaluations of Dukakis tended to be rather mild" (p. 42). The major theme characterizing network coverage, according to center findings, was that the Democrats "had succeeded in unifying their own often fractious party" (p. 42), a review of the production that would undoubtedly hearten Democratic orchestrators.

Finally, as national party conventions have become media as well as political events, academic scholars have analyzed media coverage. They, too, play the role of critics in their published findings. (See, for example, Brown, 1969; Blankenship, 1976; Paletz & Elson, 1976; Foote & Rimmer, 1983; Adams, 1985; Womack, 1985, 1986, 1988; Nimmo, 1986; Henry, 1988; Shafer, 1988; Smith, 1988). To date the key published analysis of network TV coverage of the 1988 nominating conventions has examined the sources of live interviews used by ABC, CBS, CNN, and NBC (Womack, 1989). The three over-the-air networks in 1988 aired fewer live interviews per hour than they had in 1984 (3.57 for ABC, 3.61 for CBS, and 5.05 for NBC). Not surprisingly, CNN outdistanced its rivals by airing 6.31 interviews per hour during prime time. Also not surprising is the finding that the use of white males for interviews decreased (as a percentage of total network interviews) in 1988 and that black male interviews increased; the proportion of interviewees who were women, white or black, increased for 1988 over 1984. With respect to network differences, "the networks chose their interview sources differently on the basis of race and sex," a finding that "can be directly attributed to CNN coverage, which was markedly different from other networks as far as increased coverages for white women and blacks, both men and women" (Womack, 1989, p. 674).

CRITICAL CHANTIES: THE DOMED AND DOOMED GOP IN NEW ORLEANS

When CNN's Bernard Shaw at the beginning of his network's telecast of Monday evening's session in the Superdome referred to "convention producer Mark Goode's hands-on, behind-the-scenes" efforts to "make sure" that the "convention has certain memorable elements," he was only partly correct. There was, said Goode when interviewed for this study, a "program group," not just Goode alone (see Chapter 3). It consisted of operatives of presidential candidate George Bush, notables of the Republican National Committee, and media-wise professionals such as Goode. As proposals came before the group that might, in Shaw's words, guarantee "memorable elements," within the group there "was pretty much a general decision." Goode went on, "I don't think there was an awful lot of disagreement." The candidate, party, and convention managers, in sum, agreed in their aims, a noticeable difference from what faced Democratic orchestrators Don Fowler, Mike McCurry, and others in coordinating the candidate's convention goals with the unity and futuristic goals of the convention managers.

Without "an awful lot of disagreement" to highlight instant critics of GOP orchestration confined themselves principally to saying *just that*: the convention was orchestrated. However, not moved to overplay that theme, network critics largely remained silent on the convention as a media event. CBS's Dan Rather commented on Tuesday evening: "What an interesting night at the Republican National Convention!" What made it interesting was George Bush's announcement of his vice-presidential running mate, his selection of Quayle, and so on. Interesting or not, Rather could not resist criticizing: "Things ran late tonight, partly because they slipped the convention schedule." GOP organizers allegedly knew the Quayle story would be "talked about" on network TV, and rescheduled accordingly. Moreover, the keynoter had "pulled a Bill Clinton" (running too long, something Tom Kean did not) and both the Pat Robertson and Gerald Ford addresses had come on later than scheduled. This forced CBS to stay on the air longer than anticipated—that is, the TV networks had been used. The overlong scheduling remained the principal theme of Rather's instant criticism of the media spectacle each evening, as he tried no doubt to sooth the ire of network affiliates forced to delay local programming—a bone of contention for CBS in 1984.

Network analysts' praise or blame for the GOP orchestrated media event was limited primarily to the last two evening sessions. Thus, during Wednesday evening's nomination session NBC's Tom Brokaw remarked that "not much has happened here that you could describe as unexpected." There was only a "tiny blip" of warning on the radar screen—that is, the flap over the Quayle candidacy. John Chancellor observed that "the press didn't bring this up, really, it was a matter of record," and, hence, Republicans should not blame the media for raining on the GOP parade. Later in the evening Chancellor awarded his "medal for innovation" to Republican orchestration for having six seconding speeches from the floor. ABC's instant analysis consisted chiefly of Tom Wicker's commentary about the "stylized" convention and George Will's analysis of the purposes behind conventions. ABC sounded a nostalgic note by bringing in network radio anchor Robert Trout to discuss the history of increased orchestration over the 28 conventions he had covered since 1936. At CNN Robert Novak critiqued GOP orchestration for having a convention without any sign of George Bush before Wednesday.

By the closing session of the convention instant analysis was all but gone. ABC's George Will again commented on what conventions do and evaluated Thursday's closing events; Diane Sawyer at CBS agreed with Rather that the convention had not been run well. Rather concluded that "it isn't just for play," and Walter Cronkite opined that the GOP conclave had been a "TV special." It was up to Linda Ellerbee at CNN to offer an instant analysis of the entire four-night show. She criticized the "planners" who "set out to sabotage the process" of "convention deliberation" and "who came within one night of having their way"—namely, to make viewers think they were watching the "Miss America contest instead." Both parties, noted Ellerbee, subject reporters to "the heavy hand of party manipulation." It all is "a situation that makes the planner people very happy." But, said Ellerbee, in New Orleans came the Quayle story. Then, a "convention meant to be a sing along with Mitch Miller had become, instead, a Janis Joplin concert." In the end what the planners "could not keep out of this hall was politics," she concluded, "the kind of story that explains why we're here and why we ought to be . . . a story breaking too fast for newspapers." Hence, "politics and television news are alive and kicking in the summer of '88. And so it goes."

It did not go so with media critics' reviews, in either their overnight assessments or of the GOP gathering as a whole. On a positive note the TV ratings for the RNC on the first evening were up 6 percent over what they had been for the Democrats. The total network share for the opening evening in Atlanta was 32 with a cumulative network rating of 17.7; the opening prime-time session in New Orleans had a cumulative 38 share (about half the normal prime-time audience) with a 19.9 rating—one rating point representing 886,000 households (Daley, 1988, p. 17).

Also generally positive were reviews of the address by President Ronald Reagan. Three are typical. Tom Shales (1988f), for example, noted "one could find a lot wrong with the speech" (p. D1), yet Reagan supplied something the GOP had not had before: nostalgia. However, Shales found the TV coverage of the evening's session "infuriating," noting that *what* the networks chose to cover "seemed based on whim." He singled out Dan Rather as "embedded in cement" and the ABC team of Peter Jennings and David Brinkley as "very chummy and very enjoyable" (no news but chummy enjoyability). The ABC booth was like the "Cheers" bar, a nice place to drop by." Howard Rosenberg of the *Los Angeles Times* observed that Reagan's "spirit seemed to descend from the podium and embrace" (1988b, p. VI-1) the convention. Like Shales, however, he derided network coverage: "when there is any news *everything* becomes news." Rosenberg criticized CBS's Diane Sawyer and ABC's Lynn Sherr for dealing in nonnews as news; the "Dan-and-Walter chats" in the CBS booth he found "painful to watch, the words of both men bursting like fat, empty bubbles." Ed Siegel (1988a) of the *Boston Globe* concluded that Reagan had given a "great farewell speech" (p. 63) but not one that would help either George Bush or harm Michael Dukakis. Unlike Shales and Rosenberg, Siegel did not criticize network reporters; instead he shared ABC's Sam Donaldson's judgment of Reagan's speech—that is, "Is that the best he can do?"—and seemed content with ABC's Jeff Greenfield in grading the address a C. Balancing positive reviews of the Reagan spectacle were a few negative assessments. That of the *Baltimore Sun* media critic, Bill Carter, was illustrative. For one thing, Carter (1988c) argued that speculation over George Bush's running mate upstaged Reagan on the networks. Moreover, only CNN carried intact "possibly the most slickly produced valentine ever composed for a politician" (p. B1)—the RNC propaganda film introducing Reagan. Carter granted that scheduling Reagan at 10:40 P.M. EDT "gave the party a little extra national exposure," but he concluded that it was "hard" to rank the speech "up there as one of Reagan's most scintillating performances," high points or not.

Network coverage of an orchestrated, not-so-spontaneous, made-for-television happening caught the attention of TV critics Ed Bark of the *Dallas Morning News* and Mark Lorando of the *New Orleans Times-Picayune*. That was the alleged telephone call in the Texas delegation to Bush by campaign manager, Lee Atwater, concerning the timing of the announcement of the vice-presidential nominee (see Chapter 6). Bark (1988d) likened it to the "bait" that "hooked CNN, followed in rapid-fire fashion by reporters for NBC, CBS, and ABC" (p. 5F). Lorando (1988c) called it a "news biscuit" tossed onto the convention floor by Atwater, who then "watched with amusement as a pack of network reporters pounced on it like hounddogs in headphones hot on the scent of a story" (p. B2). After network anchors and correspondents grumbled about being "teased" (Sam Donaldson) Bark sensed a double standard:

Let's get this straight. At the Democratic National Convention in Atlanta, network executives, anchors and reporters complained *ad nauseum* that the proceedings were too choreographed, that there nothing of consequence was happening. Then, when Bush gives them a story to chase [guessing the vice-presidential nominee], Donaldson and, earlier, Rather say the Republicans are creating phony baloney suspense. (p. 5F)

Noel Holston, TV critic of the *Minneapolis Star-Tribune*, was more direct: "The network correspondents were being manipulated. . . . The reporters did look like chickens. But pahleeeeeze spare us the whining. The Republicans, displaying a sense of humor they are often said to lack, were simply giving CBS, ABC, and NBC what they said they wanted: suspense and un-predictability" (1988, p. 1E).

Muting the faint but happy tunes, however, on "Ronald Reagan's Night," were several critical reviews. Not all were from media critics. Staff writers for major dailies had bylines in August 17 editions—including Thomas Rosenstiel of the *Los Angeles Times* (1988b), T. R. Reid of the *Washington Post* (1988), and Michael Oreskes of the *New York Times* (1988a)—for showcasing a problem largely unknown to home viewers—namely, the faulty sound system within the Superdome that made it diffi-cult for delegates to hear podium addresses that came across as loud and clear on TV. After Tuesday evening's session, however, that critique faded into the background as media commentators turned to TV coverage of the Big Story: the announcement that Dan Quayle would be the vice-presidential nominee. Although Mark Lorando (1988d) thought "George Bush gave away the ending and left the networks holding the windbags" only two days into a four-day convention (p. B2), Ed Siegel (1988b) wrote "as the day wore on, network correspondents became more querulous as to what virtues Quayle brings" (p. 69). Phil Kloer, TV critic of the *Atlanta Journal*, did as much as any critic to put the Quayle story in perspective by pointing out that "the surprise selection was held up to the spotlight and examined from every possible angle: the gender gap, the baby boom vote, compatibility, the Midwest's electoral strength, even Mr. Quayle's much remarked-upon, but somewhat dubious, resemblance to Robert Redford" (1988a, p. 19A). Even though the Quayle story dominated TV coverage, however, Kloer thought there was a more substantial highlight of the evening—the keynote address. Uninterrupted by the comments of anchors or correspondents it "proved that sometimes good television isn't just playing my-floor-reporter-can-beat-up-your-floor-reporter." Kloer concluded, "When the words are right, it doesn't matter if the image is 'just' a talking head." (This, of course, was the same keynote speaker judged by Dan Rather to have "pulled a Bill Clinton.")

For several media critics the Quayle story was not the story itself but which network got the scoop (Sullivan, 1988a). For Ed Bark (1988e), "CNN, 'your network of record,' scooped the 'Big Three' commercial net-works Tuesday afternoon with a live telecast of Vice President George Bush's sudden announcement of Senator Dan Quayle as his running mate" (p. 2H). Bark's comments illustrate a hazard of media criticism—that is, jumping to conclusions. He based his column on what viewers in Dallas, Texas saw. Elsewhere it was NBC's Tom Brokaw who broke the story with an interruption of the network's afternoon programming. The Dallas NBC affiliate did not carry the NBC news update. So other media critics applauded NBC's scoop in the August 17 editions of their respective newspapers: Brian Donlon and Greg Katz of *USA Today* wrote that NBC got the "only one big story" from the convention (1988d, p. 4A); Tom

Shales wrote that "NBC News clobbered its competition" (1988g, p. D1); and Elizabeth Jensen of the *New York Daily News* quoted NBC correspondent Andrea Mitchell on how she got the scoop: "I made 25 calls and then I got lucky and found someone who knew; so I called Brokaw" (1988, p. 78), who then put the story on the air *unconfirmed*. Lesson: Media critics castigate "horse race journalism," then applaud the winners of journalism's version of the horse race—the scoop.

With rare exception the overnight reviews in the August 18 newspapers by media critics concerned themselves, not with televison's coverage of Wednesday's nomination night, but with the "Quayle Hunt" (Sullivan, 1988b, p. 55). Don Kowet of the *Washington Times* observed that it "took less than 24 hours for the media to find a 'character flaw' " in Quayle (1988, p. A7). Phil Kloer of the *Atlanta Journal & Constitution* wrote that "the skimpier the substance, the flashier the tap dance. The four major news networks . . . put on their noisiest clickety-clack shows Wednesday night in an attempt to drum up a little excitement in an otherwise lackluster evening of television" (1988b, p. 32). Tom Shales (1988h) spoke of Quayle's "ordeal by anchor" and "trial by booth": ABC "ran the warmest booth," Brokaw's NBC booth was "downright chilly," and CNN's Bernard Shaw and Tom Brokaw were "very aggressive." Shales concluded that CNN's interview with Quayle "resembled a cross between an absurdist play by Eugene Ionesco and 'The Morton Downy Jr. Show.' If only the house band could have struck up the golden oldie, 'I Know That You Know.' It was turning into a tantric [mystical] chant" (pp. C-1, 2). Ed Bark (1988f) slammed ABC, praised CNN: "Jennings and Brinkley failed to seize their moments with Quayle. . . . Their interview with Quayle had more the appearance of a lighthearted chat among cronies. Shaw and Ms. Williams dared to be diggers. Journalism can be a dirty job but they did it without soiling themselves or CNN" (p. 3F).

Although the closing session of the RNC celebrated the party's nominees, critics wrote that the major TV network theme sang only of Quayle. Michael Oreskes of the *New York Times* reviewed how the Quayle story resulted in "a lost opportunity to use the convention to get a powerful Republican message out for Mr. Bush" (1988b, p. 10). Oreskes quoted Ed Rollins, manager of the 1984 Reagan-Bush campaign, to the effect that the "well-orchestrated convention plan . . . got stomped on." As additional evidence of the disrupted plan, Oreskes quoted Eddie Mahe, Jr., a GOP consultant, concerning a "time and opportunity lost."

Other media critics, however, in their columns following Thursday's session commented on the whole of the four-night extravaganza. As she had for the Democrats in Atlanta, Monica Collins of *USA Today* gave out awards: To David Brinkley of ABC for being "the commentator's commentator" who "just has a knack for the live confabs"; to Dan Rather, who Collins had found rigid in Atlanta, the "loose in the booth" and "most improved" awards—"confident, prepared, relaxed"; to Diane Sawyer for the "dumbest Quayle question"—namely, "Does your husband look like Robert Redford and do women lap that up?"; and the "bad vibes" award to the Superdome "because of the acreage of the stage, everyone appeared diminished instead of heightened by TV" (1988b, p. 3D). Ed Bark of the *Dallas Morning News,* proving there is no consensus on critical standards in judging political show biz, had other choices. His "toughest anchor interview" went to CNN's Bernard Shaw; best anchor-commentator "combo" to Brokaw and Chancellor of NBC; the "most overrated commentator" to Tom Shales *favorite,* David Brinkley, who is "a grab bag of generic insights" and "tends to dilute interviews"; "best camera work" to NBC; and "cleverest commentator" to Linda Ellerbee of CNN, "whether frivolous or fierce, unfailingly original." But, wrote Bark, let's drop "And so it goes" (1988g, p. 5C).

Again newsweeklies and watchdog groups published their critiques of the convention as a mini-series. Because of what it headlined "The Quayle Quagmire," *Time* ("Quayle Factor," 1988, p. 16) judged the convention as no triumph for Bush: "The New Orleans convention was supposed to reveal the real George Bush to the American electorate. In that it certainly succeeded, both for better and for worse" (p. 16). *U.S. News & World Report* asked if Bush could survive Quayle, and concluded that the Quayle flap derived from an intense media thirst for a TV spectacle. "Political conventions are hotbeds of bad rumors," wrote David Gergen. "There are too many reporters on hand—some 13,000 in this case—to cover too little news. . . . By late Thursday, the press reached a boiling point, and the Quayle story dominated television news" (1988, p. 27). *Newsweek* concurred: "The journalists were, in a word, bored. With the surprise choice of Quayle and the subsequent disclosures . . . there was at least something to report, stampede style" ("A Media," 1988, p. 26). The newsweekly reached no conclusion on the question, if convention orchestrators had done their job by preparing Quayle, would the "bored" reporters have had anything to report?

The Media Research Center (1988b) rated the four commercial TV networks' coverage using the same procedures applied to the Democratic convention. This time MRC ranked, in order of scores awarded each network, ABC first, followed by CNN, NBC, and CBS. Again MRC questioned the value of network coverage to the voter, bemoaning cut-aways from major speeches, the tendency of reporters and analysts (especially at CBS) to talk among themselves, and the fact that almost one-half of the 889 questions posed by the networks of interviewees over the four nights of prime time dealt with Senator Dan Quayle. Center for Media and Public Affairs findings indicated that of the total segments aired on the three major networks about Quayle, NBC had the highest proportion followed by CBS and ABC; however, of network evaluations of Quayle, CBS had the highest percentage of negative assessments. Overall, however, among network news sources and among reporters, evaluations of Bush and of Quayle were predominantly positive in spite of the furor over the selection of the vice-presidential nominee (Lichter & Lichter, 1988).

CONVENTION CRITICISM: ELEGIAC SOUNDS OF REFORM, BUT OF WHAT?

At a time when political parties were just beginning to grasp the significance of full orchestration of their conventions as media events, political scientist Karl O'Lessker (1969) reminded us that the convention is as much "campaign rally" as decision maker. That rally "is directed at two very different audiences: the party faithful, either present or watching at home, and the mass electorate" (p. 272). Media critics practice what Aristotle called *epideictic* discourse—that is, they praise or blame conventions as campaign rallies staged for the mass electorate, as well as media coverage of those rallies. In 1988 the orchestrated rallies of both Democrats and Republicans played to mixed reviews; so, too, did the star-studded, overly hyped, and advertised-based (12 to 16 percent of total convention airtime) prime-time spectacles of the four commercial TV networks.

One would assume that, by contrast, political critics would direct their praise and blame, not at the convention as a rally for the mass electorate, but as a rally for what O'Lessker called the "party faithful." With rare exception, however, such is not the case. They, too, critique conventions as spectacles orchestrated for mass audiences. This has been so since well before TV. Consider, for example, the acerbic political critic H. L. Mencken (1959) writing of the 1932 Democratic convention: "The evening session, in fact, had been postponed to nine o'clock to get a radio hookup and every fourth-rate local leader in the hall, male or female, tried for a crack at the microphone" (p. 207). A dozen years later TV was on the scene and Mencken felt compelled to describe the orchestration of the rally for the masses by relating, for example, the case of Andy Frain. Frain was a "crowd engineer" (with 17 years' experience in keeping order "among the frenzied horse-lovers who frequent the Kentucky Derby"). The GOP hired Frain to orchestrate the crowd of delegates at their 1948 convention, the first to be televised, albeit to limited areas. Frain organized a cadre of crowd controllers, "not made up of ward heelers and saloon loafers, as is commonly the case at national conventions, but of college men exclusively." He outfitted his cadre "in neat blue uniform coats and instructed them to wear dark trousers, white shirts and blue or black neckties." And, wrote Mencken, Frain provided these instructions:

No short-sleeved shirts or polo shirts will be allowed. Every usher must shave daily and see that his hair is trimmed. Do not slouch at your post. If you must smoke, do it out of public view. Our future president will be nominated in this hall. (Mencken, 1976, pp. 26–27)

What Mencken was describing was a process of glacial reform of the convention system. Democrats in 1932, Republicans in 1948—even before the nominations had been handed over to party primaries and caucuses— were *reforming* their convention rallies as much with an eye toward projecting their cordial consensus to mass audiences through broadcast technology as toward convening a deliberative gathering for the party faithful. The chanties of reform, then as now, derived from assumptions about the conventions *as media events rather than as political institutions.* (Frain, incidentally, was correct; a future president was nominated in that hall in Philadelphia. However, it was the Democrats' Harry Truman, not the Republicans' Thomas Dewey.)

As the final report and recommendations of the Commission on National Political Conventions (1990) attest, chanties of reform sing of improving conventions as media events rather than as political assemblies. The chorus responds to a lead refrain similar to that sung most clearly by political critic Nicholas von Hoffman:

the convention has ceased to have a political function [but] has its uses for journalism. . . . The mass media has . . . turned it into journalism's equivalent of the annual meeting of the Modern Language Society, where the nation's teachers of English come to look for jobs. . . . the national convention itself is a political and cultural lag, a government subsidized anachronism living on from the time of the Pullman car and the telegrapher's key. (1988, p. 27)

Not everyone who testified at commission hearings was so quick to dismiss party conventions as anachronisms. Yet in responding to Frank Fahrenkopf's task "to look at the political conventions, to determine whether or not they are still relevant," and to his commission co-chair Charles Manatt's invitation to "balance the competing needs of media in all different forms as well as those needs of our respective parties," speakers turned to their work chanting of party conventions primarily as media events not political happenings. Thus, GOP party chair, Lee Atwater, told the commission: "I do not particularly think our present system is fundamentally flawed; I do think, however, some improvements could be made." The media, he continued, "too often" cover conventions "in kind of perfunctory and almost unconscious ways." Instead, "I think the media ought to be more conscious sometimes about the symbolic nature of modern conventions and consider covering them somewhat in that light." For example, "Maybe if we could stop treating done deals as if they were novel events and get a better grip on what makes the American political party the animal it is, we could have a more useful definition of a convention"

(CNPC, 1989, p. 10). Lynn Cutler, vice-chair of the Democratic party, also took aim at how to improve media coverage and reach the mass electorate: "The question of timing of the convention during the course of the week, and using the weekends as a better vehicle, perhaps, for time to hold the convention, that more people would be able to see it" (CNPC, 1989, p. 16).

In its musical form the elegy is a mournful composition chanting plaintive cries of woe. Literary critic and social theorist Kenneth Burke (1939) writes of the elegiac as the "wailing wall" of discourse, a perfected technique rendering the complainer actually *content* with pessimistic anguish. Continues Burke, the elegiac

may serve well for individual trickeries in one's relation to the obligations of struggle—but if it becomes organized as a collective movement, you may feel sure that a class of people will arise to "move in on" it, exploiting it to the point where more and more good reasons for complaint are provided. (p. 44)

In many respects the hearings before the 1989 Commission on National Political Conventions had the tone of a collective movement. Speaker after speaker found more and more "good reasons for complaint" about the convention system. A leading voice singing elegiac chanties of reform was George Watson, Washington bureau chief and executive vice-president of ABC News. Apologizing for the absence of ABC News president Roone Arledge, Watson offered comments "which I think generally reflect his [Arledge's] views and those of ABC News about 1988, the conventions, politics, and television" (CNPC, 1989, p. 19). Pointing out things "which in our view are wrong" he began with a cause-and-effect relationship. The attempt of the political parties to make messages smoother and slicker "for the tube" may have little meaning for the voter: "Voter turnout is declining hand in hand with a decline in ratings for the conventions" (p. 20), a complaint he amplified at the close of his testimony; TV "helps us share a real national experience," but "people no longer want to share the political experience on TV because it isn't real. It is staged. It is manufactured." Falling just short of charging orchestrated conventions with the decline and fall of Western civilization, Watson concluded, "So they don't watch, they don't vote, and they don't care because they're not involved" (p. 25).

Watson's woeful chanty about the staging and manufacturing of conventions was, of course, not new. Roone Arledge had voiced it during the Democratic concert in Atlanta and, as we saw earlier, the refrain sounded in convention to convention from 1972 to 1984. Moreover, the leading lines of the elegiac composition appeared in 1988 in the sounds of instant critics, overnight reviews, and series reviews. "The Democrats had Garrison Keillor, the Republicans Tom Selleck," testified Watson, "the Democrats played Neil Diamond, the Republicans Lee Greenwood" (pp. 20–21). That a parade of such celebrities involves orchestration there is little doubt. But what Watson did *not* say, and what most critics of conventions as media or political events do *not* say, is that "ABC had Jennings and Brinkley, NBC had Brokaw and Chancellor, CNN had Shaw and Williams, and CBS had Rather and Rather" night after night in Atlanta and New Orleans; *network celebrities, not political events,* constituted the "news value" (Watson's term) of the 1988 DNC and RNC.

David Gergen of *U.S. News & World Report* also chose to, as Burke phrased it, "move in on" the elegiac chanty. Gergen acknowledged that it might be possible "to criticize the networks for the quality of their coverage"; but, he said, "the political parties have some responsibility to think about the quality of their presentations. Not the show-biz aspects of it" (CNPC, 1989, p. 99). Taking aim at the party conventions as political events he urged that a reason people "are not listening" is that "a lot of speakers do not have much to say" and "are not communciating serious thoughts or important points about the direction of the country they would like to see" (p. 99). A key reason for speakers without substance, thought Gergen, was the misconception that convention orators should limit their remarks to "five minutes, fifteen minutes at max." The 1984 Democractic convention, he argued, put the lie to that misconception. Both Mario Cuomo's keynote and Jesse Jackson's address were close to an hour in length, and "they attracted and held, not only the networks, but they held the televison audience." In fact, Jackson "actually gained audience during the time that he was speaking." The lesson? "Put people on the podium who actually have messages."

There was a lesson gleaned from the Jackson experience other than that Gergen found. Roz Wyman, the manager of the 1984 DNC, described the orchestration involved to capture a prime-time audience for the convention by *exploiting* Jackson's appearance. The DNC management staff and the Jackson management team negotiated at length on the timing of the speaker's address; Jackson supporters wanted assurances it would be in prime time. "My argument was," related Wyman, "we can get [that is, *create*] prime time that night. They [the networks] will not go off of Jesse Jackson, no matter what happens." Hence, "if we want to get a little extra prime time in, we put Jesse Jackson on the last schedule . . . for the last 15 or 20 minutes of the schedule." Concluded Wyman:

Now I must say they [the Jackson staff] were out in the trailer yelling at me, "Why is he not totally in prime time?" And I said, "Gentlemen, he will make prime time. They will stay.". . . And it was calculated on my part to put him on when we did. (CNPC, 1989, p. 133)

Was it, therefore, as Gergen said, the *political* message that attracted the alleged growth in Jesse Jackson's audience in 1984? Is that the lesson? Or, as Wyman hints, was it the calculated orchestration of taking Jackson—already a celebrity in his own right in 1984—and scheduling him as the star of the evening's *media* event? If so, is the lesson to strive for more wily, clever orchestration to, as Wyman put it, "see if you can get" the networks "to cover what you want them to cover" in the "contest" between party and media?

In any case, not every view of national conventions sounded at CNPC hearings had the elegiac tone that was the crescendo of the day. Hal Bruno of ABC News, for example, noted positive aspects of conventions as both political and media events. As a political reporter, he said, a convention "is a chance to see in person, and to talk to, the political leadership from all over the country—the city, county, state leaders," that, "in some cases, it is only every four years at the convention that we get to see them face to face" (CNPC, 1989, p. 95). Moreover, Bruno noted, there is more to a convention as a media event than network TV coverage. The needs and contributions of radio—"you have the time to almost commit journalism"—newsmagazines, and the daily press must also be recognized. And, significantly, there is local TV that emphasizes local political figures. "So the name of the game has changed," noted Bruno, "the local stations have become much more important to the political parties" and "that's pretty good, because that is where you win local/state election," through "the information that comes across from these stations" (pp. 112–13). Republican political consultant and manager of the 1984 Reagan-Bush campaign, Ed Rollins, noted that the "critical thing" about the convention is that "it is an opportunity to kick off a campaign effectively" (p. 65); Democratic consultant Bob Beckel added, "We need these conventions as parties. Leave television aside for a second. It is the only time where national parties come together, every four years, and a lot gets done" (p. 67). In short, although a muted motif, commission hearings offered the strains of an alternate view—namely, that *network coverage of conventions*, not the conventions themselves, *is the dinosaur*.

CRITICISM AS GUSH: THE BLIND MEN, THE DONKEY, AND THE ELEPHANT

A national party convention is a different performance for different critics. In some respects media and reformist critics are the fabled blind men with the (GOP?) elephant—or to be bipartisan, perhaps the Democratic donkey. One gets hold of the animal's leg and thinks it a tree, another the tail and thinks it is a rope, another the ear and believes it a leaf. Whether it be a convention of elephants or donkeys, TV critics regard the spectacle and showmanship, then review it as a *media* event. Working reporters focus on the *news* event, ever seeking a scoop, a byline, or an on-camera appearance. Network executives envision a *ratings* event, competing with sitcoms, docudramas, or soap operas. Political consultants capitalize on the *promotional* event to publicize the party and its candidates in a four-night political commercial. Party leaders ratify decisions at a once-every-four-year *business* event. And the party rank and file gather at a *celebration* event that makes of disparate factions a national institution.

Steven Aronson (1983) argues that "criticism, as it's practiced today, with few exceptions, is a form of hype"; he continues, "critics today mostly gush—daily, biweekly, monthly, quadrennially"; something that "is a gratifying activity, no doubt, but it is not an intellectually edifying one" (pp. 210–11). And what is it that critics of conventions hype? What is it they gush? Not conventions as democratic gatherings nor even as conveners of cordial concurrence. Instead they hype and gush what Burke called "individual trickeries": the tricks of party leaders for respectable standings in the polls and for financial contributions; of networks for higher TV ratings and advertising dollars; of anchors and correspondents for celebrity status; of instant critics for "insider" status; of media critics for headlined, bylined columns; of political pundits for visibility; and even of scholars for a TV appearance, a coveted journal article or book, and a sense of being "connected" with the movers and shakers outside the ivy walls of academe and "inside the beltway." For chanties of criticism the gratifying chorus is large, vocal, and often off-key.

Voices in Concert:
The Interinstitutional
Orchestration of Politics

Political, media, and reformist critics of contemporary convention orchestration differ in their complaints and in their proposed remedies. Uniting
them, however, is a fervent nostalgia for an earlier time when televised
conventions were full of fun, excitement, and doubt. If boarding a time
machine they might well choose the 1952 Democratic National Convention in Chicago, where spontaneity reigned (three ballots to nominate the
presidential candidate), network TV aired the drama on 18 million sets (all
of them black and white), viewers watched the intimate picture in record
numbers (60 million), and consumers endured scores of Westinghouse
(CBS), Philco (NBC), and Admiral (ABC) household appliance
commercials.

As Marty McFly discovered in the movie, going *Back to the Future* can
be shocking. What one thought once was, never was. In many respects the
nostalgia surrounding the spontaneity of the 1952 DNC ignores the orchestrated cordial concurrence of the gathering. To be sure, the nomination fight was exciting and made for marvelous television. After a second
ballot the outcome appeared in doubt. Tennessee senator Estes Kefauver,
who had campaigned and won in party primaries, led (362½ votes). The
reluctant candidate, Illinois governor Adlai Stevenson, having agreed after
many weeks to be considered, was a close second (324½). Senator Richard
Russell of Georgia (294 votes) and Averell Harriman of New York (121
votes) still harbored hopes. All the contenders were well short of the 611-
vote majority. Concurrence at all, let alone cordial, seemed unlikely—
most certainly not on a third ballot. However, party leaders had already
orchestrated two events that guaranteed Stevenson's victory. On a crucial
earlier roll-call vote over seating a Virginia delegation that opposed a

strong Democratic civil rights stand, the Illinois delegation threw its support behind the Virginia delegation 52 to 8. The vote came in spite of the pro–civil rights position of the Illinois delegation. "It suddenly dawned on us what was happening," said Stevenson's manager Jacob Arvey (Martin, 1977, p. 594). Kefauver and Harriman had struck a deal to pressure Southern delegations on civil rights to force a walkout. That would reduce the total convention vote, thus making it easier for Kefauver to win the party nomination. The convention seated Virginia with a 650½-vote majority, dealing Kefauver a defeat.

Yet if the Kefauver-Harriman alliance held, the outcome of the presidential roll call was still in doubt. For two ballots it held. During the first of those two ballots President Harry Truman boarded a plane in Washington for Chicago. A TV network used a split-screen picture to show the president's departure while simultaneously telecasting a vote in the Missouri delegation for Stevenson by Truman's alternate—a precisely orchestrated timing that served the interests of Stevenson, Truman, and the network (Martin, p. 597). Truman arrived in Chicago during the middle of the second ballot. Shortly afterwards he had dinner at the Stockyard Inn near the convention hall. Present were several party leaders—impresarios including Arvey, Speaker of the House and convention chair Sam Rayburn, and others. During the dinner a representative from Averell Harriman arrived. Harriman would withdraw, thus breaking with Kefauver, and support Stevenson. The switch didn't just happen. Earlier in the dinner recess Truman sent an emissary to Harriman requesting a withdrawal in favor of Stevenson. "The obedient Harriman, without notifying Kefauver as per their agreement, sent his already prepared statement" (Fontenay, 1980, p. 225).

As party leaders orchestrated the presidential roll-call drama, so too did they orchestrate TV network coverage. They had seen how the networks covered the GOP convention in Chicago two weeks earlier. Democratic impresarios capitalized on Republican mistakes and improved their own TV image. For one thing, the GOP barred all cameras from the party's national committee meeting; the chair of the DNC announced all party committee meetings would be open to the media; the Democrats, after all, were the "party of the people" (Reinsch, 1988, p. 64). Party leaders and professional consultants worked to "make sure all Democratic Convention speeches would carry a uniform theme" (Reinsch, p. 72). To improve the convention's telegenic features orchestrators located banners and signs with cameras, not delegates, in mind; painted floors, chairs, and benches gray to avoid a distracting glare on TV; synchronized musical numbers with the convention program; built a six-foot staircase to the podium so that speakers would appear to walk unrestrained and calmly to the microphones; opted against teleprompters for fear viewers at home could see them in use; and arranged for each TV network's studio to be high above and behind the convention rostrum, rather than removed from the hall. "And so ended," writes Reinsch, "the age of innocence in televised conventions" (p. 77).

ORCHESTRAL THEMES OF 1988: A REPRISE

Many an adult grown tired and weary, bored with the humdrum of daily life and disappointed at the narrowing opportunities that come with the "sunset" years, can recall memories of fleeting childhood, youth's innocence, and a time when "those were the days, my friend; we thought they'd never end." Collectively people do so in other ways. Watching a cherished film, say *Gone with the Wind*, elicits "they sure don't make 'em like they used to." And, why can't we return to "the golden days of television?" Or, "Where have you gone, Joe DiMaggio?" Where, indeed, are the shows of yesteryear? So, perhaps, critics of telepolitical conventions can be forgiven for dismissing the quadrennial conclaves as "dinosaurs." They ain't what they used to be, so dump 'em.

Reinsch is correct: the age of innocence is over. Why then remain innocent of how *lacking* in innocence party conventions have always been? More frequently than not convention concurrence, and its cordial tone, have been the norm of national party conventions from their conception in the 1830s. Single ballots and staged harmony did not arrive with the electronic era. Group-mediated, mass-mediated, and telepolitical conventions have always relied upon orchestral genius, not only for their success in selecting candidates capable of competing for the presidency but also for achieving a sense among party members, voters at large, and all Americans that *national parties exist*.

What has changed is that in preproduction, production, and postproduction phases convention orchestration has become a sophisticated, specialized, bureaucratic activity that seeks to coordinate a plurality of institutional forces. Party bosses no longer play the orchestral role they once did; professional convention managers and consultants do. Talented artists no longer freely declaim their oratorical arias from center stage; technicians schedule their appearances, draft their speeches, critique their rehearsals, style their hair, and make up their faces. Party leaders no longer stage their "show of shows" in full knowledge that TV networks will cover them; the networks obey their own commercial instincts, orchestrate their own productions, and largely ignore the party's convention (except to blame the parties for low Nielsen ratings). About all that hasn't changed is that convention critics continue doing what H. L. Mencken did—"damning politicians up hill and down dale . . . as rogues, and vagabonds, frauds, and scoundrels" (1956, p. 148).

Given what has remained the same over the years and what has changed in major ways, what can be summarized as the state of national party conventions in contemporary American telepolitics? Both critics and defenders of convention politics admit one convention accomplishment: it is the only gathering in one city, under one roof, at one time of representatives of local and state parties focusing upon party *qua* party matters as a national organization. That has always been the case, even in those years—as in 1948 with the Democrats—when party members bolted their convention. However, a telepolitical convention is a national gathering of more than elected and nonelected party representatives. It is also the only nationally televised conclave that brings diverse religious, racial, ethnic, and doctrinal party representatives into intense, intimate, and concentrated contact with candidates for office, and their organizations, at all levels; with elected and nonelected government officials of all levels; with professional political operatives and technicians; with working journalists of all types from every conceivable type of media in the nation and the world; with media moguls, executives, producers, directors, and technicians of all varieties and news organizations; and with critics, pressure-group spokespersons, protestors, entertainment celebrities, academicians, and a host of assorted political junkies, novices, groupies, and hangers-on.

A national party convention, in short, is a week-long hyped, publicized, televised spectacle that recognizes politics for what it is as currently practiced. In Bernard Crick's (1962) phrase, *"politics is politics"* [emphasis added]. *Politics* means "an aggregate of many members," representing "at least some tolerance of differing truths, some recognition that government is possible" in the "public actions of free men" (pp. 12–14). Teleconventions, in short, showcase what is normally a concealed side of the contemporary conciliation of interests, the "public actions of free men" as orchestrated not spontaneous.

In 1935 the Marx Brothers starred in a popular film, *A Night at the Opera.* Aspiring opera impresario Otis B. Driftwood (played by Groucho) wants a wealthy dowager (Margaret Dumont) to invest $200,000 in the New York Opera. In return he will "get her into society." Driftwood's employer, Herman Gottlieb (Sig Ruman) uses the money to hire a male lead to play opposite an opera starlette (played by Kitty Carlisle), thus giving the starlette's boyfriend (played by Allan Jones) no opportunity to compete for the lead or even to travel to New York with the opera company. In a sequence of predictably outlandish spoofs on opera, opera companies, and opera talent, Groucho contrives to get the money back, reunite the starlette and her boyfriend, and achieve his impresario ambitions. In the course of the movie, as with any film of the Marx Brothers, scenes unfold with seemingly no reason: Groucho and Chico agree on a contract by tearing it to shreds; Chico, Harpo, and Jones stow away on a transatlantic liner, later disguising themselves as famous bearded aviators expected to make public speeches; repairmen, stewards, maids, and assorted passengers crowd into Groucho's cramped stateroom; a furniture shifting scene to fool a detective; a madcap operatic performance featuring Harpo destroying the scenery; and a rendition of "Alone" by Carlisle and Jones.

The film's writer, George S. Kaufman, used an operatic technique, the leitmotif, to satirize opera. A running gag features the signing of a binding contract for talent and the performance, much like the numerous contracts that convention impresarios sign with other orchestrators, and that candidates undertake when they make promises in their acceptance speeches. In negotiating the contracts Driftwood simply deletes portions that not all parties agree to by tearing off each strip of paper from the contract that bears an offending clause. By the end of negotiations nothing is left of the original contract but strips of paper scattered across the floor. Everyone can now conduct operatic business as one pleases.

In teleconvention politics the various cooperative and competing interests that gather at the convention site for the week-long spectacular are akin to the shreds of a Driftwood contract. In the preproduction phase each set of partisan, media, professional, technical, and other interests that assemble for the convention has its shredded clause from four years ago scattered separate from others on the floor. Convention impresarios reassemble and rip, reassemble and rip, and reassemble throughout the whole of preproduction. Party impresarios run into a problem faced by impresario Herman Gottlieb, Driftwood's employer, in *A Night at the Opera*. After but a few bars of the overture to Verdi's *Il Trovatore* the orchestra suddenly breaks into "Take Me Out to the Ball Game." Driftwood and his pals have secretly placed the score within the pages of Verdi's music. Similarly, when the curtain rises on a national convention, party impresarios feverishly repair the unforeseen consequencs of shredding by a seemingly endless array of Grouchos, Chicos, and Harpos that televise the production, or that critique each night's performance after the fact.

Success at orchestrating cordiality, at least as judged by print and electronic journalists, is always in doubt even though concurrence on the party nominee is not. We have seen in Chapters 5 and 6 that detailed analyses of 1988 national party convention coverage content, and of televised coverage of the 1984 conventions as well, reveal that the TV networks' "nights at the opera" differ from the political parties' and from one another. The parties may set out to stage a four-night, tightly scripted, closely knit extravaganza, a mini-series in the fashion of Richard Wagner's operatic *Ring* cycle, but the networks have other orchestral forms in mind.

For example, true to its aims as a public affairs network, C-SPAN offered live, gavel-to-gavel coverage of the convention's podium activities. Yet as C-SPAN's cameras moved around the hall, and as they covered major addresses, the network provided not a four-night musical drama but an oratorio with features of the earliest forms of a Lutheran chorale. The oratorio, a dramatic but *unstaged* telling of a biblical or religious story, emphasizes solo singers, a chorus, and the orchestra. There is no dramatic action as such, no elaborate scenery or costuming. In early Lutheran chorales there were no efforts to conduct rhythm. C-SPAN's coverage, without anchors or correspondents, offered only solo speakers, occasional tunes from the orchestra, and a chorus of delegates—not in close harmony with the speakers but as a crowd separate and apart from speakers presented in bust shots or as talking heads. Action-reaction, not speaker-delegate reciprocity made up the C-SPAN oratorio chorale.

By contrast, anchor-booth chit-chat, continuing exchanges between anchors and floor correspondents, and the interactive camera coverage of speakers and delegates yielded for ABC a soloist recitative convention. Each performer sang away; an overall score permitted soloists to blend together as if instructed to "follow the bouncing ball." The melodic line was elementary, rising and falling as each anchor, correspondent, interviewed delegate, speaker, or other performer chimed in. The resulting production was comforting, troubling, or dull depending upon each viewer's taste, much like a movie-goer might find the piano and harp solos by Chico and Harpo Marx, respectively, either a treat or frustrating intrusion on the story line.

CBS's coverage enacted a conducted chorus. Just as a conductor keeps musicians and singers together by beating out the pulse of the music with baton or hands, CBS favored tight podium shots of speakers from a variety of angles. With considerable frequency, anchor Dan Rather's baton beat out the rhythm of convention events, floor correspondents' reports, and analysts' commentaries. Camera angles of speakers hovering over delegates, Rather hovering over the floor, and correspondents peering up at the CBS anchor, emphasized the conductor's role. It calls to mind a scene in *A Night at the Opera* when the mayor of New York City introduces the three bearded aviators, then interrupts by commenting on presence, appearance, and remarks. Moreover, in a conducted chorus the leader begins with a light warning beat to indicate to musicians and singers what the tempo of the performance is to be. Rather's openings of prime-time broadcasts constituted such a warning beat, setting the theme and tempo of the evening; his voice accompaniment to major addresses, floor demonstrations, interviews, and floor proceedings proved he possesses a key capacity of any conductor—to get the singer to sing a theme or motif the way *the conductor* wants it to sound.

The "network of record," CNN, gives viewers neither a chorale in the form of C-SPAN's gavel-to-gavel coverage nor CBS's conducted chorus. As in the Marx Brothers's *A Night at the Opera*, CNN's convention coverage features a large cast of performers (the anchors, floor correspondents, analysts, celebrities, interviewed delegates and party notables, focus group participants, etc.). A multitude of sequences and segments constitute the telecast—from the convention floor, podium, news anchor booth, interview booth, to candidate headquarters, downtown, and elsewhere.

They often have no apparent relationship to one another or to any over-arching coverage motifs. And during addresses numerous shots of delegates, quick cuts, and close-ups yield a sense viewers are peering through the porthole into Otis B. Driftwood's overcrowded stateroom, everyone singing and yelling, but with no discernible or harmonious purpose. For CNN a convention is an aggregation of countless singers not always on the same page of the hymnal.

Finally, NBC presents viewers an organum harmony, much like a Gregorian chant. In organum harmony tenor voices (in NBC's case the network anchors) sing a chant melody; another group (the NBC floor correspondents) sing the same melody; finally performers (anchors and correspondents) harmonze on the tune. NBC achieves the same effect in its camera coverage: very tight facial and head shots of speakers combine with quick cuts to similar shots of individual delegates to put speakers and delegates in organum harmony. Like the opera starlette and her boyfriend in *A Night at the Opera* harmonizing on the aria "Alone," a sense of unity to convention coverage and to the convention derives from what might otherwise appear to be as zany as most of everything else in a Marx Brothers's film.

THE FUTURE OF CONVENTION ORCHESTRATION AND COVERAGE

There is certainly no guarantee that each party's convention in 1992 will be orchestrated as it was in 1988, or that convention coverage of each network will follow the motifs apparent in 1984 and 1988. For example, the 1988 DNC may offer a poor guide to the future of Democratic party gatherings. There are several reasons for this. There is, for example, the party's tendency to change convention impresarios every four years. This results in the absence of an institutional memory for DNC planning. (Arleigh Greenblat's computerized program budgets and blueprints, stored away in DNC archives, may gather dust.) And there remains a reluctance, or perhaps an impossibility, for the DNC to guarantee thematic continuity in the telepolitical age, in spite of the practice, recalled from Reinsch's account, of doing so that Democrats *originated* in the 1952 DNC. Moreover, given the dissatisfaction expressed by TV executives with steadily declining viewer ratings, the musical-political productions of the networks may be scaled back and changed entirely. Finally, if the parties and networks heed the calls of reformist critics for change, 1988 may have been the close of a brief teleconvention era. Let us explore, in turn, what the parties might do, what networks might undertake, and what reformers recommend.

The party orchestrators interviewed for this study had the opportunity to talk about what the future holds for national conventions in the remainder of this century and beyond. They speculated a great deal about how television coverage might change and how the parties could adjust to shifting conditions. None seemed particularly concerned about a reduction in network coverage. Mike Miller, experienced RNC communications coordinator, said, "I think the networks will cut back some of their presence, physically, but probably not their airtime. . . . As long as they [conventions] are around, they will be covered and covered well." Don Fowler, 1988 Democratic CEO, thought otherwise: "Short of a deadlocked convention, I think the networks are going to give the parties even less time than they did in 1988, and that will make the parties search around to find new and better ways to make an impression on the public; I'm certain there will be less live coverage." Be the orchestrators Republican or Democrat, however, there was a consensus, perhaps best stated by the GOP's Mark Goode. Whatever the networks do,

we still have to go on about our business and nominate our candidate. And we have to do everything we can to give him the broadest and most favorable exposure during the convention week, and we got to do our best of directing those. Obviously the way to do that is not the same as it was in 1968 and 1972. Times have changed. We've taken a lot for granted that we no longer can.

One thing both parties plan is to continue, perhaps expand, their own TV networks. Owing to costs, the parties will probably exploit their satellite networks differently. The DNC's Mike McCurry questions the value of gavel-to-gavel Convention Satellite News Service telecasts based upon follow-up conversations he had with local TV station managers across the nation after 1988: "They all reported that the utility of a gavel-to-gavel feed would not have been great; so that has convinced me that in '92 we ought to continue to offer satellite time for our own newsmakers." Paul Byers, after directing the CSNS in 1988, said that any more elaborate CSNS programming in the future would require more facilities, more personnel, and an increase in the budget "exponentially." There could be two simultaneous feeds, one gavel-to-gavel and one for interviews. Economics did not permit that in 1988; he questioned if they would in 1992: "It would be wonderful if each party had its own floor apparatus and could at the drop of a hat do whatever it wanted and stations could pick and choose. That's not going to happen. Dollars and sense are just not there to do that."

Expansion for the RNC Network, implied Mark Goode, will probably occur, depending upon the costs of satellite time and on plans for vote targeting. From 1984 to 1988 the number of home satellite dishes in the nation grew considerably, and the costs of buying satellite time decreased. In 1988 the RNC Network took advantage of such changes to target convention broadcasts in Spanish to Hispanic areas. The party may do so for other language groups in the 1990s. Moreover, if current projections are correct, the growth in the number of home satellite dishes will not abate soon. In fact, direct-broadcast satellite television (DBS)—bouncing programs off satellite dishes to home receivers—is likely to flourish. Beginning in 1993, for example, the arrival of Ku-band frequencies holds out the possiblities for $300 dishes of small size (9 to 14 inches) capable of receiving 256 or more channels. Satellite corporations such as Sky Cable, K Prime Partners, and TVN Entertainment, Inc., are already planning to exploit DBS for entertainment programming. As home satellite receivers increase in the 1990s, both parties may consider direct telecasts to homes, thus off-setting reduced coverage by the commercial networks, not to mention avoiding competition from TV networks more concerned with staging their own convention productions than in covering party activities.

It is also likely that both parties will cater increasingly to local TV stations and to group enterprises (CONUS, Potomac, etc.) in convention programming. Party orchestrators disagree about whether such coverage itself will expand: the Democrats' Terry Michael sees "no large increase in local television news coverage in the 1992 convention," for 1988 probably "reached a saturation point"; by contrast, the GOP's Mike Miller thinks that local and group coverage "will grow." In any event, both parties will meet cutbacks in network coverage by continuing what Mike McCurry said the Democrats did in 1988 for the locals—"bent over backwards to try to get them access . . . upped significantly the number of floor passes that we gave to those reporters . . . tried to give them better and more work space."

Regardless of future network coverage the two parties plan to put on their own production, orchestrate coverage, and promote it. Said the RNC's Mark Goode:

In the modern sense you need the capabilities to be able to deliver production techniques and create those things which enhance what you're doing. If those production touches are tastefully done—it's funny to call a political convention tasteful—you need some fun . . . you need some music, you need some confetti, or balloon drops, and need some films or floor demonstrations just to keep people alive and interested, and keep juices flowing. You need to have people who have the experience and capability to deliver those sorts of things and to deliver them in a professional manner. But you should never engage in doing them just for the sake of doing them. You don't want to become all glitz and glamour, and overwhelm substance, because that isn't what political conventions are about.

And if Mike McCurry has his way (which is unlikely since he is no longer with the DNC), the effectiveness of production techniques and of the production itself will be continuously measured, with adjustments made as the show progresses:

I would like to see what a lot of the networks are now doing, a nightly tracking poll. I would like to use polling to see how our show is being received by the American people, so we can feed back some things if we need to take care of a problem. . . . I know in 1992 I suspect we'll be in a much better position to have a finger on the pulse as the convention goes along to see what people are thinking about this show that we are putting on, and what's getting through to the public.

TV network orchestrators, as might be expected, do not share the view of the future that party orchestrators voice. NBC's Joe Angotti thinks both the networks and the parties are to blame for declining viewer ratings. Taking pride in his network's "systematic approach" that "didn't rely on spontaneous kinds of stories on the floor," Angotti noted that the audience for NBC's 1988 convention did not decline but *increased* from 1984. So network orchestration is important. Too much party orchestration, however, is a problem: "They are trying to make a television extravaganza out of the convention; they are organizing them too much; they are too slick; and they are not exciting enough." Saying that he believed "contested conventions are still possible," Angotti was reluctant to predict cutbacks in future network coverage: "I think it is important that we stay as flexible as possible." ABC's Justin Friedland was more certain:

There will be cutbacks. Unless the conventions become again a vital decision-making event in the political life of the party, I can see the day when we might send a bunch of camera crews and cover it like a dead story, from 11 to 11:30, do an expanded "Nightline" on it, do highlights in one hour of what it took the Democrats three hours to do. We will cut out the dance numbers, cut out Garrison Keillor and cute kids reading postcards, patriotic numbers. It will save us a lot of money.

Jane Maxwell of CNN foresaw problems if networks cut back convention coverage. Granted, "one of these days when they don't have the money that they want to spend in that way, then what's going to happen? The networks are going to pull back." When they do, the parties may take over total control of the news event. She pondered, "Does it mean they are going to say like NASA [National Aeronautics and Space Administration], you can have only *x* number of cameras in the hall, you are going to have only two cameras in the hall, you are going to take our feed or we will not allow you to have cameras in the hall?" She said, "They could possibly do that; I mean they could try it. It is something I would fight. I wouldn't want to cover their produced feeding."

And there is another possibility. A few reformist critics have proposed that the TV networks rotate, or parcel out among themselves, convention coverage. Thus, one network might cover opening night, another keynote night, a third nomination night, and a fourth acceptance night. Or "reduce the coverage to one network," for "now that the conventions have become a form of mass entertainment, there is no reason why they should monopolize all three networks" (Kendall, 1990, p. 23). Or "one could take a shot at airing only a 10 to 11 P.M. EDT summary each night" and "another do mostly prepared analytical pieces about the issues and in-depth reports about the candidates and their positions" (Womack, 1990, p. 27). However, here too are difficulties. In the popular film *Field of Dreams* was the phrase, "Build it and he will come," meaning that if the lead character would build a baseball field in a cornpatch, his long dead father would appear. In a nation addicted to TV there might be another phrase, "Construct a spectacle and TV will cover it." Not only will TV networks cover it, they will bid against one another for the exclusive right to do so. In 1986 ABC paid $10 million for exclusive rights to cover the Fourth of July rededication of the Statue of Liberty, billed as "Liberty Weekend." That left CBS, CNN, and NBC with opportunities for partial coverage, summary, and special reports. ABC proved to be the winner in audience ratings (a 42 share on July 4) and a winner in dollars (each dollar spent on exclusive rights paid off with $3 in advertising revenue). If the commercial networks insist on arguing that the national party conventions are now *entertainment*, not news events, and thereby, to use Jane Maxwell's phrase, "pull back," what is to keep the two parties from moving toward "Liberty Weekend" extravaganzas and taking network bids for exclusive coverage? Would not ABC, or any of the other networks, willing in 1986 to risk an investment in exchange for a 42 audience share—*less* than the audience share of 1988 combined network coverage—jump at the opportunity? Perhaps each political party should encourage the commercial networks in any plans to reduce live convention coverage, air party business via satellite telecasts, and design a sideshow that entertainment networks could bid to cover exclusively—a sure-fire money raiser and promotional gimmick.

Reformist critics testifying before the Commission on National Political Conventions (recall Chapter 7) repeatedly reminded members of the possibilities for TV network cutbacks in convention coverage, even proposing alternatives such as rotation coverage and specialized segment coverage. In its final report the commission recommended that convention coverage be improved by actions that would, in effect, *reduce* televised convention coverage. First, "although continuing to encourage gavel-to-gavel coverage, the Commission recommends that the Democratic and Republican parties consider compressing the convention schedule to *four* days and *three* nights." Second, the Commission recommended that networks reallocate the three hours coverage that would normally go into prime-time coverage the fourth night "for use by the political parties to address the voting public in the fall" (CNPC, 1990, p. 11). There were two sets of dissents from the commission's recommendations. TV journalists Ken Bode and Marvin Kalb dissented on grounds that to cut back to three nights would be "futher evidence that as an institution, the modern convention has less business to do and is less worthy of continued press coverage" (p. 11). Four other commission members, including Bill Phillips who managed the 1988 GOP gathering, noted that conventions serve purposes unrelated to TV and should not be abbreviated. And as far as TV is concerned,

The media seems [sic] not to have developed beyond those halcyon days when the drama happened on the floor of the conventions and was easy to cover. We believe that the network "stars" might spend less time in their cubicle, portable living rooms interviewing each other and more time searching for the real news which tends, for various reasons, to happen backstage these days. Conventions almost always occur at a time of change in the party and of shifting in its dominant ideas. Drama and intrigue are still there. To shorten the period is, we think, an admission that conventions are purely media events. They are not. (p. 11)

THE INTERINSTITUTIONAL MEDIATION OF CONVENTION REALITIES

National party conventions are, of course, both political and media events. They are, depending upon one's perspective, also news events, entertainment events, promotional events, business meetings, trade shows, rituals, celebrations, and commercial enterprises. The perspective of this study has been upon something else—namely, conventions as orchestrated events—the orchestration of cordial concurrence. We have seen that they have been such events from their beginnings in the early days of the Republic. They have remained so through their group-mediated and mass-mediated eras of development. They are even more so in the contemporary telepolitical age.

Today the term *national party conventions* is a misnomer. We have seen in previous chapters that conventions involve the concurrence of far more numerous institutions than those that make up the membership of what people know as "the Democrats" or "the Republicans." To be sure, present are the party leaders, notables, celebrities, and rank and file. Present also are the candidates—winners and losers—and their entourages. So, too, are party technical consultants—for media, fund-raising, vote targeting, speechwriting, bite control, spin control, and damage control. With these campaign technicians are the professionals specializing in conventions—managers, entertainment directors, communication liaisons, publicity personnel, satellite network producers, even specialists in seat arrangements, balloon drops, demonstration choreographers, and "hand-painted sign" artists.

Joining this diversified company of party members, campaigners, and production personnel are representatives of nonparty institutions. From the host city are both government and private groups with a stake in the convention. There are also the superintendents and workers of the House and Senate galleries—for press, radio/TV, periodicals, and photographers. These professionals represent their own institutions, and thereby the federal government that pays their salaries, yet act as go-betweens for the political parties and the news media. And what a pluralist and diversified institutional complex are the news media! Represented are the print press—the dailies, weeklies, monthlies; newspapers, newsmagazines, and journals of opinion; publications of international, national, metropolitan, local, and county-wide circulation. Omnipresent in the hall are the broadcast media—radio and TV; network, cable, and satellite; international, national, group, and local. A national political convention reminds one of the line from the film *Casablanca*, "Everybody comes to Rick's café"; everybody comes to the spectacle, not just the partisans.

Since the publication of Walter Lippmann's *Public Opinion* (1922) it has become a truism that, politically, people reside in a "secondhand reality," a world derived not of their direct, firsthand, daily experience with politics but one constructed for them by various accounts of happenings. At times these secondhand experiences flow from the discourse, gossip, and rumor of their everyday transactions—with friends, loved ones, co-workers, colleagues, and like members of organized groups. This is the group-mediated political reality akin to the early days of party conventions. At other times these borrowed political realities originate in accounts contained in mass communication—the news, public discourse, entertainment, and so on. Such are the politics associated with the mass-mediated era of party conventions.

There is a pronounced tendency among many who criticize and some who defend national political conventions to assume that the convention remains, or should be, party dominated—that for most citizens convention politics is, or should be, group mediated. Other critics and proponents alike argue that the political realities of party conventions are mass mediated through the filters of party and media consultants, the press, and broadcast journalists. Neither viewpoint fully captures the character of the secondhand realities of teleconvention politics. To borrow a phrase from Jesse Jackson's 1988 address before the DNC, "It's more profound than that." Telepolitical realities can be reduced neither to group nor mass mediation. They are the shifting political impressions derived from interinstitutional mediation, a mediation constructed from the orchestral acts of the vast array of institutional players sketched out in this volume. We have emphasized that party, governmental, media, and technical impresarios agree, disagree, argue, cajole, and negotiate to orchestrate the show and the spectacle that is a telepolitical convention. But it is more than a dinosaur being resurrected every four years; more than a party being refreshed for electoral battle; and more than an audience-driven vaudeville being staged. Politics is happening: the orchestration of shifting alliances of a plurality of powerful institutions, and the interinstitutional mediation for citizens of what is real and illusory in their political worlds. Abolish the convention and you remove not the relic of an extinct species, or even a showcase for the national parties or networks, or the legerdemain of technological wizards. Abolish conventions and you lose instead something of vaster consequence—the single, longest running production still in existence that, in a concentrated period on a single stage, showcases a microcosm of all that *is* American politics.

References

BOOKS

Adorno, T. W. (1976). *Introduction to the sociology of music.* New York: Seabury Press.

Aronson, S. M. L. (1983). *Hype.* New York: William Morrow & Co.

Bain, R. C. (1960). *Convention decisions and voting records.* Washington: Brookings Institution.

Bain, R. C., & Parris, J. (1973). *Convention decisions and voting records* (2nd ed.). Washington: Brookings Institution.

Barzun, J. (1941). *Darwin, Marx, and Wagner.* New York: Little, Brown, & Co.

Becker, S. L., & Lower, E. W. (1977). Broadcasting in presidential campaigns. In S. Kraus (Ed.), *The great debates* (pp. 25–55). Bloomington: Indiana University Press.

Bell, D. V. J. (1975). *Power, influence, and authority.* New York: Oxford University Press.

Bickel, A. M. (1968). *The new age of political reform: The electoral college, the convention, and the party system.* New York: Harper & Row.

Bishop, J. B. (1916). *Presidential nominations and elections: A history of American conventions, national campaigns, inaugurations and campaign caricature.* New York: Charles Scribner's Sons.

Blankenship, J. (1976). The search for the 1972 Democratic nomination: A metaphorical perspective. In J. Blankenship and H. Stelzner (Eds.), *Rhetoric and Communication* (pp. 236–60). Urbana, IL: University of Illinois Press.

Bornoff, J. (1968). *Music theater in a changing society.* New York: UNESCO.

Broder, D. (1985). The presidential nominating process. In K. W. Thompson (Ed.), *The presidential nominating process,* vol. 4 (pp. 3–10). New York: University Press of America.

Bruce, H. R. (1927). *American parties and politics: History & role of political parties in the United States.* New York: Henry Holt & Company.

Burke, K. (1939). *Attitudes toward history*. Berkeley, CA: University of California Press.

Burns, J. M. (1967). *The deadlock of democracy*. Englewood Cliffs: Prentice-Hall.

Byrne, G. C., & Marx, P. (1976). *The great American convention: A political history of presidential elections*. Palo Alto: Pacific Books, Publishers.

Chambers, W. N. (1963). *Political parties in a new nation: The American experience, 1776–1809*. New York: Oxford University Press.

Chase, J. S. (1973). *Emergence of the nominating convention, 1789–1832*. Urbana, IL: University of Illinois Press.

_____. (1974). *The national party convention: Retrospect and prospect*. St. Charles: Forum Press.

Chicago Tribune. (1892). *The Chicago Tribune's history of the national conventions of both parties*. Chicago: J.M.U. Jones Stationery & Printing Company.

Cook, R. (1976). *National nominating conventions*. Washington: CQ Press.

Corse, S. (1987). *Opera and the users of language*. Rutherford: Fairleigh Dickinson University Press.

Cotter, C., & Hennessy, B. (1964). *Politics without power: The national party committees*. New York: Atherton Press.

Crick, B. (1962). *In defense of politics*. Chicago: University of Chicago Press.

David, P. T., Goldman, R. M., & Bain, R. C. (1960a). *The politics of national party conventions*. Washington: Brookings Institution.

_____. (1960b). *The politics of national party conventions*. Washington: Brookings Institution (condensed paperback edition).

Davis, J. W. (1972). *National conventions: Nominations under the big top*. Woodbury, New York: Barron's.

_____. (1983). *National conventions in an age of party reform*. Westport, CT: Greenwood Press.

Eaton, H. (1964). *Presidential timber: A history of nominating conventions, 1868–1960*. New York: Free Press of Glencoe.

Edelman, M. (1988). *Constructing the political spectacle*. Chicago: University of Chicago Press.

Ewen, D. (1972). *Opera: Its story told through the lives and works of its foremost composers*. New York: Franklin Watts.

Farber, D. R. (1988). *Chicago '68*. Chicago: University of Chicago Press.

Fontenay, C. L. (1980). *Estes Kefauver: A biography*. Knoxville, TN: University of Tennessee Press.

Foote, J., & Rimmer, T. (1983). The ritual of convention coverage in 1980. In W. Adams (Ed.), *Television coverage of the 1980 presidential campaign* (pp. 68–88). Norwood, NJ: Ablex.

Herring, P. (1940). *The politics of democracy*. New York: W. W. Norton & Company.

Hesseltine, W. B., & Fisher, R. G. (1961). *Trimmers, trucklers, and temporizers: Notes of Murat Halstead from the political conventions of 1856*. Madison: State Historical Society of Wisconsin.

Joyce, E. M. (1988). *Prime times, bad times*. New York: Doubleday.

Katz, R. (1986). *Divining the powers of music: Aesthetic theory and the origins of opera*. New York: Pendragon Press.

Kerman, J. (1956). *Opera as drama*. New York: Alfred A. Knopf.

Key, V. O. (1964). *Politics, parties, and pressure groups* (5th ed). New York: Thomas Y. Crowell Company.

Knapp, J. M. (1972). *The magic of opera*. New York: Harper & Row.

Lang, G. E., & Lang, K. (1983). *The battle for public opinion*. New York: Columbia University Press.

Lang, K., & Lang, G. E. (1959). The mass media and voting. In E. Burdick & A. J. Brodbeck (Eds.), *American voting behavior* (pp. 217–35). Glencoe, IL: Free Press.

Lippmann, W. (1922). *Public opinion*. New York: McGraw-Hill.

Marshall, T. R. (1981). *Presidential nominations in a reform age*. New York: Praeger.

Martin, J. B. (1977). *Adlai Stevenson of Illinois*. New York: Anchor Books.

Martin, R. G. (1964). *Ballots & bandwagons*. New York: Rand McNally.

Martorella, R. (1982). *The sociology of opera*. New York: Praeger.

McKee, T. H. (1906). *The national conventions and platforms of all major parties*. Baltimore: Friedenwald Co.

McNamee, G. (1926). *You're on the air*. New York: Harper.

Mencken, H. L. (1932). *Making a president*. New York: Alfred A. Knopf.

_____. (1956). *A Mencken crestomathy*. New York: Alfred A. Knopf.

_____. (1959). *The vintage Mencken* (J. C. Goulden, Ed.). New York: Vintage Books.

_____. (1976). *Mencken's last campaign* (J. C. Goulden, Ed.). Washington: New Republic Book Co.

Meyer, E. C. (1902). *Nominating systems: Direct primaries versus conventions in the United States*. Madison: Published by the author.

Murray, R. K. (1976). *The 103rd ballot: Democrats and the disaster in Madison Square Garden*. New York: Harper & Row.

O'Lessker, K. (1969). The national nominating convention. In C. P. Cotter (Ed.), *Political parties in the United States* (pp. 239–75). Boston: Allyn & Bacon.

Ostrogorski, M. (1902). *Democracy and the organization of political parties, vol. II* (F. Clarke, Trans.). New York: Macmillan.

Parris, J. (1972). *Political party platforms, rhetoric or reality*. Washington: Center for Information on America.

Pomper, G. (1963). *Nominating the president*. Evanston: Northwestern University Press.

Pomper, G. M., & Lederman, S. S. (1980). *Elections in America*. New York: Longman.

Reeves, R. (1977). *Convention*. New York: Harcourt Brace Jovanovich.

Reinsch, J. L. (1988). *Getting elected*. New York: Hippocrene Books.

Roelofs, M. (1967). *The language of modern politics*. Homewood, IL: Dorsey Press.

Schattschneider, E. E. (1942). *Party government*. New York: Holt, Rinehart and Winston.

Shafer, B. E. (1988). *Bifurcated politics: Evolution and reform in the national party convention*. Cambridge: Harvard University Press.

Stoddard, H. L. (1938). *It costs to be president*. New York: Harper & Brothers.

_____. (1948). *Presidential sweepstakes: The story of political conventions and campaigns* (F. W. Leary, Ed.). New York: G. P. Putnam's Sons.

Stout, J. A., Jr., & Rollins, P. C. (1976). *Convention articles of Will Rogers*. Stillwater: Oklahoma State University Press.

Thomson, C. A. H. (1956). *Television and presidential politics: The experience in 1952 and the problems ahead*. Washington: Brookings Institution.

Tillet, P. (1962). *Inside politics: The national conventions, 1960*. Dobbs Ferry, NY: Oceana Publications, Inc.

Twain, M. (1924). *Autobiography.* New York: Harper & Row.

ACADEMIC PERIODICALS

Adams, W. C. (1985). Convention coverage. *Public Opinion, 7*(6), 43–48.

Brown, W. R. (1969). Television and the Democratic National Convention of 1968. *Quarterly Journal of Speech, 55,* 237–46.

Carleton, W. G. (1957). The revolution in the presidential nominating convention. *Political Science Quarterly, 72,* 224–40.

Carlson, J. M., & Martin, R. M. (1987). Conceptions of representation: A study of delegates to the 1984 national party conventions. *American Politics Quarterly, 15,* 355–71.

Fant, C. H. (1980). Televising presidential conventions, 1952–1980. *Journal of Communication, 30*(1), 130–39.

Farrell, T. B. (1978). Political conventions as legitimation ritual. *Communication Monographs, 56,* 55–58.

Gleiber, D. W., & King, J. D. (1987). Party rules and equitable representation: The 1984 Democratic National Convention. *American Politics Quarterly, 15,* 107–21.

Hall, P. M. (1972). A symbolic interactionist's analysis of politics. *Sociological Inquiry, 42,* 51–54.

Henry, D. (1988). The rhetorical dynamic of Mario Cuomo's 1984 keynote address: Situation, speaker, metaphor. *Southern Speech Communication Journal, 53,* 105–20.

Lichter, S. R., & Lichter, L. S. (1988). Covering the convention coverage. *Public Opinion, 11,* 41–44.

Lower, E. W. (1968). Broadcasting the conventions: A choice. *Journal of Broadcasting, 13,* 224.

McAndrew, W. R. (1968). Broadcasting the conventions. *Journal of Broadcasting, 13,* 213–18.

McGregor, E. B., Jr. (1978). Uncertainty and national nominating coalitions. *Journal of Politics, 40,* 1011–42.

Morison, S. E. (1911). The first national nominating convention. *American Historical Review, 17,* 744–63.

Nimmo, D. (1986). Unconventional coverage. *Campaigns & Elections, 7,* 52–55.

Paletz, D. L., & Elson, M. (1976). Television coverage of presidential conventions: Now you see it, now you don't. *Political Science Quarterly, 91,* 109–31.

Pomper, G. M. (1979). New rules and new games in presidential nominations. *Journal of Politics, 41,* 784–805.

Reinsch, J. L. (1968). Broadcasting the political conventions. *Journal of Broadcasting, 13,* 219–23.

Reiter, H. L. (1980). Party factionalism: National conventions in the new era. *American Politics Quarterly, 8,* 303–18.

Ries, A., & Trout, J. (1983, March 14). The eye vs. the ear. *Advertising Age,* M-27.

Smith, L. D. (1988). Narrative styles in network coverage of the 1984 nominating conventions. *Western Journal of Speech Communication, 52,* 63–74.

Waltzer, H. (1966). In the magic lantern: Television coverage of the 1964 national conventions. *Public Opinion Quarterly, 30,* 49–52.

Weiss, P. (1988). Party time in Atlanta. *Columbia Journalism Review, 27,* 27–34.

Womack, D. (1985). Live ABC, CBS, and NBC interviews during three Democratic conventions. *Journalism Quarterly, 62,* 838–44.

_____. (1986). Status of news sources interviewed during presidential conventions. *Journalism Quarterly, 63,* 331–36.

_____. (1988). Live TV interviews at the 1984 GOP convention. *Journalism Quarterly, 65,* 1006–9.

_____. (1989). Live television interviews at the 1988 Democratic convention. *Journalism Quarterly, 66,* 670–74.

JOURNALISTIC PERIODICALS

Adams, M. (1988, October). Republicans party hearty. *Successful Meetings,* pp. 97–99.

Apple, R. W. (1988, July 17). Democrats take their convention to city symbolic of old and new south. *New York Times,* p. 11.

Bark, E. (1988a, July 18). Business vs. show business: Networks cool to producers' orchestration. *Dallas Morning News,* p. 2F.

_____. (1988b, July 18). Channel 4's first live report fails to connect. *Dallas Morning News,* p. 3F.

_____. (1988c, July 19). Early NBC interviews toss aside competitors. *Dallas Morning News,* p. 3F.

_____. (1988d, August 16). Networks bite—hook, line and receiver. *Dallas Morning News,* p. 5F.

_____. (1988e, August 17). CNN beats TV's big 3 to the big news. *Dallas Morning News,* p. 2H.

_____. (1988f, August 18). CNN plays tough, ABC plays patsy with Quayle. *Dallas Morning News,* p. 3F.

_____. (1988g, August 20). Convention coverage, good and bad. *Dallas Morning News,* p. 5C.

Broadwell, L. (1988, October). Democrats play to packed house in Atlanta. *Successful Meetings,* pp. 94–96.

Brownstein, R. (1988, July 19). Keynote speech strikes chords for the fall. *National Journal Convention Daily,* p. 12.

Brustein, R. (1988, July 24). A four-day series: A star is born. *New York Times,* p. 25.

Carter, B. (1988a, July 20). Jackson steals the TV show—almost too late. *Baltimore Sun,* p. C1.

_____. (1988b, July 21). Post-Jackson coverage loss of electricity. *Baltimore Sun,* p. F1.

_____. (1988c, August 18). Bush's choice pre-empts Reagan as spotlight on TV. *Baltimore Sun,* p. B1.

Charge of the Duke parade. (1988, August 1). *U.S. News & World Report,* pp. 12–19.

Collins, M. (1988a, July 22). At the convention, everything is news. *USA Today,* p. 3D.

_____. (1988b, August 19). Quayle captured in spotlight. *USA Today,* p. 3D.

Daley, S. (1988, August 17). For openers, ratings were up 6%. *Chicago Tribune,* p. 17.

Dart, B. (1988, August 17). From interpreters to makeup, journalists get royal treatment. *Atlanta Journal and Constitution,* p. 17.

Diamond, E. (1988a, July 18). Presswatch: CNN's pulling in the political junkies. *National Journal Convention Daily*, p. 18.

———. (1988b, July 21). Presswatch: The three wise men return, very briefly. *National Journal Convention Daily*, p. 18.

———. (1988c, August 17). How a TV pro picks faces in the crowd. *National Journal Convention Daily*, p. 16.

Dollar, S. (1988, July 17). Hollywood comes to Atlanta: Screen stars in supporting roles at convention. *Atlanta Journal and Constitution*, p. 9C.

Donlon, B. (1988, July 21). ABC's Arledge: Conventions a turnoff. *USA Today*, p. 1.

Donlon, B., & Katz, G. (1988a, July 20). Rather, Cronkite say reported rift has healed. *USA Today*, p. 4A.

———. (1988b, July 22). Comedians try to liven up convention coverage. *USA Today*, p. 4A.

———. (1988c, August 16). Reporters-Turned-Pundits now stalking the floor. *USA Today*, p. 4A.

———. (1988d, August 17). NBC: Proud as a peacock over the Quayle scoop. *USA Today*, p. 4A.

———. (1988e, August 18). Hotel breakfast menus include "Today," "GMA." *USA Today*, p. 4A.

Dowd, M. (1988, July 19). In search of pictures for home. *New York Times*, p. 11.

Elving, R. D. (1988, July 16). Democrats struggle to define their destiny. *Congressional Quarterly*, pp. 1946–48.

Fairness & Accuracy in Reporting. (1988, July 19). News release.

Gergen, D. (1988, August 29/September 5). Daniel in the lion's den. *U.S. News & World Report*, p. 27.

Germond, J. W., & Witcover, J. (1988, July 16). Dukakis's test: How he manages the convention. *National Journal*, p. 1886.

Greppi, M. (1988a, July 19). For all the bases covered, few home runs are hit. *Atlanta Journal and Constitution*, p. 17C.

———. (1988b, July 20). Early coverage an appetizer; Jackson speech is main course. *Atlanta Journal and Constitution*, p. 18C.

Grove, L. (1988, July 4–10). A mini-series called "Atlanta." *Washington Post National Weekly Edition*, pp. 12–13.

Gunther, M. (1988a, July 20). Networks ignored debate on taxes. *Detroit Free Press*, p. 9A.

———. (1988b, July 21). Local stations were LIVE!—but not always so lively. *Detroit Free Press*, p. 17A.

Guskind, R. (1988a, July 20). It's campaign time, so tune in to BeckelVision. *National Journal Convention Daily*, p. 15.

———. (1988b, July 20). The "Spin Patrol" chews the news. *National Journal Convention Daily*, p. 6.

———. (1988c, August 18). Up from the field and into the booth. *National Journal Convention Daily*, p. 6.

Hansen, J. O. (1988a, July 17). TV networks review electronic game plan. *Atlanta Journal and Constitution*, p. 19C.

———. (1988b, July 18). CNN runs with the big boys: An also-ran two elections ago, cable operation slugs it out with networks. *Atlanta Journal and Constitution*, p. 14C.

———. (1988c, July 19). Politicians finding new lives as paid media commentators. *Atlanta Journal and Constitution*, p. 17C.

———. (1988d, July 20). Anchorman, mayor get lines cross. *Atlanta Journal and Constitution*, p. 16C.

———. (1988e, July 20). With eager audiences at home, foreign media track events closely. *Atlanta Journal and Constitution*, p. 16C.

———. (1988f, July 22). Cronkite says that covering the convention with Rather has been "Delightful Experience." *Atlanta Journal and Constitution*, p. 9C.

———. (1988g, July 22). No news is bad news for TV ratings. *Atlanta Journal and Constitution*, pp. 1C, 19C.

———. (1988h, August 17). Beaming political news back home. *Atlanta Journal and Constitution*, p. 19C.

Holston, N. (1988, August 18). Running-mate "suspense" is GOP joke on the media. *Minneapolis Star Tribune*, p. 1E.

Hulbert, D. (1988a, July 18). A new stage in politics. *Atlanta Journal and Constitution*, p. 7C.

———. (1988b, July 19). Opening night as theater: A review of key convention speakers. *Atlanta Journal and Constitution*, p. 8C.

Jensen, E. (1988, August 17). NBC lands a scoop on Bush veep choice. *New York Daily News*, p. 78.

Katz, G. (1988a, July 15). Democrats focus on "TV look." *USA Today*, p. 8E.

———. (1988b, July 18). Press meets the press at 'Woodstock.' *USA Today*, pp. 1–2.

Kloer, P. (1988a, August 17). Bush's bombshell shifts media's attention to Quayle, off convention speeches. *Atlanta Journal and Constitution*, p. 19A.

———. (1988b, August 18). Networks go hunting Quayle on slow night at Superdome. *Atlanta Journal and Constitution*, p. 32.

Knight News Service. (1987, December 5). Brief 1988 Democratic platform urged. *Arkansas Gazette*, p. 5.

Kosterlitz, J. (1988, August 15). Forget politics—this is big business. *National Journal Convention Daily*, p. 8.

Kowet, D. (1988, August 18). TV drools over Quayle's "flaws." *Washington Times*, p. A7.

Kubansik, B. (1988, July 20). Less of the world is watching. *Newsday*, p. 5.

Lamar, J. V. (1988, August 1). Reaching common ground. *Time*, pp. 16–19.

Langley, M, & Davidson, J. (1988, August 19). Elephant tales: Critic of Bush flips, 'Moses' converts, Newscasters roll on. *Wall Street Journal*, p. 10.

Levin, J. (1988, July). Republican National Convention: Planning the grand old party. *Meeting and Conventions*, pp. 38–44.

Lorando, M. (1988a, July 19). NBC beats rivals with interview. *New Orleans Times-Picayune*, p. A9.

———. (1988b, August 14). ABC sticks to its guns—next time. *New Orleans Times-Picayune*, p. B2.

———. (1988c, August 16). Gun costs Robinette his credentials. *New Orleans, Times-Picayune*, p. B2.

———. (1988d, August 17). After Quayle, not much left to hunt. *New Orleans Times-Picayune*, p. B2.

Mayfield, M., & Morris, J. (1988, July 22). Parties won't cut back on conventions. *USA Today*, p. 4A.

A media "feeding" frenzy? (1988, August 29). *Newsweek*, p. 26.

Media Research Center. (1988a, August 1). News release.

———. (1988b, August 24). News release.

Merry, R. W. (1976, July 31). TV at the convention: How to bore from within. *National Observer*, p. 4.

Minutaglio, B. (1988, August 18). Director controls your TV. *Dallas Morning News*, p. 6F.

Moore, W. J. (1988, July 19). The uplink serves the hometown stations. *National Journal Convention Daily*, p. 36.

New Orleans officials may not welcome Democrats' site panel. (1990, April 23). *Dallas Morning News*, p. 20A.

Newsweek. (1988a, July 25). pp. 16–43.

———. (1988b, August 22). pp. 14–29.

O'Brian, B. (1988, July 19). Hollywood glitz experts staging no-glitz TV show. *New Orleans Times-Picayune*, p. A9.

Oreskes, M. (1988a, August 17). In Superdome, delegates are where action is without knowing what it is. *New York Times*, p. 13.

———. (1988b, August 19). Convention message is garbled by Quayle static. *New York Times*, p. 10.

Quayle factor. (1988, August 29). *Time*, pp. 16–22.

Quinn, J. (1988, July). Democratic National Convention: Planning without the agenda. *Meetings and Conventions*, p. 46–50.

Radcliffe, D. (1988, August 15). Bush's relative strength: Before the convention, reflections on home and family. *Washington Post*, p. C1.

Rauch, J. (1988a, July 19). The convention press contemplates its navel. *National Journal Convention Daily*, p. 31.

———. (1988b, July 20). Small, offbeat media jump into the gap. *National Journal Convention Daily*, p. 12.

Reid, T. R. (1988, August 17). Drowned out under the dome. *Washington Post*, p. A23.

Roll call, where homespun plugs abound, to have script. (1988, August 17). *Los Angeles Times*, p. 4.

Rosenberg, H. (1988a, August 15). TV plays host to a grand old party. *Los Angeles Times*, p. 7:1.

———. (1988b, August 17). Ronald Reagan's farewell: The power and the glory. *Los Angeles Times*, p. 6:1.

Rosenstiel, T. B. (1988a, July 21). Democrats learn to control show. *Los Angeles Times*, p. 6.

———. (1988b, August 17). Production trouble plagues convention. *Los Angeles Times*, p. 6.

———. (1988c, August 19). Snap decisions guide TV view of convention. *Los Angeles Times*, p. 5.

Rosenthal, A. (1988, July 17). Poll finds Atlanta delegates more liberal than the public. *New York Times*, p. 1.

Safire, W. (1988, July 21). 'My fellow Democrats.' *New York Times*, p. 25.

Shales, T. (1988a, July 20). Star wars: Round one. *Washington Post*, p. C1.

———. (1988b, July 21). Jackson worth the wait. *Washington Post*, p. B1.

———. (1988c, July 22). After Jesse, Democrats go to dull and worse. *Los Angeles Times*, p. 6:24.

———. (1988d, July 22). The long night of Bill Clinton. *Washington Post*, p. D1.

———. (1988e, August 15). Live from New Orleans—It's RNC! *Washington Post*, p. C1.

———. (1988f, August 17). We'll miss Gipper, and his speeches. *Washington Post*, p. D1.

———. (1988g, August 17). NBC News' scoop on the Quayle choice. *Washington Post*, p. D1.

———. (1988h, August 18). Booth to booth with the running mate. *Washington Post*, pp. C1–2.

Shapiro, W. (1988, August 1). The Duke of unity. *Time*, pp. 14–16.

Siegel, E. (1988a, August 16). A great speech but . . . *Boston Globe*, p. 63.

———. (1988b, August 17). Reacting to Bush's thunderbolt. *Boston Globe*, pp. 69–70.

Straus, H., & Hansen, J. O. (1988a, July 19). Networks are reaching out to America. *Atlanta Journal and Constitution*, p. 1C.

———. (1988b, July 22). Slick TV show hard to produce without drama. *Atlanta Journal and Constitution*, p. 9C.

Sullivan, P. (1988a, August 17). Networks quick to get the veep scoop. *Boston Herald*, p. 47.

———. (1988b, August 18). Networks go Quayle hunting. *Boston Herald*, p. 55.

Time. (1988a, July 25). pp. 16–33.

———. (1988b, August 22). pp. 16–35.

Tucker, K. (1988, July 21). With rigid packaging, networks create a bore. *Philadelphia Inquirer*, pp. 1D, 8D.

Unger, A. (1988, August 17). Show-biz producers help conventions preen for TV: Podium design, colors, music, and run-throughs get extra-special attention. *Christian Science Monitor*, p. 19.

U.S. News & World Report. (1988a, July 25). pp. 12–29.

———. (1988b, August 22). pp. 12–23.

Of "visibility whip" and the "bite patrol." (1988, August 1). *Newsweek*, pp. 18–20.

von Hoffman, N. (1988). Convention history. *New Republic*, pp. 24–33.

Will, G. F. (1988, July 20). Politics as autobiography . . . *Washington Post*, p. A15.

Wilson, D. L. (1988, August 18). When radio covers a convention designed for TV. *National Journal Convention Daily*, p. 32.

PROCEEDING OF MEETINGS AND SYMPOSIA

Commission on National Political Conventions. (1989, April 7). Official transcript [of] proceedings before Center for Democracy. Washington: Alderson Reporting Company.

Commission on National Political Conventions. (1990). *Reaching the American voter: Party conventions and the television electorate.* Washington: Center for Democracy.

Kendall, K. E. (1990, November). *Ritual in political conventions: Vaudeville revisited.* Paper presented at the annual meeting of the Speech Communication Association, Chicago, IL.

Womack, D. L. (1990, November). *Network performance at five Democratic political conventions: A critical look.* Paper presented at the annual meeting of the Speech Communication Association, Chicago, IL.

POLITICAL JOURNALISTS INTERVIEWED FOR THE STUDY

Designation in parentheses indicates at which convention the interview occurred:
DNC for Democratic, RNC for Republican.

Allen, Frederick; Correspondent/Anchor, CNN (RNC).
Ash, Clarke; Editorial Page Editor, Palm Beach *Post* (DNC).
Banmiller, Bryan; Correspondent, *Wall Street Journal,* TV (RNC).
Barnicle, Mike; Reporter, *Boston Globe* (DNC).
Barta, Carolyn; Political Editor, *Dallas Morning News* (DNC).
Bastida, Ken; Correspondent, KCBS, San Francisco (RNC).
Berry, Dave; Media Critic and Columnist, *Miami Herald* (DNC).
Brownstein, Greg; Assignment Editor, C-SPAN (DNC).
Bruno, Hal; Political Editor, ABC News.
Casey, Mark; Executive Producer, WSOK (DNC).
Council, John; Reporter, Dallas, *Daily Texas* (DNC).
Crawford, Bob, Correspondent, WBBM, Chicago; CBS Radio (RNC).
Crowls, Ed; Reporter, Austin (TX) *American-Statesman* (RNC).
Daily, Steve; Media Critic, *Chicago Tribune* (DNC).
Deibel, Mary; Reporter, Scripps-Howard Newspapers (DNC).
Duffus, Joe; Photo Editor, Thomason Chain (DNC).
Duncan, Phil; Editor, *Congressional Quarterly* (DNC).
Edwards, Ann; Washington Bureau Editor, National Public Radio (DNC and RNC).
Evans, Bill; Managing Editor, *Dallas Morning News* (DNC).
Farris, Peter; Editorial Manager, *New York Post* (RNC).
Fields, Mike; TV Freelance Reporter, Fox Network (RNC).
Follath, Erich, Dr.; Reporter, Hamburg, *Stern* Magazine (DNC).
Frank, Richard; Editor, *National Journal Convention Daily* (DNC).
Gerstle, Steve; Bureau Chief, Associated Press (RNC).
Grant, Neva; Correspondent, National Public Radio (RNC).
Gray, Lance; Reporter, Scripps-Howard Newspapers (DNC).
Greenlee, Bob; Reporter, *Hannibal Courier Post* (DNC).
Henderson, Bud; Anchor, WFTV (DNC).
Henning, John; Correspondent, WBZ-TV, NBC affiliate, Boston (RNC).
Hume, Bret; Correspondent, ABC News (RNC).
Hunt, Al; Washington Bureau Chief, *Wall Street Journal.*
Innerson, Marshall; Radio Correspondent, Christian Science Monitor Radio (DNC).
Jarrett, Rick; Washington Bureau Assistant, National Public Radio (RNC).
Jensen, Elizabeth; Media Critic, *New York Daily News* (DNC).
Johnson, David; Anchor/Reporter, WPXI-TV (DNC).
Katz, Shelley; Photographer, *Time* Magazine (DNC).
Kelly, Ed; Reporter, Washington Bureau, *Daily Oklahoman* (DNC).
Kindred, Dave; Reporter, *Atlanta Constitution* (DNC).
Kopp, Bruce; Correspondent, NBC affiliate, Indianapolis (RNC).
Kovacs, Peter; Convention Editor, *New Orleans Times-Picayune* (DNC).
Kraslow, David; Reporter, Miami, Cox Newspapers (DNC).
Loftis, Jack; Vice President and Editor, *Houston Chronicle* (DNC).

Lorando, Mark; Media Critic, *New Orleans Times-Picayune* (DNC).

MacDonell, Ellen; Producer, "Morning Edition," National Public Radio (RNC).

McConnell, Dave; Washington Capitol Hill Reporter, WTSP, CBS (RNC).

McDowell, Charlie; Reporter, *Richmond Times-Dispatch;* Panelist, *Washington Week in Review* (RNC).

Madigan, John; Correspondent, CBS Radio affiliate (RNC).

Madison, Christopher; Reporter, *National Journal* (RNC).

Marsh, Don; Political Reporter, KTVI-TV (RNC).

Matlack, Carol; Reporter, *National Journal* (RNC).

Mitchell, Andrea; Correspondent, NBC News (RNC).

Morrison, Patt; Reporter, *Los Angeles Times* (DNC & RNC).

Nauth, Zach; Reporter, *New Orleans Times-Picayune* (DNC).

Nelson, Jack; Reporter, *Los Angeles Times;* Panelist, *Washington Week in Review* (RNC).

Null, Topper; Reporter, *Los Angeles Herald Examiner* (DNC).

Palomo, Juan; Washington Bureau Correspondent, *Houston Post* (DNC).

Perkins, Neil; Anchor/Reporter, KSDK, NBC affiliate (RNC).

Plumber, Jeff; Delegation Reporter, NBC News (DNC).

Powell, Adam; Executive News Producer, National Public Radio (DNC and RNC).

Ray, Glenn; Anchor, WKBD-TV (DNC).

Reeder, Mike; Correspondent, KWTX-TV, CBS affiliate (RNC).

Rockwell, Frank; Correspondent, KTW-TV, NBC affiliate (DNC).

Roeder, Dave; Reporter, *Chicago Southtown Economist* and *St. Louis Post-Dispatch* (DNC).

Saranson, David; Associate Editor, Portland, *The Oregonian* (RNC).

Sawyer, Forest; Correspondent, CBS News (DNC).

Sesno, Frank; Political Correspondent, CNN (RNC).

Severin, Jay; News Analyst, CBS News (RNC).

Shields, Mark; Columnist, *Washington Post* (RNC).

Shoemaker, Steve; Correspondent, KMOX, St. Louis (RNC).

Silverman, Mike; Reporter, Associated Press (DNC).

Snell, Roger; Ohio Bureau Chief, Gannett News Service (RNC).

Stafford, Rob; Reporter, WFTV (DNC).

Stokes, Gary; Producer/Reporter, WNIO-TV (DNC).

Swacan, Beverly; Photographer, *Dollars & Sense* Magazine (DNC).

Sykes, Bill; Executive Producer, WAGA, Atlanta (DNC).

Teepen, Tom; Editor, *Atlanta Constitution* (RNC).

Treadwell, David; Reporter, *Los Angeles Times* (DNC).

Venable, Sam; Reporter and Columnist, *Knoxville News Sentinel* (DNC).

Watson, George; Reporter/Anchor, KATU (RNC).

White, Jack; Deputy Chief Correspondent, *Time* Magazine (DNC).

White, Keith; Reporter, Gannett News Service (RNC).

Whitworth, Myrna; Executive Producer of English Programming, Voice of America (DNC).

Will, George; Columnist, *Washington Post* and *Newsweek* Magazine; Analyst, ABC News (RNC).

Woodruff, Les; Washington Correspondent, CBS Radio (RNC).

CONVENTION ORCHESTRATORS INTERVIEWED FOR THE STUDY

Party Officials

Byers, Paul; Producer, Convention Satellite News Service, 1988 Democratic National Convention.

Cleair, Merri Jo; Assistant to the Manager, 1988 Republican National Convention.

Fowler, Don; Chief Executive Officer, 1988 Democratic National Convention.

Goode, Mark; Producer, RNC Network, 1984/88 Republican National Convention.

Greenblat, Arleigh; Consultant and Manager, 1988 Democratic National Convention.

McCurry, Michael; Director of Communications/Press Secretary, Democratic National Committee.

Michael, Terry; Democratic National Committee News and Information Director.

Miller, Mike; Director, News Media Operations, Republican National Convention, 1972 through 1988, and working journalist 1964–1968 Republican conventions.

Phillips, Bill; Manager, 1988 Republican National Convention.

Media Executives

Angotti, Joseph; Producer, NBC News.

Frey, Charles, Pool Producer, 1988 Democratic National Convention, ABC News.

Friedland, Justin; Producer, ABC News.

Maxwell, Jane; Producer, CNN News.

Michaelson, Michael; Producer, C-SPAN (Former Superintendent, House Radio/TV Gallery).

Miran, Alec; Producer, CNN News.

Reade, John; Pool Producer, 1988 Republican National Convention, CBS News.

Siegel, Lloyd; Producer, NBC News.

Towriss, John; Producer, CNN News.

Congressional Gallery Officials

Petersen, Robert; Superintendent, U.S. Senate Press Gallery.

Tate, Tina; Superintendent, U.S. House of Representatives Radio/TV Gallery.

Womack, Don; Retired Superintendent, U.S. Senate Press Gallery.

Index

ABC (American Broadcasting Company): administrative logistics, 61–62; anchors (*see* Brinkley, David; Jennings, Peter); DNC coverage, 144–46, 149–50, 153–54, 156, 159–60, 193–97, 201–2; production strategy, 40, 99–100, 163, 220; RNC coverage, 170–71, 175–77, 181–82, 184–88, 203–5, 208

acceptance speeches, 73, 126; history, 36, 40; in 1988, 118–21, 132–34, 157–62, 184–87, 200, 219

Adorno, Theodore, 10–14, 16, 26, 82, 190–91

ancillary personnel, 16–19, 52–63, 93, 110; production company management, 41, 51, 52–56. *See also* host committee; pool producers; *names of specific House/Senate media galleries; names of specific networks*

Angotti, Joe, 61–62, 85, 87, 99, 147–48, 224

Arledge, Roone, 5, 211

Atwater, Lee, 153, 170–72, 175, 178, 205, 210

Baker, Jim, 52, 55

Bark, Ed, 92, 194, 205–8

Bastida, Ken, 138–39

Bell South Lounge, 98

Bentsen, Lloyd, 101, 105, 114, 118–21, 129, 132, 134, 146, 152–53, 157–59, 161, 177, 186, 201–2

Berry, Dave, 193

bite patrol, 200

Brinkley, David, 138, 141, 145, 154–55, 160, 163, 170–71, 176–77, 181–82, 185, 193, 195–96, 204, 207–8, 212

Brokaw, Tom, 138, 141, 143, 148, 151, 154–55, 161–62, 172–73, 178–79, 183, 185–86, 188, 198–99, 203–7, 212

Bush, Dorothy, 112, 117

Bush, George, 2, 13, 65, 93, 98–99, 106–7, 110, 113–14, 123–24, 127–35, 148–49, 152–53, 159–60, 167, 169–88, 203, 205–8, 213

Byers, Paul, 47–48, 53, 67–72, 75, 93, 96, 103, 222

cameras (stills): camera stands, 89, 90; photographers, 12, 76–77, 98

cameras (television): camera stands, 89; distribution and placement, 18, 60, 62, 72, 87, 90–91, 100

Carter, Bill, 196, 197–98, 205
Carter, Hodding, 145–46, 182, 193, 196–98
Carter, Jimmy, 109–10, 115, 123, 133, 142, 144–45, 147, 193, 197
casting, 18, 65
CBS (Columbia Broadcasting System), 102, 220; anchor (see Rather, Dan); DNC coverage, 146–47, 149–50, 154, 156–57, 160–61, 163, 196–97, 201–2; RNC coverage, 171–72, 178–79, 182–83, 185–88, 203–4, 208
celebrity appearances: at conventions, 65, 73, 75, 125, 211; on television coverage, 142–43, 151–53, 159–61, 180
Center for Media and Public Affairs, 201–2, 208
central booking units, 45–46, 66, 101
central speech units, 17, 66, 93
Chancellor, John, 141, 143, 148, 151, 155, 157, 161–62, 173, 178, 183, 185, 187–88, 195–97, 199, 203, 212
Cleair, Merri Jo, 55, 57, 65, 73, 86
Clinton, Bill, 64, 116–18, 134, 155–57, 177, 197–98, 200, 203, 206
CNN (Cable News Network), 5, 78, 137–38; administrative logistics, 61–62; anchors (see Shaw, Bernard; Williams, Mary Alice); DNC coverage, 143–44, 149–50, 152–53, 155–56, 158–59, 195–96, 201–2; floor correspondents, 138, 143–44, 162–63, 167, 170, 175, 180, 186, 198; production strategy, 100, 144, 162–63, 202, 220–21; remote reports, 98–99; RNC coverage, 166–67, 169–70, 174–75, 179–80, 184, 186–87, 205–8; Special Events producers, 56, 62, 65, 85–86, 87, 98, 101–2 (see also names of specific producers); studio commentators, 139, 143–44, 152, 158, 175, 180, 184, 198, 203–4
Commission on National Political Conventions, 21, 23, 141, 189, 210–13, 225–26

computer operations (by parties), 53–54, 70, 112, 141, 151
CONUS (Continental United States Communications), 5, 12, 77, 78, 223
convention functions, 4, 6, 19, 25, 27; campaign-rally, 25–26, 29, 209; governing-body, 29, 102–3; institutional, 27, 218, 226–28; nomination, 29; platform-drafting, 29
convention history: emergence, 1–3, 14–15, 26–29; group-mediated era, 30–35; mass-mediated era, 35–41, 63, 69, 81; telepolitical era, 41–48, 59, 71, 75, 82
convention production phases, 16, 18, 52, 82, 217; preproduction, 35, 41, 59, 61, 67, 72, 82–93, 219; production, 42, 93–101; postproduction, 42, 101–3
Convention Satellite News Service (CSNS), 5, 47–48, 68, 70–71, 96, 103, 222
convention schedule, 65, 95, 123, 127, 166
credentials distribution, 59; floor passes, 94, 97–98, 125, 132; preconvention, 86–87, 125
Cronkite, Walter, 140, 143, 146–47, 154, 156, 161, 172, 185–86, 195, 198, 204
C-SPAN (Cable Satellite Public Affairs Network), 5, 46–47, 124, 137; administrative logistics, 62–63; DNC coverage, 141–43, 149–52, 155, 157–58, 195; history, 63; production strategy, 141, 162, 219–20; RNC coverage, 166–69, 174, 179, 184, 186–87

Daley, Steve, 193, 204
delegates: demographics in 1988, 108, 122–23; role, 13, 16, 73–74
demonstrations, 29, 34, 73, 96, 118, 126, 131, 133–34, 174–78, 182, 184, 223
Diamond, Edwin, 6, 77, 155, 173
Dole, Elizabeth, 106, 125, 168, 172
Dole, Robert, 129–30, 132, 171–72, 178–79, 182, 184

Dukakis, Michael, 2, 70, 93, 101, 105–7, 109–12, 114–15, 117–18, 120–21, 123–24, 126–30, 132–35, 140, 142–46, 149, 151, 153–62, 170, 172, 177, 183, 186, 188, 192–94, 197–202, 205

Ellerbee, Linda, 143, 146, 150, 152, 154, 156, 169, 175, 192, 198, 204, 208

Fahrenkopf, Frank, 123, 166, 189–90, 210
FAIR (Fairness & Accuracy in Media), 201
favorite son nominations, 26, 32, 88
Ford, Gerald, 106, 128–29, 174–79, 193, 203
Fowler, Don, 43, 52–53, 61, 64, 68–71, 73, 92–93, 96, 106, 109–10, 139–41, 195, 203, 222
Frank, Richard, 76
Frey, Charles, 60–61, 65, 70, 72, 90, 97, 108, 122
Friedland, Justin, 44–45, 55, 61–62, 70, 85, 91, 99–101, 176, 224

Goode, Josephine, 52, 55
Goode, Mark, 43–44, 47–48, 52–53, 55, 65, 67–69, 71–72, 74–75, 96, 123, 169, 202–3, 222–23
Grant, Neva, 138
Greenblat, Arleigh, 51–54, 56–57, 64, 73, 84, 86–87, 89, 91–93, 106, 113, 116–17, 119, 221

Hansen, Jane, 5, 45, 77–78, 94
Harris, Bill, 55, 90–91, 102
Herring, Pendleton, 25, 29, 134
host committees, 18, 42, 52, 68, 75, 94, 103; Atlanta '88, 54, 56–58, 101, 109; Louisiana Host Committee, 56–58, 95
hotel distribution, 18; problems, 42, 84–85, 93–94; procedures, 61, 81
House/Senate periodical galleries, 17, 42, 58, 165
House/Senate photographers galleries, 17, 42, 58, 97, 165

House/Senate press galleries, 12, 17, 37, 165; administrative logistics, 59, 68, 86, 101, 103; role, 42, 52, 58
House/Senate radio and TV galleries, 17, 165; administrative logistics, 59, 68, 86, 101; role, 42, 52, 58
hymnals, 15, 17, 66, 96, 135, 166, 221

insurance, 86

Jackson, Jesse, 4, 13, 105–7, 109–12, 114–18, 121, 124–25, 134–35, 142–46, 149, 151–56, 158–59, 162, 167–69, 186, 190, 194–98, 200–202, 212, 227
Jennings, Peter, 141, 145, 151, 153, 155, 159–60, 163, 170–71, 176, 181–82, 185, 193, 196, 199, 204, 207, 212
Jensen, Elizabeth, 193–94, 206–7

Katz, Shelly, 76–77
Kean, Tom, 128–29, 134, 149, 174–78, 188, 203
Kennedy, Edward, 13, 106, 111, 114, 129, 133, 152–54, 196–97, 200
Key, V. O., 29, 31
keynote speeches: history, 31, 36, 38, 40, 212; in 1988, 73, 107, 109–10, 123, 128–29, 134, 142, 145, 149–50, 174–78, 200, 203, 206
Kirk, Paul, 84, 93, 103, 109–10, 112, 137, 141–42, 191, 193, 200

Lamb, Brian, 141
local television coverage, 59, 71, 77, 213; consortia, 77–78; future, 223–24; independents, 77–78; strategies, 77
Lorando, Mark, 193–94, 205–6

Madigan, John, 46
Madison, Christopher, 138
Maxwell, Jane, 61–62, 70, 92, 224–25
McCurry, Michael, 43–45, 56, 60–61, 68, 70, 85, 87, 91, 135, 140, 188, 191–92, 199, 203, 222–24
media critics, 13, 16–17, 191, 209; in-

stant reviews, 192–99, 203–4; overnight reviews, 194–99, 204–7; series
reviews, 199–202, 208
Media Research Center (MRC), 201,
208
media village (workspace), 75–76; at
DNC, 90, 98, 117; at RNC, 90
media walk-throughs, 18, 59; in Atlanta, 57, 88–89; functions, 42, 88;
in New Orleans, 88, 165
Mencken, H. L., 7, 9, 35, 37, 137, 191,
200, 209–10, 217
message committee, 17, 43–44, 64,
68–69, 96, 111, 113
Michael, Terry, 47, 56, 64–65, 75–77,
87, 96, 223
Michaelson, Mike, 49, 61–63
Michel, Robert, 126–28, 130, 184
Miller, Mike, 44, 49, 52, 55, 60–61,
68, 84–85, 91, 126, 222–23
Miran, Alec, 61, 90–91
models (of convention facilities), 87,
89
multiple-ballot nominations, 2, 31–32,
35–36, 215

National Journal Convention Daily, 76,
97–98
NBC (National Broadcasting Company): administrative logistics,
61–62; anchors (*see* Brokaw, Tom;
Chancellor, John); DNC coverage,
147–49, 150, 154–55, 157, 161–62,
194, 196–97, 201–2; production
strategy, 99, 147–48, 163, 221; RNC
coverage, 172–73, 178–79, 183, 185,
186–88, 206–8
network television coverage: future,
190, 223–26; history, 38–40; ratings,
5, 45, 190, 194, 204, 211, 217, 221,
225
newsmagazine coverage, 76, 199–201,
208; photographers, 76–77; strategies, 105–6
newspaper coverage: daily activities,
98; history, 33–35; off-beat press,
76, 87; role, 46, 75–76
nomination speeches: history, 31, 36,

40; in 1988, 117, 119, 130–32, 134,
155–58, 161, 182–84
nonperforming personnel, 16–19, 52,
63–68, 93, 106; composers, 36,
64–67, 73; set designers and stage
direction, 67–68

opera: convention as, 10, 14–20, 23,
33, 36, 40, 51–52, 58, 60, 63, 67,
69, 74, 90, 107, 131, 167–68, 188,
219
orchestration: convention as product
of, 4–12, 30, 38, 51, 58–61, 66–67,
69, 71, 73, 78, 87, 103, 135,
187–88, 200, 203, 209–12, 216–17

party platforms, 2, 19, 26, 29, 34–36,
38, 73; 1988 Democrat platform, 95,
112, 114, 151, 155; 1988 Republican platform, 126–28, 167
performing personnel, 16, 52, 68–79,
93
Petersen, Bob, 44, 55–56, 59, 83, 85,
87, 92, 110
Phillips, Bill, 47, 52–56, 65, 68, 74,
85–86, 90, 93, 95, 106, 166, 226
political bosses, 26, 30–31, 33–34, 36,
51, 79, 217
pool producers, 17, 72, 87, 119; role,
58–60, 94, 100; selection, 60; strategies, 72, 97
Potomac Communications, 5, 12, 77,
223
press stands, 58–59, 87, 92
program group, 43, 65, 68–69, 96,
202–3

Quayle, Dan, 99, 127, 129–34,
138–39, 168, 172, 174–88, 203–4,
206–9

radio coverage: history, 37–39, 46; in
1988, 77–78
Railroad Lounge, 98
Rather, Dan, 138, 140, 143, 146–47,
151, 154–56, 160–61, 163, 169,
171–72, 176–79, 182–83, 185–86,
188, 195, 197–99, 203–7, 212, 220

Reade, John, 60, 72, 90, 96–97, 100–101, 108, 132

Reagan, Ronald, 71, 82, 106–7, 110, 113, 121, 123–28, 133, 135, 149, 154, 157, 167–72, 186, 204–6, 213

Reinsch, J. Leonard, 8, 37, 39, 216–17, 221

Republican National Convention Network (RNCN), 5, 46, 48, 63, 68, 70–72, 95–97, 124, 132, 138, 166, 187, 222–23

Richards, Ann, 105, 109–10, 121, 134, 142, 145, 147, 149–50, 152, 159, 177, 195, 197

roll call of the states, 2–3, 32–34, 40, 66, 116–17, 131, 182–83, 216; rules, 32, 38

Rosenstiel, Thomas, 66, 99, 206

satellite technology, 41, 77, 98–99

satellite truck parking, 59, 78, 90–91

Shales, Tom, 116, 129, 195–98, 204–8

Shaw, Bernard, 138, 143–44, 151–52, 155, 158–59, 169, 175, 178, 181, 184, 192, 202–3, 207–8, 212

Siegel, Lloyd, 61, 92, 100–101, 147

site selection, 18, 41–42, 52, 59, 61, 82–86

site visitations, 42, 82–83

skyboxes, 49, 59, 87–92, 108, 122, 137

Smith-Hemion Productions, 43–44, 53, 64–65, 67–70, 72, 75, 92–93, 96, 103, 110, 117, 195

spin operations, 64–66, 95–96

spin patrol, 191–92

stand-up locations, 49, 59, 87–89, 92

Tate, Tina, 44, 59, 77, 85–87, 91, 97

tear-down, 42, 102

television producers. *See names of specific producers*

television trailer farms, 60

Thomson, Charles A. H., 7–8, 38–40

Towriss, John, 61, 90, 98–100

transportation: as factor in site selection, 18, 41, 56, 84; problems, 42

Treadwell, David, 138

venders, 116–17

video introductions, 44, 65, 73–75, 110–11, 113–14, 132–33, 152, 159–61, 168–70, 184, 197, 205; other convention video uses, 16, 39–40, 44–45, 68, 71, 75, 114, 116, 123, 125, 168–70, 223

video-taped reports: by CSNS, 68, 70–71; by television networks, 100, 144, 169–73, 175–76, 180, 182

visibility whips, 200–201

Wagner, Richard, 12, 23, 122, 146, 167, 219

White, Jack, 76

Will, George, 134, 145–46, 156, 171, 176, 182, 185, 193, 197–98, 203–4

Williams, Mary Alice, 138, 143–44, 152–53, 155, 158–59, 169–70, 174, 180–81, 184, 188, 199, 207, 212

Womack, Don, 46, 97, 103, 125

Woodruff, Les, 77–78

work space: news media, 57, 59–61, 85, 87–88; parties, 85, 89

Wright, Jim, 109, 112, 118–19, 121, 129, 142–44, 151, 156, 191, 198

ABOUT THE AUTHORS

LARRY DAVID SMITH (Ph.D., Ohio State, 1986) is an Assistant Professor of Communication at Purdue University, West Lafayette, Indiana. He specializes in studies of presidential nominating conventions, presidential rhetoric, political and product advertising, and popular culture. His writings have appeared in *Communication Quarterly*, *Communication Studies*, *The Southern Communication Journal*, and *Political Communication Review*.

DAN NIMMO (Ph.D., Vanderbilt, 1962) is a Professor of Communication and Adjunct Professor of Political Science at the University of Oklahoma, Norman, Oklahoma. A member of several editorial boards, a frequent book reviewer, and a lecturer, he writes widely in the areas of communication studies, political communication, political persuasion, and campaign and voting behavior. His books on political communication include: *Newsgathering in Washington*, *Candidates and Their Images* (with Robert Savage), *Government and the News Media: Comparative Dimensions* (with Michael Mansfield), *Handbook of Political Communication* (with Keith Sanders), and *Mediated Political Realities* (with James Combs).